The EARLY YEARS VOLUME I

The
EARLY YEARS
VOLUME I

Jeshua

The Early Years: Volume I

First Edition

Published by:
PT. Heartfelt Publishing
PO Box 204, Ubud 80571
admin@wayofmastery.com
www.wayofmastery.com

ISBN: 978-602-9189-14-8

Jeshua Shares

I promise you this: If you become *wholly committed* to awakening from the dream you have dreamed since the stars first began to appear in the heavens, and even before that, if your one desire is to be only what God created . . . then lay at the altar of your heart with every breath, everything you *think* you know, everything you *think* you need, and look lovingly upon every place that fear has made a home in your mind, and allow correction to come. It will come. Regardless of how you experience it, it *will* come.

And the day and the moment will arise when all of your pain and fear and suffering will have vanished like a wind that pushes the foam of the wave away, revealing the clarity of the ocean beneath you. You will literally feel throughout your being that there never was a dream. Some memories will remain with you and you will know that somewhere you must've dreamed a dream or had a thought of wondering what it would be like to be other than the way God created you, but it will be such a faint echo that it will leave no trace upon you. In your heart you will smile gently, regardless of the circumstances in which you find yourself. There will be peace from the crown of the head to the tips of the toes, so to speak, and that peace will walk before you wherever you go. It will enter a room before you enter it with a body, and those who are becoming sensitive will wonder who has come into their place. And some will even say, "Behold, I believe Christ has come for dinner." And you will be that one, for that is who you are—Christ eternal.

~ The Early Years: Choose to See

Contents

Foreword

This book is a transcription of channelings given by Jeshua to public groups from the early years of my work with Him. These teachings are an extensive collection of Jeshua's wisdom, and a vital part of *The Way of Mastery Pathway.*

As recounted in *The Jeshua Letters,* after my more personal initial communion with Jeshua, my studentship and work with Him shifted to a more public stage.

During this period, from 1988 until the time He began the three year course of *The Way of Mastery: The Christ Mind Trilogy,* in 1994, He asked that I remain surrendered to Him. This included stepping into the more public role of channeling for groups, something I was very uncomfortable with in the beginning. Regardless of my discomfort, however, as word got out, groups gathered in increasing numbers at my home in Tacoma, Washington, and invitations, taking me farther and farther afield, came in as well. All this required that I surrender further and further to a process I did not understand at all!

The public phase of my work with Jeshua began with the first group gathering in which He lifted me out of my body (or what I have come to see as 'the' body), and then entered into it to communicate through it to those in attendance. I refer to this stage as the beginning of the 'channeling' phase of my work with Him, although it is important for the reader to understand what is meant by the word 'channeling.'

Here is what would always happen: I would close my eyes and initiate a simple prayer He had given me, and I would feel myself dropping into a deeply meditative space. Then, a peculiar vibration would begin, and as it increased, I would be transported out and above the body; I could see it below, along with the crowd gathered, as well as light beings fully encircling the group.

Things would accelerate, and I would experience a rapid movement through multi-colored light. I could witness the crowd, and then the house in which the crowd sat, and then further, wider, 'telescoping' out, I could see planet earth herself, and then, rapidly, the physical universe itself would vanish, even as the pulsing, vibrating colored light increased.

Then, it would stop, and I would be aware of being with Jeshua, now together with Him in a field of Light. He would teach me while I was there with Him, and yet...while all this was occurring, He was also moving into, and teaching through 'my' body to the group gathered together in my living room in Tacoma.

At some point, He would tell me, "It is finished now." I would then begin to feel a vibrational change, and the reverse of the journey ensued until I 'zoomed' downward and landed – often with a shock – in the body. It would often take as much as 30 minutes for me to be able to move a finger, or begin to make any sound as I slowly adapted to the body. After, it would be so charged with energy that I often would be up for hours, yet in an altered state. Everything shimmered in light, and often objects like buildings, trees, and telephone poles were transparent – I could see right through them! One night, I was very sick with a fever and strep throat and was sure the evening should be cancelled. He assured me there would be no problem, and – to everyone's surprise – as I 'left' and Jeshua entered, I was told later that suddenly there was no trace at all of my sickness!

Indeed, after returning, I experienced the body radiating in clarity and perfect health, only then to gradually feel it 'sink' as the strep throat returned. When I asked Him what had happened, he replied: "*I would suggest that would be a very good question for you to dwell in. Why has what you call 'sickness' returned?*"

This is the type of question He lovingly asks, in this case, to bring attention and contrast to why one might use the body for such a thing as sickness, which, apparently, His use of the body did not include!

The Way of Mastery: The Early Years are transcriptions of these messages, originally recorded live, that capture what Jeshua taught us during these beautiful gatherings. The wisdom, guidance, and sheer brilliance of these teachings are astounding; there is so much in these pages, dear reader, that will help you grow in understanding and support you to truly heal into peace. You might like to know this, as well: Jeshua shared that while this mystical alchemy I was undergoing was part of my studentship, it was also His learning curve in acclimating to 'my' body and learning to utilize the language structure of its 'brain-mind.'

Indeed, the first phases of this period would find Him often communicating in a slow, monotone voice, with no movement of the body at all. Gradually, over time, He could animate it, and seemed to enjoy using American idioms that He had accessed through this process, as well!

Our interactions were varied and amusing. I would often feel His presence as I, for example, watched a bit of television, and he would make comments on the shows and commercials. He said He was learning of my world through the part of my soul that was fixated and operating through the body, that tiny thing which I was still mistakenly thinking of as 'me.'

The Early Years are filled with ancient wisdom, timeless Love, and even prophecy. As you open to this wonderful trove of material from Jeshua, may you enjoy these jewels that He has given us all.

Blessings to you!

Jayem
July, 2021

HEALING

April 1992

Now we begin.

Indeed greetings unto you, beloved and holy children of Light divine, indeed offspring of the One Who has been called God. And if you are that offspring, indeed you are created in your Father's image and in you remains the power to heal every false perception, to leave the word of split-mindedness behind you, and to indeed perceive the real world and to abide within it. And what can that real world be if not the extension of love that need not be sent through a filter of fear. For, indeed, it is that filter that keeps the mind split and the heart at least partially yet concealed. And when you choose wholly to remember the Truth of your being, then you hold the power and the freedom to give all things over to the Holy Spirit. You can throw open the shutters of the heart and even of the cells of the body and ask—and know you will receive—that every last trace of shadow shall be released from you.

For those of you that believe that healing can come only to the mind, is it not wise to ask where the mind is? And as I have sought to teach you—the body arises *within* the mind, not the other way around. And, therefore, what you see as these lumps of flesh express quite exquisitely the patterns of belief that you have held in the mind. For the body can only serve the thoughts you choose to hold, and it will do so to perfection.

Therefore, if there has been a thought or a belief grounded in the misperception that you are separate from God, and therefore in the soil of fear you have perceived an inequality between yourself and your brother and believe that you live in a fearful world, understand well that that creates reaction in the very cells of the body; and the cells themselves become like holding tanks and you hold on quite deeply and quite strongly to ancient wounds and ancient hurts.

And though you hold the thought in the mind,

> *I am the arisen Christ,*

until you are truly willing to throw open the shutters of even the cells of the body and to let all of those little dark shadows fly away, you are still holding on to one small dark belief, choosing to claim it as your own, and you have not released all things to the Holy Spirit for healing.

You cannot know what will transpire when truly you release the hold on that last little corner of your mind that you would hold on to and claim to be your own. But you can, with great faith, trust the process that the Holy Spirit would use to release every shadow—so that even the body becomes capable of radiance.

What is radiance? It is only the Light you are without anything creating an obstacle to its expression. Therefore, precious friends, fear not the release of the chronic hold you have had even within the cells of the body. For the body is only an extension of your thought.

If you are loved wholly and in your Father's eyes you have never sinned, what then is there to fear? To fear healing? To fear release? Indeed, to fear tears? Tears and laughter are your grandest of healers and your greatest of teachers. And I confess they are far greater than I, for all I can do is come and talk to you. I can come and bring my countenance upon you, and I can stand by your side as your friend and your brother—and I certainly don't mean just momentarily as I borrow the mind and body of my beloved brother here—but whenever you turn to me, I can be with you; for indeed I am with you always.

But what your laughter and tears can bring to you cannot be measured. Therefore, fear them not and judge them not. Do not create an inequality, saying,

> *Well, I much prefer laughter over tears.*

If you have made the choice to choose healing, then embrace your tears as much as your laughter, and give thanks when they arise. Throw open the shutters of the body and let the tears create shaking in the body. It cannot destroy you because you are not the body. You are that which utilizes it as a vehicle of communication. And when you therefore hold on in the palm of your hand to that shadow, it creates constriction in the body out of fear, and you are choosing to limit what this beautiful vehicle can do. And it will do precisely what you command it to do.

There is no one here who could not walk on water. There is no one here who could not extend healing through the body. And what prevents it? That small little corner that you have been holding on to for an awfully long time.

The message that I would bring you in this hour is this: fear not healing. Yes, it feels like change, and thank God for that. Because if there has been depression, there have been old wounds from which you have been acting out and acting out and acting out, as it is called in your language. Is it not time to release it? If you would indeed be the arisen Christ, then truly have the courage to throw open the cells of the body.

Now, how to you do that? You don't. But abiding in faith and asking the Holy Spirit for the help you need, indeed helpers will come because they have been assigned to you. And it will not be by accident that certain ones will come into your life; and in Truth if you are desirous of healing, be vigilant to see who it is that comes into your life. And understand that they are sent to you because you have asked of the one Teacher, Whose guidance never errs, for healing and for completion.

Healing, then, can often feel like death because, of course, it is. It is the death of a false illusion that you have held and clung to in error. And if you would be the servant of your Father—and I say this not in a serious vein but in a very light vein, because to be a servant of the Father is to be one who expresses love and joy and laughter and play and certainty and strength and humility and compassion and patience and vision—and if indeed you would be the servant of your Father, let that death occur down to the tips of your toes. You will not taste death, but an illusion will dissolve away.

Many of you are yet hoping, fervently hoping, that you can achieve awakening by holding the thought in the mind,

> *I am the arisen Christ.*

That is a great place—and the only place—to start. You cannot approach healing as long as you hold the attitude that you are separate from God, because you will create a veil of fear and you will go through process after process after process, but you will never get to the nub of it—because you don't want to.

Therefore, when you understand in the mind, in the heart, the Truth of who you are, that becomes the very foundation and the strength and the faith to allow the Holy Spirit to completely remake even the cells of the body. Notice that I said the cells of "the" body, not the cells of "your" body, because the arisen Christ knows he is not the body and does not possess it, that he does not begin where the body starts and he will not end when the body is returned to this Earth. He knows that the body is given of the Holy Mother for nothing save the extension of the unconditional Love of God.

And from that foundation you will find your strength to allow the complete and radical transformation of every aspect of your being: it is called the personality, which is just a mask made up of fear that can be translated into a vehicle of communication; the emotional body, which is the core where you have held all of those ancient wounds; and even the cells of the body. Therefore, your Kingdom shall be made new again.

Precious friends, fear not the complete healing of every trace of illusion that you have harbored within your being. And if it feels like death, then embrace it. It is the only death that truly counts, you see.

What, then, prolongs the process of healing? *Resistance* to it, born out of the chronic holding on to nothing more than illusions. And when that illusion has truly been laid down, the body will arise, the emotions will arise, the mind, the personality will arise—but will be made new. The dreamer will have been laid to rest and the arisen Christ will finally live through you.

And I ask you to join with me in the willingness to allow that healing to occur: to embrace your laughter and to embrace your tears and to embrace every opportunity to let go of the shadows that bind you.

> *How, then, can you ask the Holy Spirit to heal you if there are dark comers which you have refused to look at, or how can you hand to the Holy Spirit what you have not yet embraced?*

Illusions remain powerful when you refuse to acknowledge them. And many yet hold the fear:

> *What will happen if I truly look my illusions squarely in the eye and acknowledge that, by God, they have been controlling me? Will they be the demons that master me?*

Herein lies the purpose of faith: to know that you are the arisen Christ, that you abide in perfect union with God in the real world, and that you are given and sent to translate this unreal world of illusions and insanity into the real world; and you do it by acknowledging that yes, you have been living there all along and it is time to heal it.

Healing really does not take effort. It takes allowing. Allowing, allowing, allowing, every day and with every breath. So that your illusion—this *unreal* world—becomes translated and becomes the perfect reflection of the *real* world. And it can be painless when your perception changes, that healing is not frightful, that it is okay to cry in front of a friend. It is okay to pick up the phone and say,

> *Lordy, do I need you tonight.*

It's okay to say,

> *There is something going on that I don't understand, but I am not going to constrict. I am going to throw the body open. And if I convulse and if I vomit and if I cry and if I scream, who cares? It's just the release of old shadows that have no place in the body and the mind and the emotions of the only begotten child of God.*

It is well and good to recite certain words,

> *I am the arisen Christ. I live in joy and I live in Light.*

But if you have not looked to be sure that you have embraced every shadow, it remains in the realm of a thought and it has not yet manifested as your living reality.

That is why so many become frustrated. They do all the metaphysical games. They even come and listen to me and say,

> *Jeshua said I am the arisen Christ. Therefore, ah, I can avoid the process of healing.*

If you are the arisen Christ—and I assure you that you are—*you will want to embrace the very process of insuring that no trace of illusion remains within you.* You will not deceive yourself. You will not lie to yourself. And when those shadows are made present to your consciousness, you will give thanks to the Holy Spirit and to the brothers and sisters that have thrown them into your face, because they are messengers of God. They are saying,

> *Here, look at this, so that you can embrace it and release it.*

Fear not shadows, because you are made of Light, a Light so powerful that it can dissolve shadows in the instant you truly choose to embrace them and acknowledge them. That is how powerful each of you truly is. And the day comes when you no longer need helpers to dissolve those shadows, because with their help you have learned it's safe to embrace them, that they hold no power of mastery over you.

The only reason there are such things as healers or teachers or masters is because yet within the drama you believe you need them; and not understanding the strength within you, you need to reach out for the strength of another. By all means do so. One who is truly awakening to the Christ within them recognizes how worthy they are of the help of the universe.

And yet, how many times—and be honest—how many times have each of you felt that you are not really worthy of seeking and reaching out for help?

> *I better just stuff this. After all, I don't want to bother anybody today.*

Anyone know that energy?

God has created you as a Thought of perfect Love in form. And when you choose to manifest that reality, do you think He sits by idly and goes,

> *Well, I don't know if you are really worthy of what I can bring to you.*

It is just the opposite. You are the one to whom the universe is given. You—you—are the beloved of God.

Therefore, when you know you need help, reach out for it. To do so is an act of power. It says that you understand your worth and you will do anything to let Christ be born in you.

The time comes quickly upon this Earth when you are going to need to have made sure that you've healed every wound and every false perception. And the wounds can only be healed to the degree that you are willing to open up and allow that healing. Not to use the power of the mind to deceive yourself, but to understand the Truth of the long journey you've been making, because it's been very complex. You are never going to really be able to look back and pinpoint the moments when a certain perception started. It's not really necessary, but you will at times be able to access certain memories that exhibit the power of that false perception. And as those moments are healed, you have healed all of them.

And isn't that a lucky thing? It would be a rather long journey if you had to heal every moment in which you let a false perception lead you astray. But in each of those moments, they are really all the same. So to heal one is to heal them all. And whether healing comes because one taps into a past life, or healing comes because they have realized that yesterday they exhibited something that was not loving and they bring the Light of the Spirit to it because they have embraced it, the healing is the same, and they have healed the whole of their past. It is not necessary to hold the belief in reincarnation and it is not necessary to go forth a thousand lifetimes backward to find what needs to be healed. Because if it needs to be healed, it is with you right where you are.

Learn to look upon all of your thoughts and all of your actions and all of your dreams and all of your perceptions and ask of yourself,

> *Is this truly the will of God? Or is there a trace of fear in it? Is there a trace of limitation? Is this something that I've seen cropping up over and over again?*

If it crops up over and over, you know it is in need of healing.

Healing has been grossly misunderstood. It's really not the fixing of anything, because to do that assumes that it is already real and that there is someone who can fix it. *Healing is the mastery of allowing.* Healing is the mastery of allowing: to allow all things, so that they can be embraced and loved and thereby transcended. Never use the mind to minimize your behavior, your thoughts. Never use the mind to do that, because to do that you will only ensure that you will repeat that perception, that behavior, ad nauseam.

You are worthy of the depth of your healing. You are worthy of seeing that in Truth the journey has already been completed, and your Father is just waiting for you to truly throw open the shutters and allow the fullness of the power of Christ to be lived through you. And that is fearful to the small little shadow you have been clinging to.

You have heard it said in your world that many fear failure. The fear of failure ensures it. But a far greater fear is the fear of success. And in this term, in the use of this term, I am not talking about success in worldly terms. I am talking about the success of living as Christ, wholly, without obstacle or block. It is that fear that leads you to hold on to the small, powerless, weak and insane shadow that you have believed yourself to be since before time began. *It takes courage to release that. It takes courage to ask for help. It takes courage to die.*

The whole purpose of the crucifixion is not that it saved anybody from their sins. It never did that. The purpose of the crucifixion was to demonstrate where you will continue to be throughout all of eternity until you are willing to truly let that small little shadow die and to claim your power, not just as a thought or a belief—although that's where it starts—but to allow that power to transform the emotions and every cell of the body. Then, indeed, the resurrection has been realized.

And if I can raise the body and ascend unto my Father, so can you. I am not saying that you have to be able to be nailed to a cross so that the body dies and then resurrected in three days and ascend before your disciples. Of course not. I am saying that that was a demonstration of what has to happen to your perceptions of yourself, which is that which makes up the ego.

A true healer knows that they heal nothing. A true healer knows that they fix nothing. The truest among them simply makes themself available and learns to speak a language that the one who perceives themselves as sick or diseased can understand. And they will abide with them and they will speak that language and they will use their modalities that they have learned, but all the while they know Who It is that will effect the healing. It actually comes from the communication of that soul or that person with the Holy Spirit in whatever form they choose to think of it. And an agreement is made that healing will come because that soul has finally chosen to allow it. And often all they need is the safety of being with a healer.

The greatest of healers are those that have understood that they have needed to allow correction to come to their own mind and their own emotions and their own bodies. And, indeed, *the greatest of healers never cease in that process.* That is what keeps them in the line of power, if you want to call it that, so that the Holy Spirit can work through them.

A true healer is one who has, in a sense, made a grand sacrifice of their life. They no longer are anxious to get to the end of healing but they enact the act of healing daily, throwing themselves open always so that they remain in communication with those that come to them, and never forget what it means to be *in* the process of healing.

Now that is very paradoxical, and I hope you will take some time to contemplate it. Because in the act of, in a sense, donning the cloak of one who is constantly working on their healing, they are actually liberated. And out of their liberation they take on the form of one involved in healing, so that they can be with their brothers and sisters and be an effective channel of healing. Does that make sense? It is very important. Very important. If ever you come across a healer that says,

> *I have already got it all licked; now let me fix you,*

please turn around and leave, because that is an unhealed healer.

There are many of you in this room who are making shifts in consciousness, and your compassion has opened. Your understanding that there is nothing outside of you has begun to open, and you have thus begun to see that your brother and sister is not outside of you and *cannot* be outside of you. And out of your compassion, you want to help them heal. You will be effective to the degree that you allow, in every day, healing to come to you; and to never shut your heart to that process. And if it means that you think you may cry tears in every day of your life for the next two hundred and forty-seven years, you will gladly do it—because that keeps you in that line of power so that the Holy Spirit can work through your humble heart, and extend the healing to the one who has asked for it but needs you as an intermediary because their strength is not yet certain enough to come to the throne of God directly.

And the greatest of days will come when all of the healers that understand what it means to truly be healers are out of work. And then they, too, will rejoice because their work will have been finished.

Please do not fear healing. But I have come to speak about that specific subject tonight because there are some among you who are creating a dichotomy within yourself. You are actually widening the split while holding on to the illusion, created with the power of the mind, that you have already gotten it finished. Hmm. Anyone feel like that? You are worthy of being healed, so you might as well get on with it. The Kingdom *needs* you to be healed.

Will you know when it is completed? Here's the rub: *when in Truth healing has been completed, you won't even care* if it's been completed because your life will become, we will use the word here, sacrificed—but I don't mean it in your normal sense of loss. It is a gift given freely by you. It is like looking at your brothers and sisters and saying,

> *Gosh, they sure are enjoying groveling in the muck and mire. Because I love them I am going to get down on my hands and knees and grovel, too. And just maybe one of them will look at me, and if they look at me at the right time, the Holy Spirit might be able to work through me. But the Holy Spirit will never be able to work through me if I don't get down on my hands and knees.*

Enlightenment, salvation, is not about keeping the mud off of your knees. It is the freedom to be in the mud without identifying with it, but allowing yourself to be there as long as the Sonship still needs you.

Now, if that were not true, when I ascended to my Father I would have waved goodbye and I would have wished you well, but you would have never heard from me again.

Understand what I mean when I say that I have never really left this world and that I work without ceasing. I can only do so because I completed my part in the atonement as a man who walked upon this plane. Therefore, that is the path you, too, must take: to let yourself complete the process of healing, so that out of your freedom you can take on the cloaks of this world and look like everybody else until *they* learn that they are not separate from God.

I am only a temporary mediation-bringer to you, and the grandest of days that will come to me is when you look past me and need me no longer. But until that day I will work without ceasing because I love you. And every genuine healer understands the Heart from which those words are spoken, because they are spoken from the Heart of Christ. That is more than any one embodiment could ever contain. I am merely one who is like you but has become identified with the Christ, and I call you to do the same.

The water is fine. Jump in. But to jump in, you see, you have to remove your bathing suit of your wounds that you have refused to embrace so that they might be healed. There can't be any dust on your body when you jump into the water of eternity.

So many of you are standing on the platform constantly repeating that prayer,

> *Holy Father, let there be Light. However, I want to keep this little smudge on myself. I want to hold on to it as my own because I put a lot of energy into creating it. My God, I've spent lifetimes becoming as wretched as I could be and now You want me to let it go? I've spent lifetimes convincing myself that I am weak and frail and now You want me to let it go? How dare You. I have used the power You have given me, Father, to create unlike You and I have been rather proud of it. I have even created the sense that I am separate from You and that took a lot of doing. And now, You want me to let it go before I jump into that lake of eternity?*

Unfortunately, yes.

Let your life be a sacrifice. Not a painful sacrifice—that's been done a thousand times. It is not a lot of fun. Let your life be a sacrifice in the sense that you realize that you are just walking around pretending like you are a body, pretending like you are just a person so that you can make yourself available to those who still believe they need an intermediary.

A teacher of God is nothing but a temporary device. Please, I beg of you, contemplate well what I have shared with you. It is very important because it is really the journey of everyone, not just a special class of species that are called "healers". You are all healers, every one of you. Learn all you can about it. Apply it to yourself. Become one who loves to heal, not by groveling in your past, but just by noticing the nuances that come when certain circumstances seem to elicit reactions. Don't pretend it isn't happening or it will only continue. And that one veil, though subtle as it may seem, may be the very veil that keeps you eternally on the wheel of birth and death in the drama of separation.

If you want to see the planet healed, then be very fervently involved in your own healing. Not by picking yourself up by your bootstraps, but by asking for help and noticing what comes into your life. It's there for a reason. If indeed nothing arises by accident, then it must be there for a reason.

Now, does that mean that you need to take upon yourself great humility and seriousness, and say,

> *God, I'm such a wretched, sinful creature after all and I've been fooling myself. I have got to dig deep. Boy, do I have work to do.*

No, it means to embrace it and move into healing with joy and with strength and with certainty. Have fun with it.

> *Have you ever spent an hour seeing how deeply you can cry? It has been said by another teacher that some of you are familiar with, that every tear releases a thousand years.*

Well, what would one hour of true gut-wrenching crying do?

Get into it, because just the other side of those tears, divine laughter comes. Some of you have experienced that—when you are truly into it, something seems to shift. Anybody experience that?

[Audience agreement]

Then, why would you fear tears? Why would you fear what you have been taught to perceive as gut-wrenching *pain*? That is just an illusion of perception. When the body shakes with tears, you have been taught to believe it is because you are weak and wretched. Those that can allow tears exhibit great strength.

I hope it all makes sense. Some of you in this room while I have been speaking about this, rather forcefully, have felt a little contraction like,

> *Oh, God, do I really have to do this?*

Yes. And your delight rests just on the other side of doing it. When you are in pain, don't deny it. Own it. It does not mean that you take on the perception that you are anything other than Christ. Even in your pain, even if memories are coming up, you can still keep your attention on the Light of Christ and bring that Light to it without blocking it, without cutting it off. It is indeed most empowering to know and to experience that you can be wailing and at the very same moment directing the healing Light of Christ right into the wailings, because those wailings are lifting the lid; and what's bubbling up out of it can then be healed by the Light that is coming to it.

The healer is just one that helps to do that for you until you figure out that you can do it for yourself. And a genuine healer will always rejoice when they perceive and see,

> *Thank God, they don't need me any longer. Now I can go on to the next person.*

So, I know that was all of a bit of a lengthy greeting but sometimes it's necessary. I love you. I love you so much that I gave my life for you. Will you love yourself with that intensity that you are willing to lay down your life for yourself? Because *you* are worth it.

Participant: Jeshua?

Yes.

Participant: Well, I was crying today in the presence of a friend but I felt myself holding back because I felt that this person was uncomfortable with it. And it seems to happen more often that way.

Precious friend, first, if you hold back the process of those tears because you sense that the other is uncomfortable, what you are really choosing to say is that their perceptions hold more reality than yours and you must acquiesce and conform yourself to them. That person who seems to resist the tears of a friend may actually need you to truly let the power of your tears come out—so that they learn that they don't have to be uncomfortable with one who is releasing and healing, that they have the strength to be present.

Never hold back your tears. Never hold the belief that someone else's need to resist those tears and to be uncomfortable with yours . . . never hold the perception that their insanity is more important that your healing. That is to take power away from yourself.

Now, therefore, first, in such a situation really let them come out, and if that one is so uncomfortable that they have to leave you, send them love and go find another friend until you find one that can be with you. That's only claiming what you are worth. And until you claim what you are worth, your healing can't truly come to its completion.

Does that make sense to you?

Participant: Yes, I hope I can remember that.

Will you choose to remember it?

Participant: Yes.

Good. That makes all the difference: not that you hope, but that you choose with all of your power to always remember that you have a right to be healed. You don't know the hour or the day when these things are going to be released. But allow them, because when you hold back in order to be conformed to the perceptions of another, you are denying yourself the opportunity to be rid of who-knows-what that may have been held for an awfully long time. And when will the conditions arise again that allow that opportunity to be handed to you?

Know you that saying, "Seize the day"?

Participant: Yes, the opportunity.

Yes. Time is given to you so that you learn to use it constructively. And if there is a shadow or weight upon the heart and an opportunity comes, through time, for you to release it and you don't take advantage of it, have you used time constructively?

Many in your world have learned to use a simple device to avoid healing. It has usually a little knob on it, and you turn it and a bunch of little dots create images on the screen. You know what I am talking about? How many times have you when you have been feeling alone, a little depressed, a little sad and confused, how many times have you turned it on? Or sought other ways to distract yourself?

That is not a very constructive use of time, and it only ensures that you are going to have to face certain conditions that must arise and to prod that stuff up again.

> *I am going to shove it back down, turn on the television, or find some other distraction.*

Participant: So, is one of the purposes of 'special' relationships to stuff our guilt?

Yes, 'special' relationships are rather interesting. Most of the time the ego will convince you that you are really looking for that one heartfelt relationship when indeed what you are really doing is looking for someone who can play your game with you and keep you from truly getting on with it:

> *Ah, we are going to have so much fun. We'll do this and this and*

that and that.

And there is nothing wrong with having fun, but a special relationship is actually designed by the ego to serve the ego, and you all know what that means.

A holy relationship is founded within two souls that have chosen to come together because they are sick and tired of not getting on with it. They don't come together to drown themselves out with all the devices of distraction of the world. They come together and are willing to allow the uniting of their energies to bring it all up and get rid of it. A holy relationship is for healing and service, not for satisfying egos.

A holy relationship is what you can offer your brother or sister every time you see them, if you would but first make the choice within yourself not to use them to fill you, certainly not to use them so that you can hold on to opinions and judgments, but to be with them openly and honestly and completely. And if they choose to be with you in the same way, you indeed experience a Holy Instant. And no matter what seems to have been going on, there is a feeling of peace that comes, and the value of that encounter makes it timeless and eternal and precious, and it will always be remembered because ultimately the Son of God will remember only loving thoughts.

Holy relationship is everything in the real world. Special relationships are everything in the unreal world that you have created in error.

Choose then, choose to be one so humbled by this vast journey that all you want is holy relationship—not relationship that serves you or gratifies you, but relationship through which the Holy Spirit can awaken both you and your brother or sister right where you are, so that you can experience that Holy Instant of perfect sacred intimacy in which you have looked beyond all illusions and have seen the equality of the Love of Christ in the one before you, and therefore have recognized it in yourself.

The habit of special relationships runs deep and it needs to be interrupted constantly. When you go to see your brother or sister, take just a moment and pause,

> *Why am I really doing this? Is it out of distraction? Is there something I am trying to glean from them? Can I choose to just be with them, to love them? And to open the place in me so that their love can be received, to create the opportunity for the Holy Instant?*

When a master walks upon this Earth—and they have many names and many of you know of many masters—what is it, what is it in them that leads those that follow them, or their disciples, or their friends, or those that study with them, to feel such depth of gratitude? Is it their teaching? That helps. But what it is truly is that a master always looks through the eyes of Christ and extends the opportunity for a Holy Instant to everyone that he contacts or she contacts. And what makes the master loved by the student (to use that term) is that the student has experienced an instant in which they, too, chose to see the master through the eyes of Christ and there was an experience of a Holy Instant.

Now, initially they will think the master did a grand thing for them. Eventually they will learn that it was their power, too, and their choice to join in sacred intimacy.

Practice, then, being masters. Not because you believe you are, but because you have the power to do so. Make a little game of it. When you rest your head on your pillow at the end of your day, go back over your day and count the times you remembered to enter into encounters—or relationships, because every encounter is relationship—how many times did you do so from the standpoint of holiness? And how many times did you forget?

At first you will be rather amazed how small the count is, but it will grow as you practice it. You have simply practiced forgetting holiness; and if you have therefore learned specialness, you can unlearn it. Time is given to you that you might learn to use it constructively. And yet, still, so many of you that have heard this same message for a year are allowing many of your days to go by in unconsciousness.

Why? Why would you want to continue doing it?

> *Well... habit.*

Holy relationship is everything, and you are the one who can bring it and give it to your brother and your sister. Now, the mind will tell you that there seems to be a dichotomy here:

> *How can I be involved with healing and yet extend holy relationship?*

Contemplate it because they work together perfectly. The one who is truly open to healing and who will hold on to no dark shadow within them, one who is willing to spend the rest of their incarnation allowing healing to occur is one who already has the power to extend the opportunity for holy relationship because there is no pretense left in them.

Makes sense?

So, have a lot of fun getting together with your friends and talking about your healing journeys and how many times you have extended the opportunity for holy relationship. See, masters can get together and can have a great time rejoicing at all the times they blow it. Hmm.

False holiness says,

> *I am perfect and I am healed.*

True holiness says,

> *Oh, my goodness gracious, did I blow that one today. Yikes! Father, I still need Your help.*

False holiness says,

> *I've got it all figured out now, Father. Goodbye.*

True holiness says,

> *Of myself I do nothing but the Father through me does all things.*

It requires a lot of humility of seeing that you've never been able to heal yourself. You don't know what a single thing is for and none of your perceptions have ever been wholly true. So why cling to them?

And when an insight comes for a moment and you extend it to your brother or sister, you might as well let go of it, because you don't really know where it came from. You don't know the purpose it's going to serve, and you can never be sure of it. But the Holy Spirit knows how to use it.

Do you know how to recognize a false teacher or a false healer?

> *Well, I see that you've got this real serious problem here and I can fix it here, and oh, yes…*

And tomorrow they will still remember telling you those things because they need to cling to their perception of themselves as a healer. A genuine healer allows healing to be done and whatever happens, happens; and then it is gone, so that they are empty and ready for the next opportunity. And they *never allow the insights to come from crystallized pictures or metaphysical beliefs about how the universe is structured.* That takes great arrogance.

Once I said to you that certain words that seem to come through me and have been written down a million times called the Sermon on the Mount, I said unto you that when those words poured through me, when that hour was over and certain of my friends said,

> *Boy, you were really on,*

I said to them,

> *What did I say?*

I couldn't even remember it and I couldn't have cared less. I was moving on to the next moment in which I might have an opportunity to extend a chance for holy relationship, and that is all.

Be, therefore, healers of the world by clinging to nothing, not even your old wounds and your old pain, and certainly never cling to the belief that you have got it all together. You are here to take on the form of your brothers and sisters who are groveling in the muck and mire of false perceptions, to take on the appearance so that they can look upon you as one of their own, and you never know how the Spirit will work through you. And when it's done, it's done. Let it go. Release the illusion that to awaken means that you get to go somewhere else and never get your hands dirty again. It's just the opposite.

How will you know, then, when you are truly awake? When you can't wait to find ways to serve and to be available always to serve your brother and sister. When you cry out to God,

> *Give me more opportunities. I'm dying sitting here in my living room.*

Then you'll know you have really begun to awaken.

> *Bring them to me, Father. I don't care. I know I can do this. I'll just be there. Bring them to me. You can do it all through me. I know you can. Bring them to me. What avenues can I use to heal this world?*

Knowing, of course, that you are not the healer; you are just the messenger. Then you will know that you have really awakened.

When you don't care if you are exhausted every day, when you no longer care whether your ego is being gratified, when you no longer care about anything but finding ways to help others heal and being available to do it, and if the Holy Spirit says:

> *Get on a plane and go here for one day and then get on another plane and travel halfway across the world to another place, and you*

will only see one client.

—and you know that that is perfect—then you will know that a miracle has been worked through you and has happened to you.

I have said that awakening comes as a thief in the night, stealing the cobwebs of shadows outgrown. And I have also said that salvation comes by your extending love to your brother and sister because *salvation can only be realized by sharing it.* Therefore, when you find yourself so passionately involved in not being able to do anything but find someone to extend love to, whatever modalities seem to work, and when you see miracles happening in others, then when you rest your head on the pillow, you will be able to remember that the thief has come in the night and begun to steal your own cobwebs, because if miracles are worked through you, they must have occurred to you. And then you will give thanks, and you will laugh and rejoice at how healing truly occurs. Indeed.

Precious friends, if I come and blend with the mind and body of this my beloved brother—who finally got so sick and tired of trying to figure it out that he just threw his hands up in the air and said, 'What the hell. I don't understand it. You do it.'—if by coming for these three short years, just one of you hears something or receives something that moves you one inch, it will have been a work well served, because when any one of you moves just a smidgen, you will have uplifted the whole of creation. And that is powerful indeed. That is a miracle. And ultimately again you will come to see that your choice for healing, the ability to take the risk for healing, comes from the power of the Christ in you because you always awaken to your own call. You have been calling to yourself. Hear your call and allow it. And in that alone you are already the Light of the world.

Now, if you really understand all of that, then, you see, there is no more time for frowns upon the face, heaviness upon the shoulders. Now, you may experience those as you are releasing and allowing healing to occur, but the rest of the time you are going to be singing and dancing because you are going to see that you are healing out of the power of Christ Himself. And if you are healing out of the power of Christ, you can rest assured that the end is inevitable. But as long as you try to heal out of your smallness, the end is not inevitable. *Claim the power of Christ as yourself and open to your healing and allow it.*

And then sing and dance and play because you have finally figured out there is nothing else to do and isn't it great? All of those demons are just little pussy cats. You might as well pet them.

Participant: Jeshua?

Yes.

Participant: I am listening to you say "of the world" and "in the world" and I have a memory of that written in the Bible, and I also am sensing that when that was spoken, it is resonating something in me that I am not aware of why. But it is important to me to ask this question.

Beloved friend, I want you to first understand that often what I talk about in these groups, while of course it is for everyone in general, it is often given specifically for one or two or five who are at a certain place in their journey, and certain words are going to resonate as an energy that gets things moving. I am not here going to address with words the answer to your question, but I am going to ask you to keep that feeling that you noticed, and as you rest your head on your pillow, ask yourself the question you just asked me—not with a rigidity of mind, but with a relaxed body and heart, letting the angel of air move deeply through the body. Ask, not trying to hear the answer, but to feel it, because what is at work here is not a concept at all. There is an energy at work that you have allowed to touch your soul, and it is going to release and heal something that you have held on to for some time. Willing to do that?

Participant: Yes.

Do you think it will be worth it?

Participant: Everything so far is.

Ah, thank you.

Participant: Even when I am over my head.

Count it as a blessing when you think you are over your head, because you will stop trying to grasp it with the mind and you will begin to allow it with the heart.

Participant: Thank you for you.

Thank you for you.

Participant: You are welcome.

And thank you for your "Thank you".

It's actually a lot of fun to sit down with a friend and just do that.

> Thank you for you.
> Thank you for you.
>
> Thank you for your thank you.
> Thank you for your thank you.
>
> Thank you for your thank you, thank you.

Spend an hour doing that.

Participant: Jeshua, I want to thank you for something. Two and a half days ago I found myself in a situation that I found very, very painful and confusing and upsetting. It took me until today and with a little help from Jon Marc to sort things out; and once they were sorted out I was really elated all afternoon, like a great weight had been lifted off my shoulders. And then I found, driving over here tonight, that I was getting depressed because I was disappointed that it took me so long to practice what you have been teaching. But while I have been sitting here listening to you tonight, I definitely got the message that I– and we- need to be patient with ourselves So that's something that I heard from you that has put me back in a relaxed state.

I am sorry to have affected your tension!

So, precious friend, indeed, be patient. As I have shared with you, I learned from the lips of a very holy teacher that I worked with when I was a child. Some of you are aware of this one who is named in certain ancient scripts, called the "Teacher of Righteousness". The Teacher of Righteousness was never born of a woman but manifested a physical form to serve as a teacher. And one thing he said to me always remained with me. He said,

> *Jeshua ben Joseph, patience is to make power slowly and certainly.*

So don't be impatient. You are worth the best you can offer yourself. Therefore, be patient with yourself. Now, on your way over here, yes, you decided to whip yourself.

Participant: Right. That's so right.

When you notice you are whipping yourself, go,

> *Ah yes, there I am whipping myself. That's a beautiful one.*

And then embrace it and love it and it will fade away because the Holy Spirit will come as the thief and will steal that cobweb from you and you won't even notice it until you look back and it will have been a week or two or three, six months or a year, and you will say,

> *Gosh, I haven't really whipped myself since, I can't even remember when. Where did it go?*

A little miracle.

Participant: That will be wonderful.

Not that that will *be* wonderful. It *is* wonderful.

Participant: That's in the present tense.

Yes. So, how are we all doing?

Participant: Fine. Good.

Thank you for allowing me to deliver that message. It was rather important, in some degree for all of you, but specifically for just a handful because of some things that are going on in your own processes.

Participant: Jeshua, would you repeat one more time what your teacher told you to do—build something slowly?

Beloved friend, I don't have time.

[Laughter.]

Well, actually that's true: I don't have *any* time.

Patience is to make power slowly and certainly.

The grandest of your artists have never hurried through their creations. And you are a great creation indeed, worthy of meticulous reshaping.

You see, *when you have truly learned to master time—to use it constructively always—time ceases for you* even if others perceive that the same body and personality is still dwelling in it. For you it has ceased. And when time ceases, all of the long journey and all of the wounds and all of the heaviness is gone. It's a rather nice feeling, by the way. But, paradoxically, then you become totally free to do what has been called, in your Christian terminology "to take on the sins of the world". That is to take on the appearance of time and to be in it as long as it takes for the whole of the Sonship to have mastered the constructive use of time.

Participant: On the constructive use of time... When I told you that I had a chance to go and stay at a friend's home on a beautiful lake, you recommended that I go, even though I had free will and could choose to do what whatever. And I chose to go, and at the time I was asking you about it, you cautioned me to use my time wisely. Now, I have been up there for the better part of two weeks, with two trips to town, and I am learning that I am not quite sure what to do with time. I have always had so many things to do with time, it feels very strange. I don't know if I need to kind of structure my time. I think I have a tendency to do that too much and yet, when I just sort of hang out, l am a little uncomfortable with that. What do you think I should do?

Does it matter?

Participant: Well, I would like to make lots of progress, more or less.

Then, do so. But understand, precious friend, that you hold the power in every moment to stop the whirlings of the mind, to set them aside and say,

> *Holy Spirit, what is the most constructive use of time that I can now employ?*

He will not hide it from you. For when you want specific answers, the Holy Spirit will give them.

For me to say,

> *Well, the constructive use of time would be not to structure it at all,*

would not be wholly true. And if I said unto you,

> *The constructive use of time is to structure all of it,*

that would not be wholly true.

The constructive use of time requires your decision to turn to the one Teacher Whose guidance is always unerring, and to trust what you hear. Although you may not hear words, you might have a feeling or an intuition. That is the constructive use of time.

Participant: What other use is there?

Ah, you've let the cat out of the bag.

Participant: I keep thinking I should hear a voice within myself.

Ah. Coming from the clouds of Heaven?

Participant: Well, at least something that is distinctly other than me.

Beloved friend, that is the illusion of separation.

Participant: I have been having such a problem with that. Sometimes it's good to say things out loud just to hear how erroneous it sounds.

The Holy Spirit is closer to you than your own breath. Now, it is important…

Participant: It is what you know in your deepest heart.

Your deepest heart *is* the union of the Father and Son.

Participant: I've got it!

Ah.

Now, some of you that can see energies that are not usually seen with the physical eyes, if you were watching in that moment, you saw a shift in the change of the color of light around this one, and what you saw would or could be perceived or described as the weight of a thousand lifetimes being lifted. Now we will find out if she lets it remain there.

Participant: Oh, I want to. I will.

Know that I love you always and I come always as your servant. I can't be anything else. I simply can't be anything else, and I don't want to be. I love you and I will love you until the whole of the Sonship has its "Aha". And those of you that choose to join with me, and understand that because I am your friend and your brother, in whatever way you choose to serve, all you have to do is ask and I will come running. When you open the door, I will join with you and together we will assist our brothers and sisters in their own process of awakening. I am available to any of you all of the time. Some of you know that.

Peace be unto you and we will see you soon. Amen.

[Short break.]

Beloved friends, what is in Truth the whole heart and essence of healing?

To share with one another from a point of equality, of seeing no one as above you and no one as below you, and seeing not yourself as more perfect than another. But to see that you *are* one another, and to realize that it is in the sharing of your journey, the willingness to listen and to love, that brings healing to the heart and to the soul. And forever the soul, which is the Son of God, is one. Though there be many bodies and personalities attached, you are but one Mind and one Heart. And when you choose to join together, you have chosen the creation of holy relationship, and even in these few moments you have extended the Holy Instant unto one another.

Therefore, always remember that there is but one thing taking place: the awakening of the holy Son of God—or Daughter, if you prefer. It makes little difference; it's all words. But you are that one, and the language that I use is used only as a point of identification so that you can recognize me.

Beloved and holy Son of God, great is my love for you, for indeed you are already all that I am. Therefore, the one known as Jeshua, that which I am that came and walked among you, could be no other but yourself. The entire drama is yours and there is nothing outside of you. Every pain felt by a brother or sister is your pain, and it is only through your extension of love that you can heal yourself of that pain. To judge another's pain or another's thought or another's behavior is to ensure that it will continue within *you*. Perhaps in a different form, but it will continue. Therefore, indeed, it is only love that heals. It is love that I am and it is love that you are. Everything else is the result of an illusion and a mistaken perception.

That is why a master greets anger with love. That is why a master greets attack with love. For when you believe you are attacked and therefore become defensive, you have asserted with the power of Christ that attack is real, and you have made sure that you will continue to experience attack.

Meet all things with love. Greet all things with love. See in the eye of even a blade of grass, yourself. Indeed, I am the holy Son of God given to the world of my Father because He loves you. Where have I come from? The Heart of God. Where have you come from? The Heart of God. We are one and the same.

Therefore, when I come forth and create a demonstration or an appearance of being Jeshua ben Joseph, it is only to animate a physical form because you have believed yourself to be the body, to teach you that you are Spirit and that you are One. The only reality that in Truth can be, is that the holy Son of God is one, united always with all that God is. And salvation is complete on Earth as it is in Heaven when the Sonship awakens to the Truth of its reality.

That is why I have asked you to join with me to extend the Kingdom to your brother and to your sister. And when you see them in error or in pain, embrace them. Offer them through holy relationship the opportunity for the Holy Instant that heals all things. You are the ones; you are the bringers of Light into this world.

I ask you only to let me walk with you. And what does that mean but to recognize that the heart and essence of your being *is* Jeshua*; is* Christ*; is* the offspring of Light divine by whatever name you choose to call it. God is Love and therefore I love you. You are the Grace of God in form. That is who you are. Embrace your brother and your sister. Embrace them with all of your being, not just your mind, not just your heart. Use the arms your Holy Mother has given you.

I am going to ask each and every one of you this week in each of your days to call someone you haven't spoken with lately and tell them how much you appreciate their being, because their being in your life has been serving your awakening. Let them know from the bottom of your heart how much you love them for that. Encourage them to be the Truth of who they are and to never deviate from listening to the voice of Spirit that speaks not in the mind of the ego, but in the quietness and the gentleness of the heart. Encourage them to follow the path that they feel they must follow, because there is a reason for it. And the reason serves the atonement of the Sonship.

Indeed, if you could look through the eyes of the Christ—and, of course, you can because that's who you are—and you would never again lament anything that unfolds in your experience or your drama because you would see the exquisite perfection that those moments are serving. Nothing happens by accident and not one of you holds an experience in isolation from the whole of the Sonship. Everything you taste and feel and think and experience is felt and touches the entire community of Christ the Sonship. Everything.

Love every moment that comes to you. Embrace it and honor it. If it means that you cry a thousand tears, then let your tears be a way in which you honor that moment. And if your brother or sister is in pain, embrace them. Don't tell them,

Why are you doing this? You are creating your own reality.

That is nonsense and it is hurtful. For well have I seen that idea being misused in your metaphysical circles. When your brother and sister is in pain, embrace them and feel it with them and allow it to be felt by them. When they are ready to think about it, you will know. Let them feel it. Tell them you know what it feels like. It is called empathy, not judgment.

Ah, beloved and holy child of God, you are one with me. You are one with me. Embrace me. Claim me as the reality of your own being. Claim me. Will I disappear from you? No. I am your brother and I am your friend and I am all that you are, and I choose to be what you are in the fullness that you have yet, for a little while, chosen to resist; and I will never cease in coming to you, because I love you, until finally you decide it's time. Then all healing will occur, and you will be brought rapidly through miracle after miracle after miracle to swiftly be all that I represent to mankind.

You shall be the worker of miracles. And that is given unto you even now. And in this hour as I stood nearby, and stood in the midst of you, you extended miracles one unto another, because in this hour and in this place you have come and you choose to set aside the perceptions taught you of your world that are wholly insane, and you choose to come together to allow love to heal.

And if not a word is said to you in the whole hour or the whole evening and you would sit there quietly, understand that you participate actively in the healing of every mind and every heart that chooses to come to these gatherings. That is how powerful you are and how precious your presence is. You can be on the floor with your best friend and still be involved in the healing of every mind and heart. Therefore, when another is speaking, let not the mind wander, but just sit there and embrace them with love. Miracles happen naturally and effortlessly to minds and hearts that choose only love.

Love and judgment can never abide in the same moment. Love is of the Kingdom; judgment is of hell. What will your choice be? You are the Light of the world. You *are* the Light of the world. *You are the Light of this world*, and it needs it so desperately.

Be love. Teach love. And therefore you will learn that you are love. Don't just expect miracles. Know that you are the one that is sent to allow miracles to be given through you. It just happens when you choose to love.

Short is the time that is given me to join with you in this rather unusual way. And when I walked upon this plane, I would have never guessed that I would be doing this work with this, my beloved brother. My Father hadn't let me in on it yet. It's probably a good thing He didn't. Hmm. Can you know what is around the corner for you? Do you need to know? The mind that is fearful looks ahead and wonders. The mind that is awake lives in this moment and it is enough, because that mind knows that it is sustained by the Love of God, and if it is true in this moment, it certainly won't change in the next.

Be at peace, then, in all things and give no thought for tomorrow, what you shall eat and what you shall wear and what career you might have five years from now. But own the presence of Love now and the future will very easily take care of itself. And you shall be more then than you think you are today.

I love you. Please do me but one favor: love your brothers and sisters, though you don't even know their names, as you believe I have loved you. And if you have felt that love, *please give it away*. In so doing you have honored the Son that dwells within you, and by honoring the Son that dwells in you, you have indeed honored me, and I give thanks for every moment you choose to extend your love to another.

I shall never leave you; and when this brief work is done, think not that I will go away from you. But I call you to quicken your choice to hear me and to abide with me always as your friend and as your brother.

I love you and I want you to be my friend. And even though you are in a body, think not that that body can be an obstacle to our communion, our communication and our celebration that we are as our Father has created us to be: the Thought of perfect Love in form. And if you seem to have the form of a body while I seem not to, what difference does it make?

There are no obstacles to minds that join in love. Forgive your brother and sister. Forgive yourself for ever having thought that you were separate one from another, that the world was a place in which you needed to be fearful. For perfect love casts out fear, which has been your only enemy. Fear blocks the knowledge of the Kingdom. Let that perfect Love, therefore, be in you, even as it is in me, given to you.

I love you, holy Son of God. Pray not to die, but to live eternally and to let your Light heal this world. Give your love away and you will never be without it. Peace be unto you. Peace be unto the only begotten offspring of God, created changeless and perfect. That is who you are. And let that power of that perfection heal every illusion ever held within your mind and in your emotions and in your body. Honor your Holy Mother by letting that healing come to the cells of your body. Hmm.

Yes, indeed, that indeed the Kingdom of Heaven might be wed with the Kingdom of this Earth, that Spirit and matter might be united as one and the love of Christ be extended as far as from the East unto the West, until it embraces the whole of the creation and *all* of us return home as one. Give your peace away and you will *never* lose it.

And what I said will eternally remain true: I am with you always. I can hardly be anywhere else. I love you, and I thank you for being willing to entertain the thought that just maybe Jeshua can borrow a body and a mind long enough to communicate with words.

But unto each and every one of you—and I speak of when you return to your abodes and rest your head upon your pillow—*I will come* to each and every one of you. Will you open the door and allow me in?

Peace be unto you. Remember, call someone each day of your following week that you haven't spoken with for a while and share from your heart what I have asked you to share. You don't have to. Don't do it begrudgingly. Do it with a lot of lightness and fun. Get into feeling how powerful the love is that is in you that longs to be given away, and it will transform the whole of your week.

Yet a little while and I will be with you no more. Cherish, then, these few moments given us, for when the form of this work is gone, it is gone. But I hope you will have used it as a bridge to come wholly to where I am, for I wait to truly embrace you without an inch of distance between us. Yet we shall work together to serve the atonement of the Sonship. We shall love every brother and sister that the Holy Spirit brings to us, and though you may not yet see the form of the work you will be doing, it will be revealed to you.

And I will join with you as your friend and your brother, and together—as one—we shall embrace the whole of creation and offer it, on the platter of the awakened Heart of Christ, back to the Father. What else is there to do?

Peace be unto you.

Amen.

THE HOLY SPIRIT
June 1992

Now we begin.

Indeed, greetings unto you yet once again, beloved and holy children of Light divine. For in Truth you are created before time is and indeed even now you abide in that which is timeless and eternal, has never been born and will never taste death.

I know that's confusing to the mind of the world; but indeed if you would know Truth, you must in a sense turn the back of your awareness on all perceptions and ideas that the world has sought to teach you. For the world is nothing but the reflection of the limited perception that the holy and only child of God can indeed be separate from all that our Father is. And from that belief the world that you have experienced many times has been born.

Therefore, if you would know the Truth of the Kingdom, turn the back of your consciousness to every perception the world has taught you. It is indeed the meaning of 'turning the other cheek'.

It does not mean that if one would slap you on the left side, to let them slap you on the right, but rather to see and understand how the perceptions of the world have created for you—and you all know what I mean by this—the experience of being slapped on the left cheek. You know what I mean—a bit of suffering here and there, a bit of disappointment, expectations not achieved—and some of you are well aware of how many times you have gathered together the molecules of dust to form a body only to find that it has not kept you safe and, therefore, it has gone back to the dust of the ground again.

Would you be willing, would you in Truth be willing to turn the other cheek? That is, to turn away for just a moment from the perceptions born of the world and to ask that Truth be restored to you? For indeed a primary perception your world would have you learn and hold is that you already know what Truth is. That it can be measured, it can be tasted. That it is like a box that contains many other beliefs about birth and life and death, the meaning of special relationships, the hope that in the body you can find freedom. *That you are here to be 'the creators of your own reality' is utter nonsense.* Utter and complete nonsense.

Let no one say unto you that you are here to create your reality, for you are here but to allow the expression, unimpeded, of the only reality that could ever be: The reality of the perfect and holy union of Father and child, of God and child, of Love and the extension of love.

There is no effort in this. Effort comes from resistance to the simplicity of the only Truth that can ever be: that you are but Love and that is all. And your function and your purpose rest solely in the extension of the Love you are. For indeed, as you give that love away, you will know that you have received it.

How can you create a reality that is the basis of your eternal being? You cannot. It is given unto you freely. For though you can be one with God, you have not created God. But God has created you, for the Son is the offspring of that Light of Love divine, and you find your purpose and your function and your fulfillment every time you turn the cheek away from the world, so that the head and the eyes of the heart turn with it and you behold a different Voice, a Voice that speaks softly, speaks gently, without fear, without longing, without anxiety. A Voice that does not tell you in the future you will find the peace you seek, but a Voice that whispers so gently, *You are already the peace you seek.*

The world cannot bring it to you and this world cannot take it from you. And yet, it is in the giving of it that you will know that you possess it eternally.

Now, what does that mean in practical terms?

It means this—and if you would contemplate this one thought daily, it will bring many shifts to your perceptions, healing to the perception. The thought is simply this: there cannot be at any time, at any place, in any dimension of this drama—this dream that some of you think is real—*there cannot be a single set of circumstances that hold the power to destroy your right to choose peace. Nothing.*

Not the birth and death of a child. Not the loss of a relationship. Not a bankruptcy. Not major cataclysms upon this Earth. Not a steak that has been cooked too long. Hmm. Not one thing can steal from you the freedom of the choice given unto you that rests in the essence of your mind and your heart to choose peace. Nothing. And if that is true—and I assure you that it is—it also means this: there can be no special circumstances you need to achieve before you can choose to be the peace that you seek.

> *Shucks. But, Jeshua, that takes the whole game away. It brings a stop to the world.*

Good. Good. For in Truth, when the world is stopped—which means the mind stops spinning in its attempt to create its reality that it thinks will bring it peace, and allows itself to become as a servant of the heart, in which stillness abides and in which peace has never been lost, and through which the Love of God seeks to be extended through you like great rays of Light that would caress and enfold the whole of creation—indeed, when the mind is set at rest and it becomes the servant of the heart, then everything vanishes right before your eyes. Hardly.

And yet, it does, doesn't it? Because what you see is an act of *perception*, and it could well be said that all you ever see and all that you ever experience is your reaction to what you choose to perceive is in front of you. And what you perceive is directly related to what you choose to believe. What you *choose* to believe.

You do not believe something because the data of the physical senses prove that it exists. Rather, the data of the physical senses reflect to you the belief you have chosen.

> *I cannot walk upon hot coals.*

Nonsense

> *I cannot possibly walk on water.*

That is nonsense, too, unless of course you believe it—in which case it would be rather wise to use a boat.

> *I cannot survive in this world unless I find someone to give me a job.*

Do you know what it is like to be in a plane, as you would perceive it, removed from this physical plane, and to look into your culture and see these buildings that you have? For every day countless thousands of people line up to sign their name on some kind of a form so that some authority sends them a few shekels of golden coins—and you call it unemployment.

No one is unemployed save by their total free choice to be in that experience. Why? Not because there are not enough jobs to go around, but because nobody needs a job unless they believe they do. Within you there is great creativity because within you the Kingdom of Heaven lies, and there is no one on the face of this planet who cannot allow that creativity to spring forth, to break through the limitations that you have held onto for so long, and indeed find a way to contribute—to extend your love into this world—in a way that provides you with a roof over your head and food for the belly. No one.

But those who believe that there is an authority outside themselves with a greater power, will hold the belief that reality means that you find a job and you go to it from nine to five until somebody tells you that you can go home. It is just a belief, and that is all it is. And that belief creates a limitation within your own consciousness, and everything you do and experience becomes somehow enmeshed with the limitations of that one simple belief.

Does that make sense to you?

And yet, what takes place and has already occurred in several of you:

> *If what Jeshua is saying to me now is true, and I happen to be one who works nine to five, knowing full well here in the secrecy of my mind, I don't really like it,*

What comes up if what I am saying is true? Is it not fear?

> *The set of circumstances, I see, have become limiting to me. I chose them at a time when I didn't know that another choice was available to me. Now I am beginning to learn. Now I am beginning to awaken. Oh my goodness, could I possibly let go of the belief that another must give me a job so that I can sustain myself?*

The question I would ask you is simply this: *what do you want?*

Seems simple enough doesn't it? What do you want? For what you want you *will* experience.That is the golden rule of how consciousness works and you are consciousness.You have wanted a job as much as you have wanted a physical body.As much as you have wanted special relationships. As much as you wanted to believe that you must eat a certain food three times a day every day of your life in order to sustain your health; you can't dare change it. It all comes from a want because the perception has told you that what you are perceiving and believing can make you safe and keep you safe.

There is only one problem: the soul you are knows that it is unlimited forever, and you can deny what the soul knows only so long. True, you could deny it for lifetimes but sooner or later a movement begins, for the soul cannot be denied forever. And it will begin to press out against every belief and perception you have ever carried, and it will make you question everything you have held to be true and valuable—and yes, that will bring up the experience you call fear. But on just the other side of that narrow ring of fear there is a perception that would see it as a blessing—as a blessing that comes directly from God. For the soul presses you to examine the beliefs you have carried that have created the world of your experience, but not your reality. And the soul asks you,

> *Allow my wisdom into the small part of the mind that clings to the belief, and if you would but trust my guidance, I will show you how to walk through that ring of fear.*

For indeed within each and every one of you lies equally what is also within me.

I am not a savior above anyone in this room, much less anyone on this planet. And if I could learn how to return and listen to that one Voice and trust It and It alone, so can you. That is why I ask you, *What is it that you want?*

For notice that I have never said there is something wrong with having a job. It's a matter of the belief you carry that creates that situation for you. Are you happy? Are you contributing all that you want to contribute? Not what somebody tells you could contribute, but what you want to contribute? It is the only place you can find freedom. The only place you can access the door to freedom is in your heart, not in your mind that is full of perceptions based on limitations and separation from God.

You are already all that I am. You are unlimited forever. There are no boundaries to what can be done through you. None at all, because that bag of dust that you call yourself is just that—it's a bag of dust called the body—and you have used the infinite power given to the Son by the Father to create body after body into shapes so that it does certain things for you. Unfortunately, it always seems to break down.

Within you, within *you* lies the very power to perform miracles. Ultimately, the greatest of miracles is to allow the Voice of the Holy Spirit to be your Guide in all things. Now, the Holy Spirit resides as fully within you as it does the one who sits next to you, as much as that one Teacher resides within and with me. And as you learn to turn every decision over to that Voice, to trust It without analyzing It, you will come to be nothing less but the perfect manifestation of the Holy Spirit. The perfect manifestation of the Holy Spirit. Here you realize that you are one with God and therefore, one with all of creation. There is no place else that you can understand that. You can *think about* it in your mind, but until you *live it* through your heart you don't really understand what it means to be one with God. Indeed.

Those of you that feel there are limitations in your life, first ask of yourself,

What has this given to me? Why did I seek it out?

Not out of a sense of blame. That has nothing at all to do with it. For you have attracted unto yourself experiences for no other reason than you wanted to—you wanted to. There is no other reason. You have even chosen to be born into a world of uncertainty, of things that change, of things that seem to be chaotic, because you wanted the experience of uncertainty and chaos and madness.

And in that place within you in which you chose to create not reality but an experience called 'this world', in that place alone can you choose anew by choosing to relinquish the world you have created in error, and ask the one Teacher to release from you every limitation and block to the presence of God's Love that dwells within you. To begin to see, to allow that one Teacher to teach you that you are unlimited forever and that indeed never once have you ever existed within a body.

Whew. My goodness, such a statement.

But, Jeshua, I know I am in this body. I can tell.

You are experiencing the effect of a perception you have chosen to believe in, and that is all. And that means you are free to choose anew, to come to see that you exist outside of the body, that the body in a sense arises within you and not the other way around; and that you animate and activate this bag of dust with every thought you think and every perception that you have held dear to yourself, so dear and so long that you have forgotten what they were.

And if that is true—and I assure you most assuredly that it is true—it means that even now you can begin to choose anew. Indeed to look out upon all that you have experienced and to acknowledge for yourself that you have never known what any of it was really for. Yes, you tried to use relationships for this; it didn't work. You tried to use careers for that; it didn't work.

It takes great humility to totally accept that if you are experiencing limitation in your life, it means the perceptions you have held so dear have failed you. And because they are not you, you are free to discard them at any time, to realize that perhaps after all you haven't been your own best teacher. And you have learned perceptions without looking at the life lived by those that would teach you, and you have not seen *their* pain and *their* limitation and *their* confusion, and therefore you have bought the things they have sought to teach you.

Why not discard all of them and start over? Why not be willing, just for the heck of it, to trust a Voice that is wholly unseen and the hearing of which may come softly and gently as a nudge in the heart? Only after much listening does it begin to take on the shape of a voice that you can have complete conversations with. Why not? Give it a try.

What would it mean if tomorrow morning when you woke up, you looked around yourself and said,

> *I don't know what a single thing is for and I am no longer under the sway of the habits of my perceptions. Holy Spirit, unseen—and I don't even know if I really believe in You, but what the heck—what is the best thing that I can do in this moment?*

Some of you will end up sitting in bed all day waiting to hear, and yet when that happens it's because you have not acknowledged that you have heard. *For every time you ask the question of the Holy Spirit, an answer is immediately given.* Immediately. It requires only your willingness to hear with different ears.

It is much like turning off the stereos in your house, asking the children to sit and be quiet, waiting for the cars that are going by to complete their journey, closing the windows so no noise enters, and when all is quiet and you have released even your need or your fear or your expectations over what the answer will be, when you become and come to that place of quiet, the Voice of the Holy One rings loud and clear, like notes struck from a crystal glass.

Those of you in this room that have been putting that into practice in your own way know what I mean, because there is a resonance as the answer is given, and you know, not in the mind but in the heart. You might find that you need to get up, take a shower, get dressed and go to work. But you might just find that you need to go and find a meadow of flowers, to lie beneath the rays of the sun, to dig your fingers into the soil of this beloved and holy Earth and just say to God,

I give it all up.

Maybe.

I cannot possibly come to you as a brother and as a friend if I come with a prescription and a set of proscriptions about what is real, what is true and what you have to do. That would mean that the power is not in you—and I assure you that it is. If you are made in the image of God, it means that you *are* the reflection of perfect freedom.

Does that make sense to you?

And that is why, no matter what you have ever chosen to dream, the One I have called Abba has never interfered with your dream; because if He did He would be acknowledging that your dream is real. That would be a mistaken perception and I can assure you that our Father does not have mistaken perceptions.

Therefore He sits gently, perceiving only the purity of your being, the unlimitedness and the radiance of the Light within you, and He waits while you utilize your freedom to dream dreams of limitation and separation from God. And that means that there is no such thing as what you call (some of you) karma:

> *Well, I'm just here because of the result of everything I've thought and done, and I'm going to have to live through this in order to balance the scales.*

If you decree it, it will be so.

It means that every single moment, and closer to you than your own breath, the fullness of the Kingdom of Heaven resides. It does not need to be earned. It needs only to be allowed. Accept it and receive.

Now, how can that happen?

If you cling to your baseline perception and belief that you are a separate entity, that you are just this little being that has been born and will die, if you believe you are guilty of any sin whatsoever, if you believe that you really are not in union with God, then when you seek to reach for the Kingdom, you only push it away.

Therefore, to allow and to accept and to receive—and therefore to manifest the Kingdom of Heaven on Earth as it is in Heaven—requires that you begin with the perception which is indeed now translated into knowledge that you are right here and right now the holy and only child of God, that you rest in perfect union with your Father forever, that you are not the body, and that space and time is not your home. You cannot earn it because it is given freely. Only when you begin with that acknowledgement can true change come to your life. And why?

Because if you have built a world in error on the perception that you are separate from God, it means that everything you have experienced in some sense reflects or is the residue or the effect of that belief, and as you choose to take a deep swallow and walk through the ring of fear and leap into the infinite pool of union with God, the water is quite fine, the temperature is always perfect and no one cares if you wear a suit or not—how would you put a bathing suit on an infinite Light? When you choose to do that, it means that something begins to move through you called Light and it must necessarily transform every aspect of what you call your experience. So, you see, those of you that have houses and cars, if you will allow this to happen tomorrow, does it all mean they are all going to be gone and you are going to be living in a cave in the Himalayas?

Not at all. It means that the Holy Spirit will change your perception of everything you think you see and understand. And what is it translated into? No longer objects, whether they be relationships, careers or automobiles or what have you that can somehow *bring* pleasure or fulfillment to you, but rather they become nothing more than tools that serve the holy Son of God as he allows love to be extended through him or her and to be given to the world, until the great ray of Light within you shines so brightly that it envelops the whole of creation. And *you* are the one who brings it back gently and lovingly and lays it in the lap of God. *You* are the saviors and the salvation of all worlds.

The question remains, are you willing to allow every limiting perception to be released? Are you willing to allow that fear that really only comes from a very small part of the mind that I have described like a gnat shouting at the vastness of space, that you have unwittingly allowed yourself to believe is the real you. That is the only place fear comes up—in the mind of the gnat trying to resist the vastness of space that is filled with God's wonder and love. Why not let the little gnat be fearful but continue to make a new choice?

You cannot rid yourself of fear and then walk on. Acknowledge that the fear is there. See what small part it plays. Acknowledge the grander reality of who you are—and *then* walk on. It is how one walks on water, upon hot coals. It is how you walk through the need to communicate with another when something is not going right. It is how you walk through having a limitation of golden coins. It is the key to everything. Everything.

I once said unto you that there are four very precious keys—keys to the Kingdom—and they are but simply this: desire, intention, allowance and surrender. Those keys are found as the foundation for every experience that you have ever drawn to yourself. Somewhere you have wanted it. You have held the intention of experiencing it. You have opened yourself to allow the molecules of this physical dimension to form themselves into that which will be the messengers of the experience you want, and then you have given yourself to it as a bride to a bridegroom. Unfortunately, sometimes you say, Why did I marry you?

[Laughter]

Desire... Do not seek to be without it but seek to understand its source. Desire is absolutely critical. Without it, there is no creation. *You* are the offspring of desire, the offspring of Love, which is our Father, to extend Itself infinitely. That is what has created the rays of Light called the Sons of God, and you are a ray of Light. Nothing more and nothing less. Desire, then, is always the first factor in awakening or changing anything.

Intention... Only when there is uncompromising intention can you begin to draw the resources to you that can begin to carry you from where you are to where you would be, whether you are talking about getting a new job or awakening to your oneness with God.

Many of you have mastered those two keys. Some of you are just beginning to see how the use of those two keys wittingly or unwittingly has always formed your experience.

But the transformation begins with the use and the subsequent mastery of the third key of *allowing*. When your desire has been for nothing less than the unlimitedness that comes from your acknowledgement of your union with God—total and complete remembrance of who you are in reality—and when your intention is for nothing but that, the whole of your life begins to serve as the means that will carry you through each illusion that has been blocking you.

And when your choice to become vulnerable—for indeed your safety can only be found in your choice to *be* vulnerable—to be innocent of heart, to acknowledge you have never known what a single thing is for, when you begin to allow that unseen Intelligence that I have called the Holy Spirit to reshape everything in your experience so that it becomes the means for your awakening, then miracles begin. Some of you know what I am talking about. Suddenly resources come to you. Masters come to your life who are well to be heeded, and indeed you don't even know how it happened, and yet it has been the direct effect of your desire and your intention and your willingness to allow a different Teacher to teach you. And as you begin to rest in the mastery of that key of allowing, something rather magical happens that can in no way be explained completely in the languages of your world.

For *allowance* itself slips gently into *surrender*. It is nothing you have done; but out of your choice to allow, the one Teacher given of the Father takes the final step for you. And allowance becomes surrender, and in surrender the peace you are becomes manifested in every moment of your experience.

Others begin to see it and feel it and are attracted to you, and when they ask you,

> *How did you get to where you are?*

you just shrug your shoulders and go,

> *Hmm, I'm not too sure. Somebody must have done it for me, because of myself I can do nothing; but I have learned that through me, my Father can do all things.*

Surrender. . . Surrender is the state that everyone in this world truly desires above everything else but they have forgotten what it is, where it comes from, and what it would mean. For only in surrender can peace come to be known fully.

What, then, begins to change? You will look into the mirror and you will not see yourself any longer. You will not even say "my body". You might say "a body".

> *I suppose I should put some clothing on the body since there are some in this world who still actually think that to look upon a body without clothing is an embarrassing and sinful thing.*

Have you ever been embarrassed by looking at the dust of the ground? Hmm. Odd perceptions.

But if somebody looks at the real me without my clothing on…

No one can look at the 'real' you save one who Is awakened to the Christ that dwells within them, who will look well past the body anyway.

Indeed, precious friends, something quite magical happens. It is something felt and known cognitively. That is, your perception has wholly been changed and though the body seems to move about much as it always has—or perhaps not move about, it really doesn't matter much—there is a new intelligence if you will, an awakening that is infusing the use of that body. It no longer becomes used as something that you seek to draw power or pleasure to yourself through. It no longer becomes something that you think can keep you safe. You no longer seek to beautify it just so others will smile, so you feel you've been accepted—called self-worth. The body becomes nothing but a bag of dust formed by the Mind of Christ into a tool for the extension of love—not to *receive* love, to *extend* love—and only because the world in which you find yourself is totally wrapped up in believing in the reality of bodies. That is obvious.

Love can never be received through the body. Never. It can be *extended* through the body so that another who believes they are a body can understand or feel the reflection of that love.

But truly, love can only be received through an open heart and a quiet mind. And it will not be received from the objects of your world . . . it is received by the descent of grace into your heart.

For ultimately the only relationship that is real is the holy relationship between the Son and His Father—or between the Daughter and the Goddess, if you will. I really don't care what words you use, and I'll let you in on a secret: my Father doesn't care either.

Is all of this making sense to you?

It means that every time that you are not at peace, every time you know doubt, every time you taste loneliness, it is because a part of you is choosing to withhold your love. It is the only thing that is causing it. And you are choosing to listen to the little gnat shouting at space,

> *I can't be happy until this person,*

singled out of the whole of creation, comes and bows down before me and says,

> *'I love you.' Then I might choose to be happy.*

While all around you there are hearts and minds crying out for you, the arisen Christ, to extend your love.

Some of you well know that in the moment you choose to set aside all your worries and concerns and be busy extending your love, suddenly all the problems go away.

> *Where did they go? I still have to make that mortgage payment.*

It's still there, but the reaction to it is not there. It will be taken care of as long as you are busy never allowing yourself to restrict the extension of your love. For the lack you are experience in your life is the effect and the direct result of the choices you have made previously to withhold your love.

I'm sorry, but that is the simplicity and Truth of it all. There is no other answer. It is not because of your parents. It is not because of your upbringing. It is not because you were born black in a white man's world. It's not because you were born a man in a woman's world.

Participant: Jeshua, I'd like a specific example.

Of what?

Participant: Jeshua, I need some sort of concrete example here. If I am in a place where I have grown to be something that I have looked at

and said, "Oh, I don't want this". Right at that point am I to turn away from it and start extending love?

There are two things here. First, you have created a vast generalization.

Participant: Yeah, I was trying not to be too wordy.

But, by so doing, you have overlooked the simple fact that what you experience is right in front of you. Do not make the logical mistake of extending to generalizations.

Now, that's the first thing. By turning away—and I use the analogy or metaphor of turning the cheek from the world—I am talking about turning your consciousness from the perceptions you have chosen to believe in. It does not mean that if you are driving your car and there is someone in the wrong lane coming at you, and you say,

> *I don't want this,*

that all you need do is turn the other cheek. Do you see? Obviously you need to take action to correct that.

In the sense of lack you are never without knowingness about the road you are headed in. Does that make sense to you?

Participant: Yes.

Therefore, to look and see the car that's coming down the lane at you and to take corrective action means already you have turned your attention from the perceptions you have held that had begun to draw that experience to you. It may be, for instance, that money is the root of all evil, therefore I'll live in lack because that is more spiritual.

> *Well, yes, it would be nice to turn the heat on in the middle of winter, but after all that would take money and money is evil.*

Very well, have fun shivering.

I am speaking, precious friend, of looking at the *perceptions* from which your world of experience has been built. To look at it honestly and openly, not by beating yourself and saying,

> *Oh, my God, what have I done? What a jerk I have been. Oh, gees, I'll never get this straight.*

Not at all. Look at it with the innocence of a child. When a child in a sandbox begins to build a castle—and if you've seen one—they sit back and they look at it and they go,

> *Not right, [motion of knocking it down]*

and they start over. They don't beat themselves. They don't go in and say,

> *Father, whip me for I have sinned.*

They just start over.

Participant: I get confused, I think, when it comes to relationships.

You are not the only one.

[Laughter]

Participant: I know. I know. We all have lots of trouble with relationships, but you have been teaching us especially strongly the last couple of weeks that relationships are the avenue of the greatest growth and understanding, and today I have reason to believe that someone I love very much, one of my children, has stolen from me. And things like that have happened in the past but I thought they were long past. And driving over here I was really upset for quite a few miles. It's a good thing I have a long way to drive.

Anyway, I was really upset for quite a few miles and then I suddenly realized that I didn't have to do this. I didn't have to make myself upset because I didn't decide to do the thing. Someone else decided to do the thing. I felt like what I needed to do was just let it go. But then I get confused because I feel hurt because it is someone who is my child and who I raised and loved. And I don't want to judge him and say he is a horrible person and he will always be a horrible person, but I do feel like I need to move out of the way of this kind of treatment. I can do that without being judgmental, can't I?

Can you?

Participant: Well, I seem to have a hard time knowing when exactly to do that—to let it go and not feel heartbroken that my son would do this to me, his mother. I want to let all that go.

Now you are beginning to get to it. Listen to what you said and say it again. What you just said.

Participant: I want to let go of this being hurt.

No, that's not quite it. The sentence with the words "son" and "mother".

Participant: Well, I have this feeling. I feel so badly that my son has done this to me, his mother, who loved him so.

Is that perception not the source of your hurt?

Participant: Yes. But is he not my son? Is that just my perception?

Yes. It has been said in many forms and ways that your children are never your children. They are your equal. They are a soul. They happen to have a bag of dust for awhile. Within this world, ones that come from your womb, you feed and clothe them, you nurture them/They are never yours.

That's the first mistake of perception: to use the word "my"... It is a word of possessiveness. You cannot possess a soul. You cannot possess the body.

Participant: Is there no special bond? More special than any other bond?

When you seek a specialness of a bond in one relationship over others, you will have already decreed that you believe in separation from God and that you are in need of something that only a certain other can bring to you.

Participant: Right. That's right.

Yes, it is. Now that doesn't mean—I am not drawing the conclusion therefore—that you go callously in the world. Of course not. But everyone in this room has been your mother, your brother, your sister, your father, your grandparent. You name the relationship. You have all enacted them a million times.

The point here, beloved friend, is exactly the whole point of our theme tonight.

Are you willing to release every perception you have learned of the world and to allow the one Teacher to re-teach you? Your pain comes always and only as a result of how you react to your perception of what you think you see.

Does that make sense to you?

Participant: Yes.

Let me give you a concrete example. I would be willing to bet that if I asked everyone in this room and everyone on the planet, if an angry or fearful or judgmental thought or perhaps a victimhood thought like, "Why me?", if I were to ask them if such thoughts were to arise if one of your own friends kissed you on the cheek as a way of identifying them to your government, and then the government took you and tied you to a cross and then pounded nails through your hands and feet... In that experience would such thoughts arise?

Participant: Yes.

Had there been a trace of identification in my mind to the perceptions that the world would believe in—that such a thing is barbaric, that it ought not be done, that it is a cruel thing and how could they do this to me, anyway? All I wanted to do was pat them on the back and love them—if one iota of such a thought would have entered my mind, *the whole demonstration would have failed miserably and I would have died a death like anyone else.* There would have been no resurrection, no ascension and I might not even be here to blend with this mind to communicate with you. That is how powerful your perceptions are. And your pain can come only from the soil of the perceptions you have believed are true because you believe they would bring you something that you are lacking.

There are many, many in your world who actually believe that if they come together and create a baby, that somehow the relationship will become happy. Hmm?

Participant: Yes.

It usually doesn't work!

Now, precious friend, do you see how essential this is? What you are bringing up is not just yours. The dilemma, if you will, of every single mind that has bought into this little spinning vortex called your world and gotten caught up in it—which is only to get caught up with believing certain perceptions—the relationship of a son to a mother will never, under any circumstances, hold the key to the mother's fulfillment or peace. And we can also say it is the same for the father, of course.

The one who has stolen is not your son, but is our Father's son. And that act is a cry for help. For in Truth an awakened, healed, sane mind knows it need never take anything. Hmm?

Participant: Yes.

That is the act in itself. The hurt you are experiencing must always come from the perception that you've described.

> *How could my son do this to me, his loving mother that has done so much?*

And you have.

But, precious friend, though it may seem a little confronting, I don't mean it that way. Let me ask you this. How could you begin to hold the perception that because you have sought to extend love to another, they must repay that by behaving in a way *you* would conclude is an inappropriate expression of love toward you? Do you see?

Participant: I don't think it is so much that as my question to myself is: Why would he hurt me? It's like a deliberate hurt, as opposed to ignoring me or just going off and doing his own thing. I have not felt like I've held on to the children who were born through me, like I was clutching them to me.

Precious friend, clutching has nothing to do ultimately with the emotions or with the physical hands. It has to do with your perception. And the clearest indication that you have clutched is the very description you used:

> *Why would my son do this to his loving mother?*

The hurt does not come from the act. It comes from your perception of what the act means. Do you see?

Participant: How can I let it go?

By choosing to do so. To begin to see—and this is why I have talked about vigilance—to see that when an action takes place in your experience, to notice your reaction and to see that it must come from your perception of it.

Let me give you an example. Two people are asked to stand before a crowd of ten thousand and to give a speech on the meaning of love. The first walks on—and they don't have time to prepare, by the way—the first walks onto the stage and looks out and does what you would call the wetting of the pants...

[Laughter]

...and has to literally be carried off the stage, stiff as a board, barely breathing. The second comes and stands on the stage and looks out on all those sea of faces and goes,

> *They are just like me.*

Then says to the ten thousand,

> *I love you. That's the meaning.*

And walks off skipping and singing, and everyone stands and gives him an ovation.

Nothing has been different except their perception. Nothing at all. The situation is the same. Nobody did anything to change anything except the infinite power of one mind chose a different perception. And you have a saying in your world: 'that made all the difference in the world.' The perception of separation and fear has created a lot of differences in your world.

And you are being asked now to choose a different way of seeing, a way that doesn't ignore what's taking place but sees through it and beyond it, to choose only peace no matter what, to understand that none of your perceptions have ever been wholly true, and that is why you need in each situation to ask the Holy Spirit to teach you the meaning of your experience. He will not keep it from you whenever you are willing first to acknowledge that you are reacting not to what happened but to your perception of what happened, and to ask it to be replaced.

There is something for you to see in this experience, something you would be asked to do in this experience for the soul—who is actually crying for help and doesn't even know it, who lives in a state of consciousness of the virtual lack of self-worth, lack of power, is totally confused, sees the world as threatening and overwhelming; and because of his perceived powerlessness, believes that he must secretly take what he thinks will bring some pleasure. Totally insane perception. The act is a cry for help. Nothing more, nothing less. And your son has not hurt you, because your son cannot fulfill you.

The questions that you have asked and asked often, if you were to go through and lay them out one after the other since first we began to communicate, you would find that there has been a progression, a movement to subtler and subtler levels of the same question. And in this moment, beloved friend, you are getting about as close to the hub of the wheel as you can. You are just beginning to touch the place of truly seeing—that's not thinking, that's a seeing that involves the wholeness of your being—that your perceptions have created everything you have experienced, and your perceptions are the only thing that have been creating limitation in your life, and that *you* are *not* your perceptions. That is the great point of freedom. And you have come to understand that you are not, never have been, the thoughts of the world. You just got a little entranced with them, that's all, and you are free even now to choose anew.

Guidance will be given in how to deal with that situation, for turning of the cheek doesn't mean that you let the car hit you head on. It never meant that. It means that you choose to listen to another Voice rather than the reactivity of your perceptions to know how to deal with it effectively.

Sometimes dealing with it effectively means you have to turn the tables of the money-changers over rather than asking them to reconsider. And indeed, you may be asked to confront wholly this other soul who is not 'your son' and to say,

> *I'm sorry. That's enough. If you choose to be in a disrespectful relationship to me, you therefore cannot be in relationship to me, because I am a child of God and I am to be honored as such.*

That would create a little shockwave in that one's mind.

> *Are you trying to tell me . . . ? But you're my mother. You are supposed to always be here, no matter what I do.*

Why? Who said that was true? Do you see?

Participant: Yes, but what is the price to pay? That was coming to me just before I drove up here.

Now, do you know why it was beginning to come to you?

Participant: Yes. No. Why?

Because, as you stated earlier, you began to shift, did you not?

Participant: Right.

And that shift brought you into a place of openness where a friend of yours could begin to whisper and indeed said unto you,

> *You know, this would be a very good thing to bring up tonight. It will help a lot more than just yourself.*

Participant: You know, I didn't hear that part.

[Laughter]

Participant: Right.

Are you okay with all of that so far?

Participant: Yes. Fine really, thank you.

There are a lot of others in this room that are thanking you for bringing it up.

Participant: You know, I think a lot of us have read or heard that children that come to us—and significant relationships with the opposite sex—that we might have had relationships with in past lives and we need to work out whatever problems it is that keep bringing us back together, which has always tended to stop me from saying, "Okay, that's it. Enough is enough." Because I felt like if I didn't resolve whatever it was in this life, it would come haunt me in another one.

How do you resolve anything?

Participant: Forgive it? Somehow, reach some understanding that, is this an appropriate behavior and we just don't do this to each other? I don't know.

Stop right there. It is very important.

The statement you just made comes out of at least a loosely held perception indeed that resolution must require an agreement reached by two infinitely free minds; and that only when an agreement is reached that precipitates a change can there be a resolution. That already is to create a limitation.

What if you resolve within yourself to not participate in that energy any longer? For indeed, that which you call the drawing back of souls to keep playing the same old circles of dramas over and over—and some of you know what that's like even in this life, you keep drawing to yourselves relationships and somehow they all have the same flavor to them—it is because something in you believes that you are supposed to draw that to you. Which means to say that you want it because you are unwilling to accept that you are worthy of the fullness of the Kingdom.

What if you were to resolve that simple perceptual error? And to understand that if that other mind wants to continue they are going to have to find somebody else to play with, because you are in a sense taking a quantum leap and only choose to allow those who resonate in the understanding of what it means to extend love—that those are the only beings you want in your life? That is not a selfish thing. That is called wisdom.

Do you see the difference there?

Participant: That's really mind-boggling.

I hope so. For when the mind is boggled, the wisdom of the heart can begin to seep through its cracks, finally.

Participant: You mean, that no where is it written or said by God that we have to resolve all issues together? We can resolve them in our own mind and that's enough?

It could be said that the only place *you* can resolve it is in your own mind. And because all minds are joined, as you heal your misperceptions you have already enlightened the weight of *all* minds. And you have made it easier for other minds that, in the moment it may appear that you are walking away from and they have to find somebody else to play their games with, you have given them something that they witness. And what is it? The freedom to make a different choice. And the seed becomes planted, and guess Who comes along to start watering it? So that eventually that seed will also break through the soil of the mind and begin to flower, and that mind will begin to make new choices.You may not physically see the effect of the new choices, but you will feel it at the level of the soul.

When I have said that relationships are the grandest and most significant of things you have, it is because they will reflect to you every perception you have ever held. And when you are willing to extend love to embrace the one in front of you unconditionally, without need or expectation of any kind, then you have used the very soil that you created in error—that is, bodies floating about in space—you have allowed it to become translated into the means through which you manifest the power of a new choice and therefore experience the healing of your own mind.

It takes great courage initially to begin to see that sometimes in letting go and walking away you have done the grandest thing you could do for yourself and for another. God has never etched into stone that you have to pound on each others' heads for lifetimes. Your purpose and function is to extend love, to allow yourself to receive love.

Therefore, look well at your life—and do this honestly, of course, so that you are not falling into the trap of trying to please the gnat, but be very honest—to see

> *Where am I not allowing myself to receive the beauty of God's love and where am I withholding it?*

If that means that the picture surrounding you has to be shaken up and changed, if you are moving toward love at the guidance of the Holy Spirit, you can rest assured that the changes that come serve the highest and best for everyone. I almost said "everyone concerned" but then you would think it's just those limited minds involved in that one situation, and that is not the Truth. All minds that exist are affected by everything you think and do.

Hmm... what a responsibility. And it seems like it until you understand that all you are asked to do is to live as though you are not an ego. And the only other choice is to understand that you are just a—to use your popular word—channel for God's love and that there is one Teacher that knows and will guide you, and Whose guidance is certain.

Fair enough?

Participant: Yes, very fair.

Does all of that help?

Participant: Yes. A lot to chew on.

Rather, just embrace it a lot. The mind likes to chew; the heart likes to swallow.

[Laughter]

No bad. So, how are we all doing?

Participant: Great.

Look, then, around yourself. Now, just take a moment. Allow your eyes to rest with the eyes of another. If that means that three of you need to do that, that's fine. Allow, truly allow yourself to let the bag of dust relax. Stop holding it as an armor that would separate you from your brother or sister. Block not the angel of air; it is the presence of the Holy Spirit.

It doesn't require any talking.

Who is before you? What you are looking at is not a body. It is not a body. Allow your heart to see through your eyes and through the eyes of the one in front of you. Look deeper and deeper still. Look beyond the body. Look beyond the personality that you think is attached to that body. Look beyond any imagined or known history associated with that being, that body, that mind, that personality.

And if you would allow yourself, you can begin to see the reflection of rays of Light. Allow those rays of Light to shine ever more brightly and let the attention of your seeing be only on those rays. And if thoughts arise in the mind, they are just clouds passing through the sky. They don't mean anything.

Look deeper still. Look without fear. Look without expectation. Look without a perception of any kind that you would cling to. And in your own way in this moment ask your Father to show you the reality of the one before you.

Is it not Love that waits to be recognized in the one before you? Is it not the Love in you that waits to be unleashed, to recognize the Love in the one in front of you?

In your vulnerability is your only safety. Let Love rejoice in the perception of Itself given wholly as a ray of Light seeded into each soul since before time is. You are that Light and you are that Love, and from Its power you can see the Truth in everyone and everything. And, right now, know that as you allow yourself to see the love in the one in front of you, you are providing healing for them because they can rest in the vulnerability required to see you as you choose to see them. And in seeing them as the holy ray of Light that is the Father's Son, you have finally seen yourself.

Love alone is the essence of all that is real. Choose, then, love. And abandon perceptions born of fear.

Are you your brother's keeper? Oh yes, because you are the one you see. Love them as your Father has first loved you and *you* are the Light that lights this world and returns the whole of creation into the hands of the One Who has sent us forth. The Kingdom of Heaven is no further from you than your choice to see your brother through the eyes of Christ.

Now, indeed because the Holy Spirit translates everything you have ever created in error, it means that even the body has already been translated. Would you not then reach out and place your hand upon the heart of the one in front of you? Indeed.

And who said miracles can't come through you? The hand, look at the hand you think is yours. Look at it. It's not yours. It's made of dust. It's nothing more than a means of communicating the Love you are. Allow, then, that infinite Love to be transmitted through your hand. Let that Light penetrate the heart of the one in front of you. Embrace the Heart of Christ . . . with the Love that *is* Christ. Let it go. Let the perceptions of separation go. Let the veil of the world go. Reclaim your innocence. Reclaim your union. We are infinite and unlimited. We are the Thought of Love in form. The world can bind us no longer, for we choose to see with different eyes, the eyes of an awakened heart that rests in vulnerability; and through us the Father does all things.

And to you who sit in front of me, you are the presence of my Redeemer and I give the fullness of my Love to you in gratitude for your beauty, your wisdom, your strength, your courage. I see you as healed and I see you as perfect and I am with you always. For though bodies can be moved from place to place, minds that join in Love cannot taste separation.

And now all things are made new again and our union is restored on Earth as it is already in Heaven, and therefore *we* bring Heaven to Earth with our choice to extend and teach only Love.

Indeed. Some of you are feeling some heat and warmth in the area of the heart, to put it mildly. Those of you that know how to open the inner eyes and see not just physical bodies, the room is full—helpers, guides, teachers, call them what you will; masters indeed. For wherever two or more are gathered in my name, there I am in the midst of them, and therefore we come and we will give you our strength until yours is as certain as ours. It is called friendship.

There. Now there *is* Light. And there is really nothing left to do except to give one another a big hug.

Now, I have a favor to ask all of you. And the favor is simply this: you need not make it public, but some of you had some rather interesting experiences just then. As you return home this evening please don't make the mistake of saying to yourself or to another,

> *Oh, what Jeshua did tonight . . .*

But rather say unto yourself,

> *Oh, what I, the holy Son of God, have* allowed *tonight.*

For healing can only come when you use the power given unto you, even as power was given unto me, to choose to be the fountain which spreads the healing grace of Love into this world. To see no one as above you ever again, for right where you are—and this is the Truth of reality—you are not in the body. You are as much with me above this world as any master has ever been. You are as much with me now as this my beloved brother is when he allows himself to let go of the limitations of mind and therefore sees me and feels me and sits down on the bench with me. You, too, are there now.

And the only barrier—the only barrier—between you and the fullness of the miracles that would be manifested through you into this world, the only barriers are the obstacles called perceptions that you have not learned in the Kingdom but in the world.

A very good exercise to do is to sit down with a piece of paper and just begin to let yourself, allow yourself, to list perceptions you have been taught and have believed. Look at them and ask yourself,

Is that limiting?

And if the answer is yes, rest assured the Holy Spirit did not teach it to you. And then on the other side of the page draw a line and write the belief or perception that would be the antithesis of the limited belief. Not a new exercise by any means, but a very powerful one. And if it speaks to you of unlimitedness, if you allow the cells of the body to feel joy, rest assured you've been listening to a new Teacher.

You are already everything I ever represented to anyone, and in reality you are but a brother, a sister, a friend who comes to everyone you see in your life as a messenger from God. And God is but Love and therefore has but one message to deliver. Never limit what I can do through you, for if you would but choose to join with me—and I am but a manifestation of the Holy Spirit—understand well that there are no limitations to what I can do through you when you are willing to be the witness of miracles in your life. And when you have seen those miracles, you must then acknowledge that they have been done unto you.

No one comes save but to answer their own call to awaken. You have come unto this hour, some of you many times, some of you for the first time, but understand well the level of the soul: you have come to answer your own call, and you have chosen me to be the brother and the friend through whom you will be finally willing to receive the reflection of the Truth that lies in you. Because in a part of you, you know that there is safety in abiding with me and you have not yet extended that sense of safety to abiding with yourself.

And that is why I have said that in all things—and I give this as my promise unto you—I will give you the fullness of my strength until yours is as certain as mine. And then indeed we walk together. And where two of us have gathered together the power of Christ becomes unlimited forever.

Walk with me then with every breath, every thought, and I shall not leave you until together every mind and every heart has reawakened to the presence of Christ that dwells within us all.

Remember that miracles shorten the need for time. Think not then that together miracles cannot bring an end to the need for time itself.

And when you have chosen with me to embrace the whole of creation as your very body; when you have seen that this planet is not outside of the need of your love; when you see that your brother or sister or your sons or daughters are but aspects of your own self and need to be embraced with the Love of Christ that dwells with you, and you are the only one that can bring it to them; when you join with me in embracing the whole of all worlds that have ever arisen; then indeed together we will translate those worlds into the reflections of the Kingdom of Heaven—and time will be no more. Suffering will have been forgotten. Birth and death shall be no more.

And for a brief moment that is wholly out of time, all things will rejoice and reflect the Light of the perfection of God's Love for His creation. And His creations will have reflected what He intended when He brought you into being, and then the purpose of creation itself will have been fulfilled and there will be naught but the Light, and Light eternal: that which is, that which was, and that which forever shall be. Heaven waits on your choice to believe it, to acknowledge it and to live it. The only barrier between your world and the Kingdom of Heaven is the choice to hold on to perceptions created not in Heaven but in the world.

And your brothers and sisters wait for you to arise from sleep and to never tolerate error in yourself again, so that *you* become that one who walks through this world as the presence of Love and thereby extends to everyone you see an opportunity to make a new choice. For if you would have your brother and sister awaken from the chains that bind them, you must release your own first. You are your brother's salvation, as he is yours.

Join with me, then, on the park bench, and indeed I will come and I will talk with you whenever you want. Isn't that right? And indeed, through you, if you are willing, we will awaken every mind of our brothers whom we love. Hmm. Why not? You've tried everything else.

[Laughter]

Wherever you are, wherever you are, the fullness of the Kingdom is present. All power is given unto you in that moment to be the Light that lights the world. You may think you will have to be a little crazy at first. Perfectly okay.

It may feel like you are dreaming just a little bit. When you have been asleep dreaming this long, waking from the dream *seems* like a dream. Don't let it stop you. Don't say,

> *Oh, I've got to get my feet back on the ground. Only angels can fly.*

Hmm. That's just a perception. The angels know better.

Precious friends, let there in this evening then be no more questions that need to arise, for all questions have already been answered. And if you have come here with a question, ask it of yourself and then touch the place provided for you by the glance of your brother's eyes and his or her hand upon your heart, and go to that place; and there the one Teacher Who also taught me is waiting for you, and there you will find the answers that you seek.

And yet, when all questions have been asked and they have all been answered, there is still but one choice left to make:

> *Since I am in Truth the holy child of God Himself, will I choose to live it?*

I have said elsewhere that there is only one question you need ask of yourself: what do you really and truly want? When you are clear about that, everything else falls into place. What do you truly want?

Some of you know that in this evening you have already experienced or had reconfirmed for you the answer that you have always known. And when I said to those of my old buddies that some have called disciples—what a term of specialness that is—

> *Ah, yes, the grand apostles. Boy, they were chosen by God. Did you know that? Whew, maybe if I hadn't sinned so much in my last life, God would have chosen me, too.*

Saint this and Saint that. Why not Saint Judith? Why not Saint Edith? Why not Saint Marilyn? Why not Saint Hank? Why not? You are already saintly in the eyes of your Creator. You might as well live it.

What do you truly want? That is the question that requires an answer, and from it every other question and every other answer will be but servants that bring into manifestation, in and through you, the fulfillment of your heart's desire.

Be at peace in all things, for I am with you. And the promise that I gave you then in the drama of time has never changed. I am with you always. All you have to do is open the shutters and look through the window of your perceptions and you will see me sitting on that bench—legs crossed, palms open, smiling—and you will notice that there is space on it for you. All I have ever asked is that you allow me to be a friend. No false piety is required. No great chants and no great cathedrals. You are the temple of Christ. And because I love you—because I love you—I abide in unlimitedness so that I can be with you always. I can be with all of you always, as you can be with me always. And nothing—*nothing*—is impossible to minds that have joined in love.

My peace I give unto you. My blessings I would shower upon you, and do. Some of you like to deflect it a little bit. That's okay. Somebody else will pick up the spray. But I do want you to know that no matter what choice you make, I will never stop the shower of that love upon you. Sooner or later you will give up the game of the ego and accept it, and then all things shall be made new. No longer a journey to the Kingdom, but the glory of a journey within it.

Carry, then, peace in your hearts—and give it away, for in your giving you will receive. Love the world as yourself and you will have manifested the knowledge of what it means to live as though you were not an ego. Indeed.

Peace to the precious and holy and only begotten offspring of Light divine, the One that I call Abba, because that Love is so personally yours as it is mine.

Peace to the great rays of Light that shine forever and touch every corner of creation. That is who you are, nothing more and certainly nothing less.

Be, therefore, who you are and your Light will light this world, and together you will know that there has never been an order of difficulty in miracles.

Amen.

AWAKENING

July 1992

Jeshua

Now we begin.

Indeed, once again, greetings unto you, beloved and holy children of Light divine. In Truth, once again I come forth to shower my blessings upon you; and yet I can do nothing but shower those blessings upon you which *you* would choose to receive. Therefore, my giving them to you is *your* giving to yourself. And I do not say that lightly though, indeed, it is given in Light.

For in Truth that which I have given unto you is your own giving to yourself. It must mean that everything I have ever represented to the consciousness of mankind is in you now. And that which was once called the incarnation or the Word made flesh, when it is said that God came and dwelt among us, that must have been your gift to yourself.

How can that be? For you believe that you have perhaps been born in this body for a short time and, if you are lucky, have a good time and then the body will degenerate and you will experience something called death. And the one that was known as Jeshua ben Joseph is said to have been here some two thousand years ago.

How could that incarnation have been a gift to myself?

Quite simply, you are not the body and you are not the personality. What you are transcends all space and all time, and all lives that have ever been lived arise within *you*. And in this drama, this scheme of space and time, even as you have all together as one mind chosen the perception that you are separate from God and therefore separate from one another—so too, as you have been the creator of your world in error, you have been the creator of the form of salvation. And every master and every teacher that has come and given you grand words or brought healing to you, or inspired the heart to look beyond its limitations, each and every one of them has but come as a reflection created by the soul you are, to mirror back to the conscious mind the Truth that necessarily lies within you. And that Truth is not difficult to find. It is not far from you. It is not far from you. Indeed, the Kingdom of Heaven can be no further than the distance of a single choice.

How then to rediscover that Truth? To touch that place that some of you believe that I mirrored so perfectly? How could you see that perfection if you did not already know that that perfection is in you?

How then to rediscover that Truth? Not by striving. Not by seeking. Not by mastering a plethora of techniques. But by wanting above all things—*by wanting above all things*—to become, once again, the Thought of perfect Love in form. To be willing to release every perception you have cherished because once upon a time in your long journey you thought it would make you safe or bring you some greater good. To be willing to give each day back to God. To be willing to become innocent. To set aside and imagine what it would be like if in each day you were to set aside every and each perception you held about what reality is, about where you came from, about what your purpose and function is, about what the brother or sister in front of you means.

To abide in an innocence and a faith that trusts what appears to be unseen, and be willing to allow that unseen love to guide you moment to moment, to teach you anew until each and every perception that has been created in error has been released as a veil from before your mind, before your heart. And then you will not see what you have created. You will see what you have always been. And you will know that there is no such thing as separation, and time and space cannot be a barrier between minds that are joined in love.

To be the Thought of Love in form is to choose to incarnate Christ. Not to wait for another to do it. Not to hope that it has already been done two thousand years ago so you can skip around the corners, but rather to choose to allow your life, what you call "my life", to be transformed—gently perhaps, a moment at a time; and at times not so gently—you call those major breakthroughs. The only reason it feels so major is the thing that you are releasing is something you have been holding on to for so long that you couldn't comprehend being without it. And yet, it has only been a perception—something so flimsy, so thin that it holds no power and does not distort the Light that comes to your soul. But you have looked upon it as something to be cherished and treasured and have made it part of yourself, and have believed that it holds a power to keep you separate from God, or that you have needed it to remain safe in an unsafe world. And that is most interesting because the perception that you abide in an unsafe world is just that—a perception—and it, too, must be released.

Therefore, precious and holy friends—and I do say friends, you who were created with me before time is—you are eternal and unbounded, and within you and before you and all around you lies that wisdom that is available to you in every moment and with every decision you believe you must make. But what seems to be so difficult is the habit of the mind that has believed itself to have been separate from God and must make its own way. It must be the grand maker and doer. It must cling to certain perceptions about what life is and how it ought to be lived. That little habit cannot believe that it could be so simple; and yet it is.

And there is no one in this room who in this moment cannot be crucified, dead and buried in the mind, resurrected and ascended to join in perfect union with the Mind of God. It is available to you now.

And all that is ever asked of you is that you make the simple choice to be at peace. To relinquish, to let go of your striving, your grasping, your anxieties, your fears, your doubts. And therefore to begin—and I mean begin every day, until it becomes the beginning of every moment—to begin in the recognition that in reality,

> *I and my Father are one, now.*

Not in the future. Not in a distant past that I somehow managed to throw away by accident with the garbage. But now, right here and right now.

There is nowhere to go and nothing to achieve save to use the power given unto you to acknowledge:

> *I and my Father are one. And I walk in a safe world. And as I walk, that One walks with me, and I walk only in Love, and each step I take takes me into the extension of Love. And I choose to think only loving thoughts. And when my mind is given to memories, I choose only loving memories and I release the rest because everything that has not been loving has been born of illusions of fear.*

Can you imagine what it would be like to live one day in which each step you take, you feel it? And each thought you think, you witness it and you are with it? No more idle thoughts just running about in the mind—but you direct them wholly from that place in you that is Love. What would it be like to begin from this moment and to allow yourself to recognize that no matter what the circumstances seem to be around you, you hold the power to be the presence of the peace of God? What would it be like to live one day, just one day, in which everyone you thought of, everyone you looked upon, you embrace totally with the Love of Christ and did not let a single perception of your own making boomerang on you, to create in you the illusion of the belief that another could hold the power to change your countenance? What would that be like?

And if you can accomplish one day in that manner, rest assured that when you rest your head on the pillow that night, it will be Christ that is going to sleep. One day without a negative or fearful thought. And then indeed you touch that which is eternal, that which has been within you since before time is, has never been tainted, cannot be taken from you. You touch reality.

Now, there have been many that have begun the spiritual path, many that would even seek to follow me—though I would prefer that they follow themselves—and when they begin to discover that awakening isn't going to bring great brass bands to play for you, your neighbors might not even notice it, you may not wake up with winning lottery numbers in your head, you may not even transcend what is perceived as illness in the physical body, that just perhaps it is not quite what you thought the journey would be... Many throw in the towel and say,

> *Well there's nothing to all of that. I might as well go back to the way I was. Perhaps the thrill is yet around the corner.*

When that takes place, remember it is the voice of the ego that does not want you to awaken, for when you choose to awaken, its purpose has been completed and you will put it away as a child puts away an old toy now outgrown.

Awakening is a simple affair. Being awake is a simple affair. First understand that you *are* awake now—*you are awake, now*—and there is no one in this room but Christ. Yes, there seems to be the appearance of many bodies, but underneath them and just behind them there lies a Love, a Love that is available to you whenever you choose. A Love that throws open the shutters of the heart so wide that you feel your arms could embrace the whole of creation, and you smile no matter who you think about or look upon. You cannot help but smile because you have chosen to be awakened from the dream of the dreamer himself, or herself. You have chosen to just relinquish the grand drama that would lead you to feel that if you hold onto anxiety that it gives life some purpose.

Eventually you will give up the grandiose notion that you must do great things in this world in order to be happy, and you will become happiness itself. And when you become happiness itself, rest assured that grand things will be done through you. Because you are like a Light that just dances in this plane and wherever you are—and I mean this as deeply and profoundly as I can—wherever you are, miracles are taking place in the minds and hearts of those who encounter you. You may not see them visibly but rest assured they are occurring. Because when you choose to be that Happiness with a capital "H"—not an egoistic happiness but just Happiness, the love from which creation has come forth—right where you are, every mind that encounters you witnesses that Light. How it chooses to react to it is its own choice, but the Light is seen, and when Light has been seen it seeps in and begins to work its miracles. And it may be next week, it might be next year, it could be next lifetime, but that mind will begin to be attracted to the Light it experienced through you.

And that is why I have often said to you—and please, please take it deep within your heart: *There is no such thing as separation, and the thoughts you choose to hold within yourself affect the whole of creation.*

Are you then your brother's keeper?

Yes. Not out of moral sanction, moral duty. You are your brother's keeper for the simple Truth that you are your brother. And the thought you choose to hold will allow your brother redemption or damnation—to use those kinds of terms—to experience a movement toward freedom or to feel held back. That is the responsibility you have and it's not a burden. It can be done very lightly since you are the presence of Light itself.

Does all of that begin to make sense to you?

[Audience agreement]

Good. Then we are just going to sit here and bring a lot of Light to this world. Are you ready to do that?

Participant: Yes.

Remember that right here, right now, though you hear a voice that seems to come through something called a body, a bag of dust, and that indeed a mind that was associated with one known as Jeshua ben Joseph seems to be directing those words, remember what I said when we began: you are only hearing and seeing a reflection of the Truth you are. Which means you are talking with yourself, right now. And there is only one Mind here if you choose to acknowledge only Christ.

Therefore, allow the eyes to close for just a moment. Imagine that by so doing you are turning away from the roar and the din of the world, choosing to relinquish how you may have perceived this day.

And with the eyes closed, allow the angel of the breath to move through the cells of the body like a gentle stream of golden light, unlimited forever, given to you freely and eternally, as though you could ride on the crest of that golden Light, that breath.

For is it not written that God breathed into man the breath of life? That is how close you are right now to the One Who has created all of us. And with each inbreath you are receiving life eternal and with each outbreath allow that golden Light to be extended beyond the form that you think you are, like rays from the sun that reach out to every comer of the universe.

Allow images perhaps to come into your perception of ancient friends, family members, children, lovers, enemies. Imagine that you could allow the whole of mankind to come into your inner view and still the rays of your Light shine all around them, envelop them and penetrate them. See them becoming that Light itself. But do not strive at this, allow it. Feel the beauty and the simplicity and the joy of embracing the whole of creation with the love that you are. That love is eternal and unbounded and there is not a single obstacle that can impede the extension of your love.

Witness within yourself, creation becoming that Light. See other minds awakening and remembering. And think not it is your imagination for you cannot imagine what you have not experienced somewhere along the way. Begin to feel that joy ever deeper and deeper as you see creation awaken to the Light of its only reality. Feel that joy as though it can begin to lift you out of your chair. Feel gratitude and beauty. Say "yes" to that Light. Indeed.

And if yet you think there is a single shadow left within you, right now turn it over to that Light. Just turn it over. If it's a fear, a doubt, an old hurt, turn it over. It can no longer serve you to hold it. Every chain that has been upon you melted and dissolved. Light of very Light. Truth of all Truths. And the Light grows brighter and brighter and brighter, more and more radiant.

And every solar system is enveloped in your love, and it is expanding to touch even other dimensions that are not physical at all. Embrace them. Embrace all beings upon them. Imagine that you could embrace every master that has ever been. For some of you that communicate with masters on other planes, embrace *them* with the Love you are and see that they have arisen within *your* beauty and *your* Truth.

And look now upon all dimensions and all worlds and all time frames that have ever been and every brother or sister you have ever known—and you have known all of them—and feel the meaning of these words as yours:

> *I am one with all of life. I am one with my Creator and I embrace every aspect of creation as myself. For I have learned the only lesson I have ever needed to learn: that there is nothing outside of me.*

And then in your own way, abiding in that Light, simply feel the energy of eternal gratitude . . . eternal gratitude:

> *I am that Light. I am that Light. As it was in the beginning, is now, and forever shall be. And being that Light, I choose freely—freely—to begin to take on the appearance of a single personality, a single mind. And I will don the cloak of what seems to be but one body and I will choose this time frame on a planet known as Earth, and I am the Light that becomes that form that I would call "myself". But from this moment forward I will utilize that vehicle for no other purpose than to extend the infinite Love that I am, and to give it to this world.*

Coming down then, beginning to feel the flesh of the body. Delight in it. It is not your prison. It holds no power over you. It is a vehicle through which Christ can communicate. And begin now, as though for the first time, to allow the eyes to open. And as they do, look around you. Who do you see that you do not know and love?

Welcome to this moment of a rather interesting drama called 'space and time'. And you, the Word of God, have just chosen incarnation. I would call it rebirth, and that rebirth will continue to be the foundation of everything you do unless and until you choose to reach back into an illusion and bring back to yourself a perception of lack, of limitation, of fear, of guilt. It is not just an exercise that bides your time. It is your own reality remembered.

What do you think, Firewalker? How does it feel to be incarnated as the Word made flesh?

Participant: It feels like it is the only game in town.

Have you tried others? Anyone here tried out a few games that didn't quite work out well?

[Laughter]

Freedom, indeed, can be expressed whenever you remember that you are not the doer or the maker of your experience and you don't need to be—and thank God for that. But you can be that one who learns to live without effort and without planning, as your world would see planning, if you become one who begins each day remembering who you are, opening like a flower to the Light that is in you and allowing that Light to be your teacher and your guide. It really doesn't matter what words you use. It's the feeling and the knowingness that matters.

In my language that identifies me relative to the time that I walked among you, I would simply say:

> *Holy Father, what would You have this day be for? I am Your child and therefore I am Your servant, for I know that where I walk, You walk with me and nothing is impossible to me. For of myself I could never do anything, but You, Holy Father, through me, can do all things. All I need to do is to be out of Your way. And each time I choose to be the presence of Love, I have given up the illusion of separation and You can live through me. This world can bring nothing to me of value. Not a single thing. Not an object. Not a bank account. There is nothing here that holds any true value for you.*

> *Therefore, there is nothing that I can draw to myself, but there is everything that I can give to this world, for I have tasted of the only thing that holds value: Love. Just Love. Just Love. Just Love. Love is all things. Love embraces all things, allows all things, trusts all things, celebrates all things; and continually gives itself away.*

And the arisen Christ lives each day, though in the appearance of a body—or so it would appear to others—knowing that there is not one thing this world can do to tempt you. There is nothing in it that can bring you happiness or fulfillment because you as the arisen Christ have realized it is only in the giving and extension of the infinite Love you are that you can receive what you have prayed for.

So that makes it, you see, very, very simple. You don't need fourteen hours a day of burning a certain kind of incense. You don't need seventy-two years to wait for the tape to change. You don't have to wait for seventy-two years in terms of learning some foreign language filled with an infinite number of chants. You don't have to learn how to direct energy into your body. *There is nothing you have to do to be who you are.* Nothing. Not one single thing you have to do.

None of it will bring love to you but, rather miraculously, when you simply decide to do nothing but give your love away—to be only love no matter what other minds may choose to be or what game they may choose to play—you will find that what you have been seeking to get from the world all this time is yours now. And then indeed miracles can begin and life can begin to shift and change, because what you experience can only be the result of what you insist on perceiving and believing in.

If you believe there is lack as you perceive it in your life, it must and can only be because somewhere previously you believed that lack could exist. Or perhaps worse, that it must exist for you.

> *How could I be unlimited?*

And when you begin to acknowledge the Truth of who you are, that alone is when you create the new vibration that changes everything.

Does that make sense to you?

If you seek to grow and believe that you are in lack, and you've got to work and strive to learn all the techniques so you can become plentiful and abundant, have you ever noticed that it seems to take forever?

Participant: But Jeshua, that's what almost all of us learned from our parents. So you could say, almost from infancy onward we were taught that.

Yes, and I know that you've just been a victim of others. Hmm? Beloved friend, it doesn't matter. Understand this well: every time you use the word 'but', what you are really saying is,

> *I choose to resist my unlimitedness now and I will find some way to explain why where I am must continue.*

Does that make sense to you? Do not blame your parents. Do not blame your great-great-grandparents. Do not blame your government. There isn't anybody to blame. There is just everybody to love.

Participant: I didn't really feel as I was blaming anyone when I said that. My meaning was only: no wonder it comes as such a surprise to us that our thoughts create our abundance. It's not surprising that it is a big surprise to a lot of people.

Reality seems shocking when you begin to see it.

Participant: Right.

But, precious friend, look and understand what I am talking about here: the power of the mind right now. As soon as the thought entered the mind,

'But' we've been taught this,

you have turned your attention to a perception that somehow others have affected where you are now. And what I am trying to share with you is that *there is no one at any time who has not chosen moment by moment which perceptions they will take and make their own.*

If it were true that you are formed, let's say, by your parents, by your educational systems, it would mean that people who have similar experiences—let us say being born into a ghetto and nine hundred and ninety-nine out of a thousand of them become addicted to drugs and one becomes a world leader, a teacher, a doctor—if it were true that all were affected by their environment, there would not be a doctor that would arise out of that thousand. Each brings about their experience by the choice that is made in the mind in each and every moment.

The greatest lesson that you must learn is that you are free now. The power is now— not tomorrow—to insist on choosing to live only in unlimitedness, only in vision, and only in the present and not in the past. It is the only time healing can come. The only time.

Therefore, precious friend, as you are learning, learn well: there can never be such a thing as an idle thought. Never. You are choosing to indulge in an illusion that has limited you before and will continue as long as you choose to hold it within your mind.

That is why I have said to you that vigilance is so critical. Vigilance. What am I choosing to think, now? Some of you indeed would laugh and chuckle because perhaps you have cursed at the person that runs the stop light in front of you. There is no such thing as an idle thought, and though you may think you are doing it in jest, your body is responding to your judgment and all the chemistry in it has changed immediately to respond to negative thought. And the thought you think is not separate from all other minds. It is so critical to play at choosing only loving and unlimited thoughts and to learn how to abide in (what we will call here) that frequency, constantly.

That is the only way you can awaken the Light that you may perceive as yet dormant within you: to practice in every moment to be that Light. It's the only way anything changes, you see. It's the only way Heaven can return to Earth: for you to choose, with me, to think only thoughts that are unlimited.

Does that make sense to you?

And, you see, that's the great power. That's the gift given unto you—that no matter what has happened in the past, no matter what thoughts you have held, no matter what actions you have done, no matter what anybody's done, what your Father extends to you in every moment is the freedom to think anew, now. Right now. And though you might not see it, every time you have had a negative thought, if you would look back at perhaps a two or three year period or a lifetime, whatever you want to look back upon, and see it as a time of heartache or struggling or loss or what have you, it doesn't matter, all you are doing is looking at a movie that you have brought with you. The experience has already been dissolved in Light.

That is called Love. You could say that your Father is like a grand street sweeper, and though your horses seem to leave a little muck and mire in the street, He comes right behind you and sweeps away all of its effects and waits only for you to understand that there isn't anything to feel guilt over, nothing to bring a heaviness upon your countenance, because the past has already been washed away—it no longer exists.

And when mankind chooses to stop writing history books, it will begin to understand that the future is present now, dependent only on what thoughts are chosen now.

> *Well, we've got to keep our armaments up, because, you see, there have been wars. You hurt me once. I remember. It may have been last week. It may have been ten thousand years ago, but I remember*

> *and I am not about ready to forgive you.*

And then you can't understand why there is something in you that doesn't feel forgiven.

You are your brother; and with what measure that you mete unto them, so, too, shall it be meted unto you. That's how it works. Does it mean that if you judge another, somebody is going to come along with something called karma and hit you over the head? You have already done it to yourself. And when you hit yourself over the head, you then prove to yourself,

> *I must only deserve being hit over the head. Yes, it's a tough world.*

Do you begin to see how it all weaves together? It's so important. Give your forgiveness to the world wholly and as quickly as you can. Let everybody off the hook—you know, all of those beings that you have hung on the hook in your basement?

> *Good, you are going to stay right there and I am going to remember.*

Let them all go. Release them from their cross. Let them go. For as you release your brother, you have released yourself. There is no other way.

When fear seems to come up to prevent you from doing something, remember it's not even your thought. It's an echo of a past that has already been dissolved. And if there is a phone call you have been waiting to make, if there is a presentation you have been wanting to do, if there is an old friend that you have just been missing, if there is a job you want to apply for, by all means go and do it. It's just a drama. That's all it is. You've been playing a game and you took it seriously, and part of the game has been the creation of guilt and pain and suffering and limitation and lack. And right here, right now, you can choose to put a new game piece on the board. You can choose to live unlimitedness and you don't even have to know how to do it. That's the great thing.

Does not a loving parent take their child and say,

Here, I will show you how to cross the street.

Your Father will show you how to cross this *universe.* You don't have to know how to do it. All you need to do is give Him your willingness, no matter what. It is called throwing in the towel of separation and understanding that your will *is* your Father's will.

For there are many of you in this room who have felt the desire for abundance—what we will call here material abundance—and yet, you have blocked it at every turn because somewhere you have perceived that it is not really good to desire material abundance. That is just a thought in your head. Throw it out the window.

Heaven waits. Heaven itself waits on your acceptance, and your brother waits on your acceptance for him of the Heaven that lies within you both. Heaven waits on your acceptance. What if indeed you are the one? What if you are the one that holds the key? You are what they would call the one hundredth monkey? And if *you* choose to adopt that new perception, then suddenly in the twinkling of an eye the whole of mankind will sit up and go,

My goodness gracious, there's no one here but Christ.

What if you were that one? Please join me in not waiting any longer for somebody else to do it. That is the whole essence of the Second Coming of Christ—your choice to turn the key to the Kingdom of Heaven that dwells within you, and to understand you don't have to know how to walk around as a living Christ. All you need is to be willing to ask before every decision and you will have the guidance that you require.

And some of you indeed can join me now and can see that as I speak those words—I do not so much see bodies, by the way, I don't find them to be very interesting—but those words met a certain resistance in some because it means giving up the game. It means assuming complete responsibility for every feeling you have; and realizing completely that there is no one outside of you who can affect you unless you allow it.

When your Light so shines before men, before mankind, that its radiance cannot be limited, you will then know and understand—to use some Biblical words, since some people seem to like them still—that though you walk through the valley of the shadow of death, you need fear no evil. The rod and the staff of the Love of God is in you, within you, and around you—always. And there is no one there in that valley save yourself, the face of a brother or sister who asks *you* to help them awaken from the dream.

Now, how do you do that? Well, of course, you slap them around a few times and tell them to wake up. No, you don't fix anybody. You can't fix anybody. It's impossible. All you can do is be what you would choose to teach them. That's it. And allow them to choose to see the Christ in you. For to do so will mean that they must have begun to recognize that Christ in them, too, because only Christ can recognize Christ.

That means that the only thing you are asked to do in this dimension is to live as though you are not an ego; and to live as though you are Christ.

I can't make it any simpler, and only you can make it difficult. Sorry about that. What do you think? Is all of this making sense?

Participant: Yes.

Well, then how do you choose to live right now? This moment? Who are you? Nobody knows yet?

Oh, but if I say it out loud I feel a little self-conscious.

Participant: The arisen Christ.

Hmm. How do you know that?

Participant: I know it because I choose to live my life that way.

Ahh. Well, one out of a room isn't so bad.

[Laughter]

Who are you? Stop whispering. Let's go! Who is sitting next to you? What do you want to create on this Earth?

Participant: Heaven on Earth.

Well then, don't wait for somebody else to put the spade in the ground. What would it be like to live each day . . . when you walk into your grocery store, you are just beaming with the radiance of Christ and somebody thinks a negative thought and you reach over and you put your hands on their shoulders and you say,

> *Oh, my precious friend. Oh, no. Please, no.*

[Laughter]

Participant: The men in the white jackets are ready to take you away.

They won't come and take you away unless you fear it.

What if you looked that one in the eye and say,

> *I know you, even if you don't know yourself.*

Tell them that they are doing what is called playing out or watching a re-run, and there is a new show in town. Ask them if they perhaps have failed to go to their mailbox? The invitations have been sent and the party is beginning. The party is beginning and everybody is invited.

That's what it's all about. It's all it's ever been about. You are the one who has been here throughout all of time and all of space, and you have danced with one another in a million different ways. If you can think of a role, you've played it. Whether it be a role that could be said to be wearing a white hat or a black hat, if you can think it, you've played it. Oh, isn't that embarrassing?

So who are you going to judge? Somehow, in some way, because of the love I see in you, you could say I am like one who looks upon this world and sees parched land; and then I look at each of you and I see this infinite reservoir of the most nurturing waters that one could ever comprehend, without end and without a bottom. Sparkling clear. Radiant Light. Such a perfect water. And all I ever really try to do is to find a way to let you let me open the door and take a glass of it out, so that we together can pour it upon this world. One glass of your love is all it takes. Hmm.

And in everything that I have ever said to you—whether it be this odd form, or the other two thousand and three that I am currently doing similar work with, or through any of the hands of an infinite number of healers that I also communicate and work with, whether it was a single word or act that I ever did through my Father's grace when I walked among you—nothing I have ever said or done has ever been designed for any other purpose except to help *you* open the floodgates to the Love of Christ that lives within you.

So the cat is out of the bag. And as I have said to some of you: if you want to wait, I can outwait you.

So, does the world need saving? No, the world is an illusion; how are you going to save it? All you are asked to do is not to fix anything, whether it be on a macrocosmic scale or the microcosmic scale as you would perceive it called your life. Stop trying to fix what may have occurred in the past. Simply begin now to think with different thoughts. Not to say,

> *I wish I could be unlimited. If only I could get rid of this, whatever it might be.*

Participant: Sometimes it's a person.

Or a ghost.

Yes. But indeed begin now to put the fullness of your attention on being the unlimitedness of the Love of Christ through Whom anything and everything can be accomplished. And remember, it's easy because *you* don't have to do it. You only have to allow it.

So [addressing someone present in the room], within thirty days I would like you to deliver a speech in front of at least two hundred people about the Kingdom of Heaven. Now, if you don't accomplish that, it will mean at least ten thousand more lifetimes.

Participant: Ohhhhh. I know you don't mean that.

You do, huh?

Think about it though. Begin to imagine and visualize yourself giving that talk. Feel it until it is as real as it seems to be now that you are sitting on the floor. Okay? It's your meditation for the next thirty days.

And listen to the words you speak. Feel the effect of the words and realize it is the Holy Spirit speaking through you and open to it. Hear your words and watch and feel that experience as though you are indeed witnessing it, and yet feeling it at the same time. Okay?

Don't worry, because if you think you get stuck, I'll hang a few . . . cue cards I believe they are called.

[Laughter]

Participant: Oh, great.

Hmm. How are we all doing?

Participant: Great.

Hmm. Life is really very, very simple. Lament nothing that comes to you. For all that can come to you is either the result of a thought you *used* to think, in which case you are watching it pass you by because you are no longer thinking that way, or you begin to witness the miracles which are the effects of the thoughts you've begun to learn to think. Does that make sense? Those are the only two possibilities.

Think with unlimitedness and miracles will come to be your way of life, and you'll just be shaking your head with a smile on your face:

I used to think I was limited. Well, it was a funny movie.

Now, please do not think that to be unlimited means that you are going to have what you call forty-seven Rolls Royces in the garage. Of course, that's not quite what I am talking about. You can abide with five dollars in the pocket and be totally at peace and know that the path you are walking is absolutely perfect; and you can love every moment of it, and you are as abundant as the richest man that ever lived. But be honest with yourself. If you'd rather have ten instead of five, admit it and begin to do something about it by beginning to allow yourself the feeling of living in unlimitedness, referred to you in the former measurement of golden coins. That's all you are doing. It is just an energy, after all. It's really no different than what makes your heart beat. *It's just an energy.*

Those of you that have ever taken a glass of water to your lips—and in any day of your life is there anybody here that has ever done that? Receiving abundance is really like drinking water. You make the choice to allow it to enter into the sphere of your experience. You may not know how and that doesn't matter. All you need to do is be willing—to imagine, to visualize, to feel that abundance, and to ask the Father to set all things in motion so that it is created around you and through you. And then miracles happen. Perhaps a phone call from an old friend. It could happen in a million ways, but it will be there for you. Isn't that right?

Participant: Mmmm.

So. What would it be like? What would it be like if you chose to step to the front of the crowd and be the leader that shows everyone else how to live in the unlimitedness of Christ? What if you got so crazy that you abandoned all of your fears, or at least chose to walk through them? Or so crazy that you are willing to stand in front of a crowd of two hundred people and say,

> *Well yes, I'm an expert on the Kingdom of Heaven. Here, I can show you how to create abundance. (Father, how do you do this?)*

Why not?

How can you know what your Father's will is for you? When you are truly willing to be honest about what seems to be the burning desire in your heart. And if you look at that desire and it is not caught up with the manipulation or hurting of anybody, not the taking of anything because you think you need it, but just a burning desire that seems to have been with you no matter how often you tried to ignore it, it's a safe bet that you might as well go for it. And if you do, many miracles will come. Many miracles.

And what you thought was your heart's desire will have been realized to be only a stepping-stone that the Holy Spirit has placed before you, because your Holy Spirit knows what's in your heart, you see, and creates then that desire because you will be attracted to it. And as you step upon it, like a flower it opens up, and you realize that it really meant something else, and you've become something else. Perhaps in your pursuit of abundance you discover that you are asked to be a teacher of God. Does all of that make sense to you?

Allow yourself to step lightly and with joy upon the stepping-stones that are placed before you. Not one thing arises in your day by accident. It only waits for you to turn your attention to it and embrace it and say,

> *Well, if this is here, there is a purpose for it.*

And in that moment you hold the power to discern its purpose if you are willing to embrace it with your love. Learn from it. Step upon it and go on. And everything serves, *everything serves* what could be called here, your becoming. For as you have lived in time and have created the dramas that would draw you into the perception of separation from God, so too now, as the arisen Christ, you allow time to be used as the device through which you witness the flowering of the Light and Love you are.

You walk through a magical kingdom. There is nothing realistic about this world. Nothing. Someday you will understand that even the body is not realistic. You walk through a magical kingdom. Everything is being formulated for you out of the thoughts and perceptions you have held, and *when you choose only God, please rest assured that everything quickens and a new power comes to form everything.* And every experience that comes to you is given to you as a stepping-stone, as a touchstone if you will, that leads you ever more into the fullness of the Christ you are. Hmm.

Contemplate what that must mean and see how it asks you to change your perceptions about what you experience. Now, the grand thing is this: if you forget, all you have to do is remember and the game goes on.

And the last thing that I want to say to you before we allow the bodies to have a bit of a break, the last thing I'll say is this: it is absolutely impossible to regress on this journey once you choose to begin it.

So the next time you go,

> *Ohhh, God, I'm really gonnnne...*

—Nonsense. Pinch yourself and wake up and walk on. You can't go backwards, you see, because the past has been washed away from you. There is nowhere back there to step. So even if you experience doing something again—you call it the pattern that goes around in a circle and you can't seem to break it—you are not stepping backwards. You are fully choosing in the present to create that experience. It is not coming up from behind you to bite you in the butt.

[Laughter]

Take a nice deep breath—the breath of God—and exhale and let your Light radiate out in all directions. And then remind yourself that after all is said and done, *you* are the Light of the world. How about that! And even now many of you have felt in the last twenty-nine and a half seconds the descent of like a blanket of peace, and though this may seem a little fantastic to some of you, to others it won't—I never come and do this work alone. I have some friends, just as you are my friends, but these don't have a body; and they come with me whenever this work is done. And that blanket—how many of you felt it?—is bestowed upon you by what you would perceive as several masters, though I am not so sure we like the term. Think of them as friends that love you deeply; and know that you are not separate from where they are. And that peace is available to you with one breath, any time you choose to receive it.

Know you the term, some of you, 'The Ascended Masters'? Perhaps 'The Great White Brotherhood'? Think not that they are unavailable to you. Think not that this my beloved brother has what you call a red phone on the desk. Hmm. There is no one special. And that love and that peace, that opportunity, descends on each equally. What creates the appearances of differences is the willingness to receive it and to enact it. That's all. That's the only difference.

Remember, and breathe that peace. Just play at it. You might even want to gather with one or two in the corner and just take a nice deep breath together and feel that blanket of peace. It's there for you. And, as you say in your world, practice makes perfect.

Peace be unto you, and thank you for me allowing these few moments to create a mirror for you of the Truth that lies within you.

Amen.

[Break]

I want very much for each and every one of you to truly, to truly embrace this simple fact—and I speak unto you now, each individually, if you will. I give thanks to my Father for *your* presence. I bow down before your Light and your Love and your beauty. I cannot possibly find words in any language that can possibly express to you the gratitude and the love that I feel, the joy I feel, when I look upon you.

It isn't what you do. It isn't what you say. It's who you are. And throughout all of eternity I have and will remain in awe at the stupendous Light that you are. Thank you from the depth of my being. Thank you for the Light that you bring to creation.

It's a rather joyous state, you see, to be in a place where constantly, with everyone that comes into your experience, the feeling that I just expressed to you is there—is there always. And yet, it is not a feeling that is peculiar to just me. It simply comes of itself unto any mind or any heart that is truly willing to relinquish the perceptions that have served to do nothing but veil the presence of the peace of God within you.

And what I have just shared with you in words you could just as well share with anybody you saw on your street. Not just as an exercise, but as a Truth, a reality. What is called existence, which is really the practice of awareness, is rather incredible when every moment is lit by the fire of gratitude for the radiance of the being who is before you—even if they are giving you what you call a ticket for moving your automobile too quickly. Indeed.

And as you give, you receive. So if you feel at any time there is maybe a little bit of a drying up of the river of love, find someone to give your love to. Find a way. The situation may not call for the words that I just used as I spoke to each of you individually, but find a way to give the fullness of your love to them. And that fast [snaps fingers], you will see how quickly you can change your own countenance, because as you teach, you learn. And as you give, you receive.

Therein lies the whole of the laws of creation. That is why, you see, our Father receives so much—because He gives so totally of Himself unto the infinite reaches of all that creation is. And therefore, God being but Love, never experiences anything but the unlimited radiance of Love. For He that gives all, receives all. It does seem rather simple, doesn't it?

Hmm. Well, enough of all of that. I just wanted to express my love to you.

Participant: We love you, too, Jeshua.

And it is received without a trace of resistance.

[Laughter]

Look well then, for if you perceive a difference between yourself and me, could it be that perhaps there is something in you that feels it should resist, at least a little bit, the overwhelming Love that is the presence of God? Resistance is what makes this world. That's a rather good line. Hmm.

So, some of you that have been around for the past year, have you not noticed that in many ways the form of language has changed?

Participant: Yes.

And there are reasons for that. What needed to be said in terms of correcting certain Biblical perceptions has been established, and even though what seems to be different bodies and minds are here to some degree than when we started, the message is being received by all. So that as we moved along, certain walls have been melted, even in those that have come for but the first time. Does that make sense to you?

Participant: Yes.

Now, if that is true—and I assure you that it is—it means that every time *you*, in the course of your own life, your own experience, every time *you* choose to be the presence of Love and to teach only love, rest assured you are extending it unto the whole of creation and uplifting it. You could say that you are like one who stands before what seems to be a very long and very high and very thick wall, and your Father has come to you and said,

> *Take down the barrier between creation and Myself. Here is your chisel and here is your hammer.*

And you have put it up against that wall and one thought has been,

> *Oh, my goodness gracious. How will I ever tear this wall down? It's a hundred miles thick, four thousand miles high, and who knows how long?*

And yet when you place the chisel on the wall and tap it lightly with one loving thought, the vibration is felt throughout the whole of that wall. And as you choose to be the presence of Love, you are chipping away at the wall that surrounds the heart of someone on the other side of this planet.

How valuable are your loving thoughts? Hmm. It is that which cannot have a price tag on it. How powerful are your negative thoughts? Hmm. Those of you that would envision a world transformed, a planet radiant with Light in which all of mankind lives as a brotherhood—or perhaps it's time you start saying as a sisterhood; but if you understand who you are, masculine and feminine terms really don't matter much, they are just forms of language—for those of you that would envision such a world, and there are many in this room that don't just think about it, the vision is pressing upon your heart. Almost so that there is a quickening. Do you know that feeling? As if Light is descending down into the core of your heart so that at times it feels as if it is going to burst? Do you know the feeling?

Be you therefore the one willing to tap the chisel with every single loving thought that you would hold, and choose only loving thoughts. Step back just a little bit and abide in what you could call, some would call, cosmic consciousness. That's an interesting term. It only means that you are aware that separation does not exist. Nowhere. And each loving thought affects the whole, and you can learn, you can literally learn, how to do whatever you do in your life and at the very same moment—which is truly outside of time—to hold the whole of creation in your awareness.

And whether you are laying your hands on another's body, whether you momentarily seem to be blending with the mind of one individual amongst many to speak to a small room of people—friends —you can know that in that moment you are addressing or laying your hands on or giving a smile to the whole of creation, and you can literally feel the Truth of that and know it. Not just as a hope, not just as a dream, but as a living reality. And as you practice that, something very miraculous happens. For when you are in relationship—and whether it be with your lover, your mate or the gas station attendant, it doesn't really matter—when you are in relationship and you look into their eyes, you literally see the whole of creation before you and you embrace them with the Love that you are.

That is how vast you are. And that experience, that reality, is really open to you in every moment. It requires only your choice to allow what you have thought to be the mundane and ordinary moments to be translated by the Holy Spirit into the means through which Christ enlightens creation.

That is the power given unto each and every one of us before time began. That's how powerful you are. And all it requires is seventy-two lifetimes in the monastery.

[Laughter]

You have already done that. And that didn't work.

All that is required is that you, in the quiet and the peace of your own heart and mind, make a simple decision:

> *I will be the presence of Love. I am the one sent of my Father to share the joy of unconditional Love in each moment and with every breath.*

That choice not only can transform your entire being, it will transform this illusory world into that which shall reflect the Kingdom of Heaven on Earth. *That choice is the Second Coming of Christ.* That is why I said earlier that Heaven waits on you. Ahhh. Thank God it's no longer *my* responsibility.

[Laughter]

What do you think? Perhaps one of these evenings as we begin and everyone is sitting in silence, and hopefully you are not expecting or looking forward, hopefully just abiding in that place . . . perhaps I won't say anything at all and we will just be Christ. But be you therefore vigilant for you will not know the hour or the day in which I might choose to do that. And in that hour would you become impatient? Would you let the mind create thoughts,

> *I wonder what is going on? It's been forty-five minutes. Has Jeshua left?*

Ah, the one that you would call Jon Marc, who I prefer to call Jon (but that's another story)

> *Oh, the poor thing. He will be so embarrassed.*

[Laughter]

Or would you allow yourself to realize there is nowhere to go, nothing to achieve, that I cannot be separate from wherever you choose to abide together in love? For where two or more are gathered in my name, guess what happens? It might be fun.

Participant: It would be great transcribing.

[Laughter]

Participant: You want twenty dollars for that booklet, right?

It would be worth a thousand. So, how are we all doing?

Participant: Good. Great. Fine.

Are you happy to be here together?

Participant: Yes. Very happy.

You could be out doing what they call celebrating the independence.

Participant: We are.

Frankly, I haven't seen a whole lot of what you call independence in your culture. Inter-dependence in a way that really isn't all too healthy. But that's going to change. Do you know why it is going to change? Because we, the Ascended Masters, are going to make it happen.

Participant: Ha!

And on your next Fourth of July I am going to descend in a chariot of fire and land on your White House lawn and take over the government.

Participant: I'd vote for you.

Would it be okay if I run on what you call the Independent Ticket?

[Laughter]

The whole point of that, of course, is that there is no group of masters that does not already include *you.* Let no one tell you that there is some group called Ascended Masters that are so far over your head, literally and otherwise, that it will take you lifetimes to go through many initiations to become as grand as they are. It is time to let go of the myth of progression because it is a myth born in time and therefore a language or model that has simply been used because that's all you could hear. You are already in the club . . you are already in the club . . . and I want to let you in on a little secret: those of us to whom many of you have given labels or allowed others to give labels to us called 'Ascended Masters' have just been waiting patiently for you to realize that where you sit in any moment to ask for help from us is inside the clubhouse. You're already there. Does that make sense to you?

You are—and listen carefully—you are *already* an ascended master. It's already been finished. Your resistance to it comes only from the belief that that's not true. You've misperceived that the journey is already finished, and the joke's on you. You are already that Light. It doesn't matter what shape or form your body is in. It doesn't matter what age you are. You are an ascended master. You already awakened. The game is over; you are just watching a re-run. I know that seems almost simplistic, but anyone who chooses, even in this moment, to accept that fully, realizes that I am not kidding. There is nowhere you are going. Nowhere at all. You are already back home where the long, long journey that's never been, began.

I and my Father are one, and there is nothing to do except allow that love that you are to be given away in any number of infinite forms. If you want more forms and more ways in which to give it away, just ask your Father; He will provide them to you.

> *Oh, but if only I could become a great artist, then I'd be happy.*

Be happy and you *are* a great artist. What could take a more delicate touch, a more creative stroke, than to master the art of being the presence of happiness itself? Hmm. Yes!

Well, so here we are together in this experience called creation.

What on Earth shall we do with it? Anyone have any ideas?

Participant: First, let's clean it up and make everybody happy.

Let's play while we are doing it. Let's give away God's love to one another.

Well. Indeed, play well and laugh well while you are repainting the canvas. That's all you are doing: repainting the canvas. In your own life you can repaint the canvas any time you want to start.

> *I don't like that color. Hmm. A little boring.*

So, change it.

Indeed, play—and play well. And yes, of course—play fair.

So, in all of that I've had my piece this evening. Actually I have my peace always, but . . .

There is really not much else to be said. But if you have questions, we can entertain them. Now, I don't mean to make light of a question that someone feels they have that is a serious matter to them. And yet, all we can do is entertain questions until the soul itself finally comes to the point of being willing to acknowledge that it *is* the answer it seeks.

I regret to inform you that I have never answered a single question in a way that has made any difference whatsoever. It is the willingness of the soul to accept what it already knows, since all I do is read the book in your heart—and I just know how to read well. And when you receive it and go,

> *Ah, yes,*

that's when change occurs. Does all of that make sense to you?

Participant: Yes.

You have been taught that I was created to be the savior of the world. Hmm. Actually, my Father said,

> *Do you know, Jeshua ben Joseph, I hope you don't mind, but I am just going to make you into a mirror. Go around and let people see their reflection. I know it sounds a little boring. It's not too royal or grand. But that's what I want you to do.*

So I said,

> *Fine. Make me a mirror.*

And He did. And I said,

> *Whoa, look at that.*

That fast I became a mirror with nothing to do except reflect. And it's not a very boring way to exist.

So, do you have any questions? Or better yet, do you have any statements?

Participant: Jeshua, I have a question since nobody is jumping up to say something here. In what we perceive as time and in what we perceive as having lived many lifetimes, what the soul learns in a lifetime does not seem to be carried forward into the next lifetime on a conscious level. Does that make sense? I really want to know if our souls, as we go through lifetimes, if our souls remember the Truths that we learned in each lifetime; and if we do, does it impact our consciousness in that next lifetime or many lifetimes?

Now, we are going to give you an answer in two different ways. First: what the Son decrees, is. What does that mean? You are the one. You *are* the one. And what you decree, that is, what you select to perceive and believe, will be your experience. That means that if you hold the perception of a model that souls go through many, many lifetimes and learn lessons that are added to their luggage, and they carry them with them so that they are progressively becoming wiser, then that will be your experience; and you will believe it because you will have wanted to choose the experience of a progression through time. So far, so good?

Participant: Yes.

Therefore, if you ask me, given this model, does this follow? What I will say to you is: do you want it to follow—that the soul gains knowledge that is carried?

Participant: Well, now I am confused. I thought I understood you to say many times in our evenings that we have gone through countless lifetimes because we never get it straight.

That is absolutely true, but that does not deny the fact that you are the one choosing on insisting that you are a soul that has gone through many lifetimes and haven't got it right. That's what the whole point of this evening's talk has been: that you are the one clinging to that perception, and I am a mirror that reflects it back to you. Do you see?

Participant: I'm completely lost.

Good. Now, we can make some real progress.

I have indeed talked about other lives. I have even used the model of language about progressively getting on with it. But in all cases in which I have done that it is a teaching tool given to the one to whom I am speaking, or perhaps to several in a group, because it is a language that they are insisting on seeing things with. Do you see?

Participant: So we only live progressive lifetimes if we believe we live progressive lifetimes?

Yes. And all of that is still within the realm of the dream. *Your reality is that you are the only begotten Son of God and you exist wholly outside of time.*

You embrace the whole of creation and it arises within you, and the model and the perception of lifetimes is part of that which has arisen within the Mind of Christ as a free choice. It is like looking at clouds in the sky and deciding that you see animals or what have you. You are the one creating it. You are the one creating the clouds. Even your scientists know that there is no such thing. That is, they are created according to your perception, according to this apparatus that you have created. Does that make sense to you?

Participant: Yes.

Precious friend, come to understand that awakening will never come as long as you insist on adhering to a model in which you see yourself as having had a beginning, going through a chain of lifetimes, getting better and better, hopefully. Except for the times that you regress. Hmm.

Do you understand what I am saying? It doesn't mean it's not okay to have fun talking and pretending about all of these incredible lifetimes you've had. But if you want to be Christ, which is to accept who you are, you are going to give up that model because Christ abides in what is eternal and timeless, changeless and unlimited forever. And that is really the goal of every soul that perceives itself progressing through time—to become timelessness, to become unlimited.

Does that make sense?

That's what's pressing against you, you see. It's the feeling of being constricted. That's what you are trying to overcome. You may interpret it in a million different ways, but what you are seeking is to be unlimited. And it won't happen until you are willing to begin with a new perception:

> *I am unlimited—now.*

And with that, what unfolds is the releasing of every perception that is not in accord with unlimitedness.

I have said many times that you live the life of every being. *That* is reality. It is part of the highest Truths, if you will, that can possibly be uttered. And when you truly rest and let go of that resistance, you will find, incredibly, that that is true.

Some have said to me,

> *Boy, you seem to know me so well. Better than I know myself.*

Only because I chose my unlimitedness, and therefore I embrace you. I use the word brother and friend because it is a way of communicating at a place where your mind still is.

Precious friend, this whole gathering tonight has been about the power of perception. Actually, we started a little while ago, even last week. The power of perception is what creates what you experience; and the only difference between where you are and where you think I am is that I chose to perceive only unlimitedness, while you have chosen to perceive that unlimitedness is something you will gradually grow into once you have learned all your lessons. And that's perfectly okay. Just enjoy the journey.

What would happen if you were to begin to constantly practice the perception that you *are* unlimited now? That everything you see, every brother, every sister, every blade of grass is arising *within you*?

Participant: So what I'm getting is that the whole concept of reincarnation is part of the dream.

Exactly.

Right where you are, you are already home. You are not the body, you are not that personality your parents told you that you were. You are that consciousness, that awareness, that Love, that vast Light in which all of creation is arising—and the holy and only begotten child or offspring of God is eternally one.

Where else can you possibly find a greater freedom than to realize that there is nothing *outside* of you, but there is everything *inside* of you?

When you lay your head on the pillow at night and you dream countless dreams, when you awaken in the morning don't you realize it just took place within your mind? All of this is occurring within your Mind, the one infinite Mind that is Christ. And the dream is shifting. I have called it elsewhere the transference or the translation of an unhappy dream into a happy dream. The reflection of Heaven on Earth is still part of the dream. But it will reflect perfectly what your reality is and that is why at that moment creation itself will no longer be required. What you call 'creation' manifests forms in time. It is very difficult to talk about what that will be like. In fact, that isn't possible because it transcends the dream itself.

Oh, precious and holy Christ, you are eternal. There has never been a time that you have not existed. There has never been a world that you have not sojourned through. You are the one that has made it all up. Every lifetime. Know you that called the Book of Life? It is a term from your Judeo-Christian religion. You are the Book of Life; that's who you are. That is why when two minds come together and are willing to accept their enlightenment, there is really hardly anything to do but have a very good laugh. And create from the infiniteness of your being; to play in the drama and choose to play with unlimitedness, when you realize you have been playing with limitation.

I once said unto some of you within the drama of the dream:

> *Fear not for I shall be with you always.*

And those of you that were a little bit attached to that aspect of the dream have clung unto it. Some of you still hold that your greatest sense of identity is who you were then. Hmm. And when I said:

> *Fear not, for I shall be with you always,*

I did so with a twinkle in my eye, for I can hardly be anywhere else. And when I say I have waited patiently, it means that I simply sit on a park bench in eternity, waiting for you who are in the bus in time to choose to stop and get off, and sit down with me.

Is all of that making sense? It is rather important.

So, it's over. The time is at hand. I have never ceased weaving myself in and out of your dreams and dramas to whisper in your ear,

> *Precious one, remember. Remember.*

"Come home" means nothing else than to open the eyes of your heart and realize the Truth of who you are. Has the drama seemed long and vast? Oh, yes. But the more you choose to identify with your unlimitedness, the more the weight of the dream is forgotten—just as when you open your eyes in the morning and for a moment you shake your head and say,

> *Oh, my goodness,*

and your heart is still palpitating. You know that feeling? And then you realize,

> *Wait a minute. I'm just sitting in my bed. Ahh.*

And by the time you get up and take a shower and have a bite to eat, you have forgotten what you even dreamed. Is that not true?

Participant: Yes.

That's what awakening is like. When it first hits you, you go,

> *My goodness, how amazing. I can't even put it into words.*

But by and by, you forget all the weight of the dreams, and you actually become better and better at finding ways to communicate, to teach in an artful way that prods the minds of your brothers and sisters, which are really but aspects of your own Mind, into the recognition of who they are. But even that is part of the dream. Miracles are valuable only within a dream, and the choice is simple. And I've used this analogy before, and when I have, some have smiled, some have chuckled. It's very, actually quite literal . . .

It is as though every moment you are walking up to one of what you would call one of your movie theaters which has many movies going on at the same time, on different screens, and you select which ticket to buy. That's really how simple it is.

One of the movies has been that you are only born once and then you are going to die, and thank God that God sent His only begotten Son to die on the cross and save you from your sins. And there are many that cling to that movie and love it, and that's perfectly okay. One of the movies is that I am an infinite soul and boy, have I gone through a million lifetimes and oh, my goodness, when I was in Egypt; and all of the rest. That too is a movie that many would cling to.

But your reality is simply this: you are the one standing outside the theater and so much power is given to you that you can watch them all at once without buying a ticket. You can allow all of them. You can embrace all of them. You can look at the people that are sitting in the little rows, entranced with the movie, and you can *love* them into awakening by being the one who is awake. Does all of that make sense?

And that is what you are called to do. Now, who is doing the calling?

Participant: You are calling yourself.

Exactly. You will awaken to your own call and no one else's. And if you are here in this room, it's because you have at least begun to hear and answer your own call. And I am but that aspect of you that is a mirror of the deepest Truth that lies within you. And you brought me forth.

Whew, try preaching that on a Sunday morning.

[Laughter]

You might have to say,

> *Oops, wrong theater.*

Make sure you duck before the eggs are thrown:

> *No my dream is so important. I have to insist that my dream is real. Everybody else's is false.*

A dream is a dream is a dream. And nobody is doing better than anybody else if they are still dreaming.

Have you ever had the thought that, perhaps some of you have said,

> *You know, a long time ago I used to believe this certain way but now I know I am really an infinite soul that's been incarnated a million times,*

and you've believed you made progress? I am sorry to say one is either dreaming or one chooses to be awake. There is no other choice and nothing else is occurring. Some of you have been taught,

> *Well, there are gray areas.*

In this sense there is but white and black, on or off. Love or fear is another way to put it.

And therefore I echo to you your own call to choose to be awake now!

And now is all there is. Have you ever played the little game: during the course of a day, every hour, stopping and asking yourself, where are you and what time it is? You are always here and it's always now.

And the very same choice is in front of you now as was in front of you when you were a priestess in Egypt. A warrior in the Steppes. A yogi in a cave. A monk in a monastery. A drunk in a Western town. Sorry about that one. And it's the same choice that is right in front of you now:

Will I choose to be awake?

Do you see what we are coming to within the perception of the dream? *This is the highest form of teaching that can be given because there is nothing beyond it that can be put into words.*

It's the last level, if you will; if you want to play that game, it's the last level. And this is what you are coming to because you have chosen to awaken to your own call and to hear it and follow it.

Some of you have heard me say that the bell has been rung. I didn't ring it; you did. Or another level: we rang it together. And as you go out into your journeys, really think about this for a moment . . . you know your journeys called your lifetimes? Aren't those really very much related to the body? Is it not the body that gets into this car instead of that car and into this bed instead of that bed? That eats this instead of that, and all the rest? The Mind that you are is embracing all such journeys and all such dramas, and that is what again you must come to allow yourself to remember. Those of you that have studied my little work called *A Course In Miracles* will remember this: the only lesson you have to learn is that there is nothing outside of you. That's it. Learn that and the game is over.

Does that bring an end to time? Will the body just crumple to dust? Who cares? Who cares! When you are awake, you are awake, and if the drama goes on or if the drama ends, who cares? When you are so busy being the presence of Love and giving it away, who cares? Who cares if there is going to be an earthquake tomorrow? Who cares if the Earth is going to flip on its axis? Who cares? It's just a drama. And you are too busy delighting in being Love to take on a drop of seriousness about it.

Do you understand that it's that level of freedom that allows some of you to walk upon the hot coals, called the firewalking? That's the very same freedom. You just haven't allowed yourself to recognize that that's the same level of freedom that I manifested when I made a bit of a dramatic appearance. Hmm. It's the same thing. And every time you walk through a ring of fear to embrace your brother and sister as yourself and give them your love, you have done the same thing that I did when I allowed "them" to crucify me. I walked through a ring of fear that was nothing more than a perception: that having nails driven through physical hands could somehow separate me from God. And I demonstrated that that is not true. And if *that* ring of fear can't separate you from God, there is *no* ring of fear that can separate you from the Love that you are.

Whenever you are in a situation and you feel that little bit of constriction and you have something in your heart that you are burning to share or whatever it might be, what you are feeling is a little ring of fear and that's all. And it's a blessing. It is such a blessing. My goodness, you've confronted it a million times in your dreams; and all you have to do is walk through it, and it begins to shatter like pieces of glass falling out of a window so that the breeze can blow through.

Fear is a blessing. Walk through it. Those of you that have walked on the hot coals know perfectly well what I am saying. Those of you that have ever allowed somebody to kiss you with passion know what I am saying. Remember that first kiss? My goodness, you've all walked through those rings of fear so many times that it's old hat. And the only thing that now prevents you from walking through what you think are your rings of fear is that you are choosing to perceive it as a wall a hundred miles thick. And as a curse instead of a blessing. That's the only difference.

Do you begin to get the freedom of it all? Good. So now I can return to the place from whence I have come, sitting at the right hand of God, surveying all below me. Seeking out the poor and wretched sinners who need me to save them. Boy, aren't I hot stuff?

[Loud Laughter]

Hmm. I think I'll just rest in reality and be right with you in your own heart throughout all of eternity—as an aspect of yourself that is your brother and your friend as long as the happy dream is necessary.

They once tried to get rid of me and it didn't work. And now you can tell your friends Christ is indeed returned, because that Mind is awakened within you. And so if one comes and says,

> *Do you believe in the Second Coming?*

say,

> *Well, of course. Behold, I stand before you.*

[Laughter]

In other words, lighten up and have some fun.

So, what I am going to ask you to do now, tomorrow—this is very important—I want you to do whatever and only what you truly *want* to do. Whew. Think about that. So, right away, you see, we've collaborated to create some rings of fear. And if you are willing to accept them as a blessing, you can walk through it. Just use tomorrow as the one day that you are choosing to do only what you truly, from the depth of your being, want to do. Hmm, I wonder what that might mean? It will be a very interesting day.

Are you willing to try it out?

And if some of you have a certain work that you go to that inwardly you are not so pleased with, if in the morning when you wake up what you really want to do is go sit on a rock overlooking the ocean, call your employer and tell them that something's come up. You don't have to tell them that awakening has come up. And do it, go walk through your fear and sit on your rock.

Now, will consequences come from that? Perhaps. Are you willing to really walk through your ring of fear? Are you willing to let the illusion shatter and allow your life to be reformed by the One Who has sent you forth? Oh, my goodness. It's entirely up to you; so keep that in mind.

Love one another as your Father has first loved you. And He has loved you with unlimitedness and with joy. He sees the perfection of your Light wherever you are. You are free to don the cloak of time and yet be beyond time.

You are the one that comes to bring Light to this world. You are infinite. You are eternal. You are the beauty. You are the beauty of every ray of Light that dances a thousand diamonds across the waters of this planet. You are the beauty and the light of every star. You are the vastness and the silence and the power of space in which all things have arisen in your little physical universe. Hmm. You are the brightest of colors and the deepest of tones. You are the perfect melody. You are the song, the instrument and its composer, and you are the one that delights in the song.

You are all that I am and we are one: Christ eternal, unbounded oceans of Love and Light and perfection . . . perfection.

You are the Prodigal Son that has journeyed through all of time and all of space and all worlds, and now has returned to your Father's sacred place. Start chowing down on the food and the abundance that's on the table. For the feast has been prepared for you. The time is at hand and the journey is over. Welcome home. Welcome home, precious and holy friend.

Peace be unto you as you dance your Light into this world and work with me, play with me at translating the unhappy dream into the happy dream. Each of you is a miracle-worker because the miracle has been accepted in you, by you:

> *I and my Father are one.*

Peace be unto you. And indeed Heaven and Earth have been joined in you and extended as far as from the East to the West.

Amen.

THE HOLY INSTANT

September 1992

Jeshua

Now, we begin.

And indeed, greetings unto you, beloved and holy friends. Indeed, greetings unto—*you*, the only begotten offspring of the Father, of the divine, of Love. In truth there can only be one Being present. In truth there can be only one Reality present. In truth there can only be what is true.

Remember then, always, that regardless of what the eyes of the body show you, you remain as you are created to be. Made indeed in the image of all that God is, and God is but Love. Made in the image of all that the divine is, and the divine is that which extends itself infinitely and eternally from its desire to reveal Love. This is why in each and every moment when Love is expressed through you, innocently, purely and without attachment or investment, you have always experienced a state of peace, a state of ease.

And in that moment, the Holy Instant, you have remembered the truth of who you are. You have seen beyond the body in that split second. You have seen beyond the distance between you and your brother or sister, and you have reveled in the bliss of perfect union. Your life has flowed, in that moment, effortlessly. It has flowed in that moment with absence of anxiety, for there is no thought of tomorrow. There is no memory clung to of the past. There is only this freedom, in which Love, the essence of your being, the essence of Spirit, the essence of all that Christ is—that essence has flowed through the perceptions once held in the mind, the patterns, some of which you might call karma. It has seeped through the blockages in the cells of the body, and the body itself has gestured in such a way that Love has been extended into the world.

It is in just such moments that the fullness of the spiritual journey is completed. For that journey is only completed in the act of remembrance of what you have always been, that which alone you must always be. In a very real sense then, there is no evolution, there are no strategies that can get you to God, except forgetting that you are separate from God. And that forgetting, that moment, again that Holy Instance that brings you into the fullness of your being, into that state of remembrance is *in those moments* when Love has flowed through you to the world, in any of its myriad expressions, and there has been no thought to cloud it. That thought being

> *I wonder what I will receive from this giving? How will I be able to shape the universe around me in order to extract what I believe I need by being loving?*

In those moments of pure love, there is only perfect union, perfect innocence. Forgiveness itself cannot even enter such a moment, for there has been no condemnation.

In each and every moment then, when you choose to surrender the self and allow Love to be present, you have elected to live in the Kingdom. And *you* are the one who *receives* the joy, the enjoyment of witnessing Love's effects. And where do you experience the effects of Love if not *first* in your own being?

As Love flows from Spirit through the soul, through the basics or the matrix of the persona, the personalities, as it moves through the emotional field and out through the body and into the world, you must be the first that receives it. And this is what brings us to the heart and soul of what we would seek to share with you in this hour: It is not your doing that can establish you in the Kingdom. It is not your accomplishment that evolves you into the consciousness of God. It is first and foremost in your willingness to receive the reality of the Kingdom, which is the experience of Love flowing through you.

This is what I meant when I once said, 'Seek first the Kingdom within and all these things shall be added unto you.' For in every striving that the mind enters into, based on its forgetting of who it truly is, what is sought is not money, not fame, not what you call your soulmates, not the accomplishment of great tasks; what the mind is looking for is Love. That is the only thing the mind can seek, for that is the only thing it was designed to give.

Know then, that in all tasks you choose to undertake you will be motivated by only one of two things: Love or fear. Fear can come with many masks, it can even wear a smile. Fear is born, and accesses your matrix or conduit which propels your activity, when you have forgotten to seek first the Kingdom. When you have forgotten to open and receive the Love that is forever present for you, in every moment and *under all conditions.*

As you choose then to cultivate the decision to seek first the Kingdom, the tasks that you enjoin can be flooded with the Love that would flow through you, as That Voice guides your creativity, your choices, your decisions. And yet Love colors things a little differently than does fear. And this is a very important distinction. Fear will seek the results of the task, for fear believes that by the accomplishment of the task something will be received that the egoic mind believes is lacking. Love will extend itself into the task, knowing that the true treasures are the moments of relationship that arise along the journey, that become those moments in which souls can heal through learning the practice of forgiveness—of looking with innocence, of looking the shadow in the eye and choosing Love instead.

So Love is not results-oriented, Love is Love-oriented. Fear is results-oriented. This can only mean that when you enjoin any task and you find yourself depressed, frustrated that the result has not been achieved, the mind or your awareness has slipped over into the territory of fear.

Fear is an energy that believes Love is lacking, that union with God is lacking. It is run by the beliefs such as

> *I must earn my union with God. Performance is what will bring it to me,*

and all of the rest. What would it be like then, if you learned to look upon each of your days through new eyes? What would it be like if you looked upon each of your days as merely the opportunity to discern and distinguish which of those two camps your awareness is falling into:

Is it fear that is propelling me, or is it truly Love?

How again to know the difference? If you are feeling frustrated, anxious, depressed and all of the rest and you notice finally that the mind is fixated on the results you have decided should be achieved are not being achieved, and therefore a feeling state emerges, you know that you have entered into that task from fear.

Now, what then do you do? Well, it is very, very simple. You get one of those whips and you take off the shirt and then you beat yourself with it. You take out an ad in your newspapers with your picture, saying,

Behold, an unworthy one!

You have all taken out those ads in your papers, you know.

In truth, because Love does not condemn, and because Love makes all things new, even as what would be birthed from fear is arising, all you need do is stop and seek first the Kingdom and abide there until you feel restored—until you are sober, you are in your right Mind, you have received Love for yourself for no other reason than that it is good to do so. And then, as you bring your mind to the task, simply ask that Love guide the way. That Love restore your mind and awareness to the reality that the great jewels that will be presented is not so much in the result that the mind would picture, but the moments of relationship in which Love can change a pattern of perception that has been running that mind: yours, or your brother's or sister's.

Those moments are referred to as Holy Instances, and they are the crown jewel of creation. For only in such moments—and they always occur in relationship—in those moments does the reality of Love come to be more solidly established as the basis of your consciousness. And this can be nothing more than a return to what is true.

The message then, that we would seek to share with you in this hour, is a message that can transform your life. Even if it is flowing beautifully, it can flow more deeply, for there can be no limit or bottom to the depth of God. Paradoxically then, because you are the created and not the Creator, you—just like I once had the opportunity when I walked your planet as a man—you have the opportunity to translate how you see time, what you perceive its value is and utilize it to deepen your direct remembrance of the Presence of God . . . by cultivating the choice for Love, the remembrance of Love, the dedication to Love, the surrender to Love, by learning to seek first the Kingdom and allowing each of your tasks to *flow* from that choice.

When you awaken in the morning, there is a task before you. You are going to have to lift the head from the pillow, you are going to have to put your feet on your floor and you are going to have to decide which direction those feet are going to carry the body. Is that not true? And yet, how often have you awakened in the morning and immediately the mind has gotten busy with all of your to-do lists and unbeknown to you, at times the voice for fear has been the main magnet that lifts your head from the pillow, puts your feet on the floor and you're off, running scared. Hm.

> *If I don't get this done, what will they think? Oh my God, what about that? Oh!*

And it goes on and on and on.

Once, many years ago, I spoke to this, my beloved brother, that one of the greatest things he could ever learn to do was to 'wait on the Lord', which means to seek first the Kingdom before the eyes opened fully. Just in that moment when you know you have awakened from your slumber, something is going to be activating the body—a thought, an impulse—and in that moment, before the eyes open, to remember God. To choose Love. To cultivate feeling it as it penetrates your soul, your mind, your emotions, your personality, and even the tissues and cells of the body. To make sure you are not bringing with you anything that you took to sleep with you, that is a judgment of a brother or a sister. To make sure that what is going to move the body that day will not be fear but Love.

Now that sounds rather simple, doesn't it? Hm. I would then challenge you to keep a list, a calendar by your bed and when you have gotten up in the morning, and you have taken your shower or done whatever you have done, or made your coffee, or made your fourteen phone calls before you eat—before you leave the house, pause and ask yourself,

> *Did I remember to abide in Love before I opened my eyes this morning?*

Keep track! It will be most humbling, for this simple act is the most difficult to achieve. To learn to choose for Love at the most subtle moment, as consciousness is beginning to focus into the physical domain every morning. To remember Love *then*, is indeed a difficult task and yet the mind can be trained more and more to make that choice.

Would you be willing to enjoin such a challenge? Remember, we will be watching!

[Laughter]

And always, beloved friends, without judgment, without condemnation.

The mind that has awakened comes to each moment anew. The mind that has been fully established in the remembrance of the Truth that is true always, comes to each moment fresh and anew. It is not possible for such a mind to lose patience with a brother or a sister, for lack of patience can only arise from fear. From a mind that has forgotten the Kingdom and therefore is keeping score, adding up the past, it has the results about what it thinks the future should be, and this other one obviously isn't fitting in quite right.

But Love looks with innocence upon each created being, for Love sees that they look not upon another but upon themselves. This can only mean that you are your brother and sister's keeper because you *are* your brother and your sister. This is why I have often said that your greatest saviors are those that really push your buttons. For do they not call you to the task of patience? Do they not call you to the task to uncover more deeply within what must be preventing Love from showing up? For Love also provides you the wisdom to know what to do with each moment. Luckily, and by grace, it is not given you to know what your brother or sister needs. Luckily, by grace, it is not given for you to be the *caretaker* of another but the *keeper* of another. And what could that mean?

To *keep* another means to hold in your consciousness the image and remembrance of them as the perfection of the truth that they truly are. And within each soul is the spark of Light, which is the Christ Mind, which is that Mind, whole and complete, made in the image of God. To keep another is to be the *friend* of that one. And a friend indeed is one who sees the other as Christ in the journey of remembering Christ and holds them in that Light until they can hold it for themselves.

A friend is one who does not condemn or judge. Therefore, the greatest state of consciousness is to be a friend to the world. But because it is not given to you to know what your brother or sister needs, you are released from the burden of believing that *you* must know. And in any moment, as you cultivate the ability to remember first the Kingdom, to receive Love, to abide in that place, where Grace can speak to you, the Holy Spirit—that part of the mind that remains perfectly united with God and is heard when all the other dimension of your being are at peace (and peace requires non-attachment to the world)—in that moment, the Holy Spirit will guide your words, your gestures, your choices and decisions. You might find yourself speaking, you might find yourself being silent. There is no handbook, you would say, for each moment arises fresh and pure.

Seek then, seek within your own consciousness to desire the Kingdom more than anything else. More than any result you have ever imagined. More than any richness or fame or what have you. Above all created things, seek to nurture within yourself the passionate desire to have released from your consciousness anything that impedes it from being entrained to seek first the Kingdom. So that more and more and more with each moment, even as you live in this physical dimension and the body moves about on your planet, and decisions and bills to pay and all the rest arises, but the mind goes

> *Oh, I think I'll just receive Love. I'll just receive Love. I think I'll just abide in the remembrance that only Love is real.*

Ah, drink that sweet, sweet, clear water, if you will, and *then* enjoin the task before you. For in that way you'll begin to access more and more clearly the guidance and wisdom of the Holy Spirit.

But what might arise in the mind that could prevent it from wanting the Holy Spirit to hold authority over the mind? Fear. Fear. For the guidance of the Holy Spirit is not circumvented by the rules of the world. It is not contained in the guidelines that you have learned from the world. In this sense then, *wisdom is radically free.* To be guided then by the Holy Spirit is to grow into a state of being, which could be called 'radical freedom', in which no part of the mind is caught up in fearing what the perceptions of the world might be. The body-mind itself, the personality, the soul itself, becomes fully the servant of something invisible, something quiet, and yet something which in its wisdom knows how Love can serve this moment, whatever that moment may be.

To embody such a state of consciousness is the true goal that you are all seeking. It is the true result that the soul wants. It is the result for which the fearful mind creates substitutes or idols, by translating the results of its plans, its endeavors, forgetting that only Love is real. That the very purpose of time and creation is but the creation of contexts in which Holy Instances can arise and Love can be remembered and restored to the minds and hearts of friends.

Peace then comes into your life and into your relationships, into your nations, and eventually into the world when only friendship exists—true friendship—whether it be between political leader and one casting a ballot, whether it be between husband and wife, man-man, woman-woman, man-dog, cat-dog, it doesn't really matter, all forms of relationships—when they are established in friendship—*then is peace restored. Then can Heaven come to earth.*

As you learn then to want Love alone to be your guide, as you learn then to recognize that it is only in those moments, when Love has successfully (shall we say) out-shouted the voice of fear—and you know you have had thousands of those moments, in which Love has been enacted through you and you are left with the sweetest, most sublime feeling of fulfillment—when you want more and more those moments, until those moments are established as the ocean from which the waves of your life emerge, you become the gift to this world that can transform this world and *is* transforming it. Rest assured, indeed, beloved friends, each and every one of you in those moments, when through your desire, your cultivation, your practice, if you will, you have remembered Love—you have already begun to transform this world. You have taken up the cross of crucifixion, which is a symbol of the burdens of this world, and you have demonstrated that there is another way. You have literally become the embodiment that models to each brother and sister that behold, we don't need to spin in the same circles. There *is* another way and that way is Love.

Take a moment then—and I would indeed ask this of all who would hear these words now—to take this moment and turn your awareness within and imagine that you are speaking to yourself, to your very soul. Pause right now, and give yourself deep appreciation, deep gratitude, honor yourself for every single moment when only Love has led your way, when only Love has been extended. And then ask of yourself this simple question,

Would I desire more of such moments or fewer of such moments?

If the answer is 'more', simply say, "Yes," to that desire. Invite the Holy Spirit to become increasingly the authority of your consciousness. Ask It to become the magnet that pulls your attention to It before each decision. For the Holy Spirit can only come to you to the degree that you invite It in.

You are beginning to near a certain time upon your calendar, called the Christmas Season. As I have shared with you many times before, rest assured it was not the month of my birth into the world, but it became a symbol, a symbol for the birth of Light into the world, even as my life has become the most universal symbol in the human psyche for what *must* occur within each created mind. For that which alone can truly fulfill the journey of the soul, the remembrance that only the truth can be true, the recognition that Christ—which is simply a word for the purity of consciousness untainted by fear, resting in the remembrance that only Love is real—the symbol, then, of my life, celebrated at this time of Christmas should be enjoined with prayer, with silence, with celebration with true friends of the Heart, those who would be willing to join with you in celebration of every loving thought that the two of you, or the four of you, or the hundred of you, have experienced in your lives.

Imagine a Christmas celebration in which you tell stories, one to the other, of the moments in which you knew that Love had acted through you. You have in your phrase, where you are living here on this speck of earth, the 'talking of the story'— 'talk story'? What wonder stories those would be! If you would come together at that time of Christmas and listen to each other share the moments in which they know in their heart and soul that God, Who is but Love, moved through them and spoke or gestured out into the world. Would that not be a Christmas to enjoy? Would it not be a time of great celebration as you honor the great courage of each and every one of you in that group, to have chosen the courageous act of enacting Love instead of the products of fear? In which you set aside all remembrance or trace of thought of the moments in which you think you failed and did only one thing, to celebrate those moments of Love—for in those moments, you were enacting the incarnation of Christ. You were literally living what the symbol of my life is all about. The moment in which Christ came to earth, to the body and to the mind, and was birthed into the world. For each Holy Instant is Christmas.

Would you be willing to have such a gathering? Does it not create within you a tickle of excitement and enjoyment? What indeed if you wrapped your presents of your gifts to one another and placed only in them a piece of paper, or several pages, in which you write to the other all the moments you can remember in which you were the recipient of love through that other? Hm. Would that not be to give a precious gift?—to help remind your brother and sister that they have indeed succeeded, probably far often than they even know.

Would you be willing to do that? Does that sound as like it would be a good gift to give to another? What could you possibly give from the material plane that could possibly create such a permanent gifting? What could possibly match the gift to another's consciousness that *you have experienced the gift of Love through them*? What could inspire that soul to know the truth of who they really are, to be inspired, to cultivate even more moments in which they have been the birther of Christ?

Therefore, we would leave it up to you, everyone hearing these words, to set about, to take what you call the initiative, to experiment with this whole new approach to your Christmas Season. Rest assured, it will not look good on your gross national product but is it not time for the national product to cease being so gross?

[Laughter]

Is it not time for it to shine with the brilliance that can heal the wounds and the fears, the distrust, the judgments? Is it not time for Christ to be birthed into the world? To truly celebrate, to be celebrated, to be praised? And how can you praise Christ? Certainly not by attending your functions in which all attention is put on me. But rather that you create those functions in which the attention and praise of Love is offered to the brothers and sisters through which Love has touched your soul. This is to truly honor the Christ that must come cosmically. I am indeed one who looks forward to the day when the life of Jeshua ben Joseph has been entirely forgotten by everyone, for they are too busy *being* that one, celebrating the living Presence of the Christ Mind amongst themselves. So that if my name comes up, someone says,

> *Oh yes, that was a brother. I think he was here a long time ago. Let's get back on with what we are doing.*

That would be different indeed.

I have looked upon that which is called the religion based in my name. And rest assured, it has brought sadness to my heart and soul, *for my message has not been heard and received.* They have projected their praise onto the messenger and not the message.

In your Christmas Season, when so many gather in their buildings to remember *me*, to turn their attention to a historical event that occurred so long ago, what I see occurring in their souls is the attempt of fear to project the Christ Mind *outside of themselves*, to keep it at a safe distance; and when they leave those buildings, no transformation has occurred. If you would remember me on that day, please remember me only as a friend of the world, a brother equal to each and everyone of you and not above you in any way. If you would honor me in any way whatsoever, please remind your brothers and sisters of the times in which they have been the bearers and gifters of Christ to you, the times that your soul has been uplifted and inspired, the times that you have healed and transformed in their presence as they took the courageous act to let Love be given through them. In this way, my heart will indeed be gladdened. This is the transformation that must come to your planet and to your human consciousness.

Only fear projects the essence of truth outside of you and keeps it at an arm's length. There is not anything that this world has to offer that you need. There is no material thing that can fulfill you. Indeed there is no relationship that can fulfill you. There is nothing that can fulfill you. You are already fulfilled in your perfect union with God. Your only task is to cultivate more and more the remembrance of that, for it is again in those moments, when Love has flowed through you, that you have experienced your deepest peace, your greatest joy, and your deepest certainty of who you are. That is the sublime state, that is the sublime drug that you are seeking with every results-based picture, dream, endeavor. Does that make sense for you?

Christmas, the mass of the Christ. Why not be a mass of Christs, celebrating each other? Hm? And then some day a critical mass will be reached and no more criticism will be necessary.

Indeed beloved friends, there are times when many of us would wish indeed, to merely find the way that we could blow what you call the veils of ignorance, or forgetting, away from you. We see when you suffer, we feel when you suffer, because we are one with you, because you are an aspect of the Christ Mind, the one and Holy Son or offspring of God. And yet in your sovereignty, there is no one who can remove those veils for you. They remain in place only because you choose them. Look well then to see, with great innocence, what must be at work when you choose to move from fear and not Love. For everything that arises, arises only within the sovereignty of your own awareness. And you can only see outside, what you have chosen to see inside. And you can only place a judgment on what is outside because you have already placed it on yourself.

When you experience impatience with a brother or a sister, it is because there is a place within you that has been impatient with yourself. There is a place within you that is calling for your own forgiveness and love. And as you find that place within and bring it to Light within, and extend that Love to that part of you, you will suddenly find yourself feeling only patience with another. Any time you look upon anyone or anything with judgment it can only be a projection of that reflection within *you*, that you have judged.

When you perceive lack in the world, it is because in that moment, you have chosen a perception that lack lives within *you*. What then restores consciousness to holy sight? By now you should know—the decision to choose for the Kingdom, to simply stop and to remember. To drink that Love for yourself, to drink it well into yourself and then, as you open your eyes again, suddenly, the world you see has changed. For Love indeed does change and heal all things. And this is the *one and only purpose that time and space can have.* There is nothing here to be accomplished, save this: The restoration of the memory of God in the seat of the soul, so that it becomes perfectly centred as the conduit through which Love creates.

Then indeed, as you enjoin your plans, you know that you are merely creating contexts in which Holy Instances can arise. Reasons to celebrate! Reasons to dance! Reason to give praise! Reason to give thankfulness! You are looking for moments as excuses to have a party. You are not solving world hunger. You are not ending child abuse. You are looking in all the contexts you enter into for the moments of relationship in which Love is restored to the minds of those, in that moment of relationship. And of course, *that* is what ends world hunger, that is what ends child abuse, that is what ends everything that is not Love.

Look then, in all of your endeavors, not to achieve a result that *you* have decided, but rather allow Love to be the stream that carries you and energizes you for that journey within that context. And be vigilant for the moments of connection with another, playing with you in that context, in which the remembrance of Love can occur.

We would end then this simple message with one more exercise, if you will. When you rest your head upon your pillow at night, and you notice that the body's tiredness is beginning to call your attention to fuzziness—as indeed the soul begins to retract its focus on the physical domain and journey into other dimensions while the body sleeps—in just that transition time, just before you drift off to sleep, ask yourself this,

> *How many Holy Instances did I give myself permission to experience this day?*

Rest assured there will be times when a big fat zero is the answer. Know you those days? Doesn't it look then like the world is very bleak? [Jeshua chuckles] You can only see on the outside what you have seen already within.

That indeed is a very, very powerful exercise and I do not give it lightly for, hear me well, that very question was given to me by one of my Essene teachers when I was but fourteen years of age. And it was given to me, to my fourteen year old mind, *every day* for two years! "Have you remembered, last night when you went to sleep, young Jeshua ben Joseph, you who think you know all the answers? Did you remember to count the moments of your Holy Instances?" And as you well know at fourteen, there are often many zeros and many 'No, I forgot again!'

And yet, as finally I began to taste the transformative power of that remembrance, I began to realize the wisdom of my teacher and more and more, each evening, I *relished* that time, just before consciousness slips away, the remembrance of the Holy Instances I had experienced that day. Those moments became the sweetest of candies, they became the most valuable moments in my consciousness. And from about the time of fifteen and a half or so onward, it became the foundation of my purpose for rising from my sleep each morning. To cultivate contexts in which Holy Instances could arise. That is what fueled my entire ministry, as it has been called, that is what fueled my entire field of desire until it was so established, so deeply established, that I couldn't shake it off. And everything in my field of consciousness, the sovereignty of my own soul, just as you have your own field of sovereignty, became fully enjoined, aligned with, dedicated to, committed to one thing—the taste of the Holy Instant. Everything in my mind, everything in my gesturing became willingly transformed to serve the experience of the Holy Instant.

Let me give you a little proof of that. Have you ever wondered why I have ceaselessly sought to join with minds, such as this my beloved brother, in order to find contexts in which I might communicate with and join with my brothers and sisters? Is it because I see you as, shall we say, deluded? In need of fixing? Hardly! The impetus of all the work that I do to reach into the field of human consciousness is born of the taste and the knowledge that the Holy Instant is as a pearl beyond all price. *For in the Holy Instant is the perfect remembrance of God.*

So now the cat is out of the bag!

Imagine this... Imagine that you are walking this earth of yours, associated with a bag of molecules you call the body, for the last time. And everything in you is oriented only to the creation of contexts in which the Holy Instant can be experienced between yourself and your brothers and sisters—that is the only thing that lifts your head from your pillow each morning. What would such a life be like? Hm. Something worth pondering, is it not? And it is perfectly okay that you have had occasional moments when you wanted something else. [Jeshua chuckles] Proof of your guilt, proof of your depravity, proof of your failure, proof that the world really is a bad place—and all of the rest. Those are just movies in a theatre—you know, those theatres you have, where you go and watch the movie and there are ten or twelve different screens and you get to select which images are going to vibrate in your nervous system? All of those choices in the mind are just movies. Just movies. Just movies. Sooner or later you get tired of looking at the screen and you put down the popcorn thing that you have been eating out of. You dump your napkin on the floor and you leave the theatre and you go outside, back to Reality.

And Reality is the Presence of Love. The great joy of relationship. Those moments in which two have come together—and this is of course the great, great height of possibilities you have—when any two or more have come together in my Name. What did that mean? In the vibration of recognizing that only the Holy Instant could possibly hold any value at all, as a means to justify celebration and praise. The reality of the Presence of God.

Between the time of now and the day of Christmas, you have a certain number of days, in which you are going to be lifting your head from the pillow and placing it on your pillow again that night. What if you were to dedicate the time between now and that day of Christmas to enjoin the practices I have suggested for you in this hour, in which you learn to relish and desire with great passion the cultivation of attention on the making of Holy Instances with your brothers and sisters. Might it not carry you into a celebration of Christmas unlike any other, in which you will be able to relish the degree of wisdom and the depth of joy that you have allowed to grow within your consciousness, as you have trained it to not settle for movies?

This then in truth completes the message that I would seek to extend to you, those of you that are here present, and those of you that will be present when you hear these spoken words.

Christmas is indeed a precious gift—if it is held in the right frame of mind. If it is utilized for its right purpose: the Mass of Christ. To join with brothers and sisters in celebration of every Holy Instant that has shined through you into the darkness of this insane world. For remember, the world was birthed in the desire to try to create something that is opposite of the Kingdom. And from that very moment Love has worked to transform that dream, to restore reality.

Celebrate your successes, celebrate your Holy Instances, by celebrating each other's loving thoughts, loving gestures, the moments in which each of you has birthed and expressed Christ.

And so to those of you who are present in this hour, how are all of you doing?

Participant: Good.

Hm. Hm. Good!

Would any of you then be willing to commit publicly to becoming an addict of Holy Instances? You can have what you call your support groups.

[Laughter]

And who would want recovery? See how much more addicted you can support each other to become! Indeed.

And with that, actually, a suggestion has been given you not by accident, though it sounded a bit 'tongue in cheek', I believe you say. This is only a phrase I can use; I have neither tongue nor cheek.

What would it be like to transform the purpose of your friendships, your relationships, so that the primary goal was to support one another in remembering to cultivate Holy Instances? Hm. Would that transform your business meetings? For this is truly the power and the gift of your relationships and your friendships. To find and seek out, to attract to yourself and to settle for nothing less than relationships based in the holy desire to cultivate the ability to remember Love, so that Holy Instances can be increasingly experienced in the moments of your coming together. Would that be a worthy goal?

[Audience agreement]

Well, it's up to you! It's up to you!

Heed well, then, what was just said. That you would seek out, that you would desire to attract to yourself, and that you would be willing to settle no longer for less than relationships based in that commitment.

> *Well, there goes my grandfather.*

It does not mean that you reject another. It means you look wisely at where you place your time and energy. Which relationships that you know in your life now really begin to (what you call) fit that bill? Which ones could fit that bill if only you extended yourself a little bit and set up a 'business meeting' for the business of talking about how your relationship can be transformed and cultivated into one that helps grow each other's capacity for experiencing Holy Instances. Rest assured, if you let your attention even now begin to sift through all the relationships you have, you'll see right away which ones perhaps you should be giving less time and energy to, and those that could indeed bear much good fruit with just a little bit of exertion on your part. Would you be willing to do that?

And so, there are a few among you who have questions being held in the mind. In fact, a few of those questions have been held so much in the mind that what was being shared at times was bouncing off the questions. [Jeshua chuckles]

Which of you would then would like to ask a question that can be explored? Hm. Not going to ask it then, huh? Hm. And is it not because there is a part of you that knows the answer has already been given? This can only mean that there is really never a time that the questions being held in your mind are really 'private'. Did you know that when something is going on in your life and you have a question turning over in your mind and you walk into a room of a party, everybody instantly already knows what's going on in your consciousness? Now, through social training, they will pretend they don't. There is no such thing as privacy, for all minds are but fragments of one Mind. There is nothing unknown by everyone. Ha!... Hardly then worth the effort trying to hide.

Indeed...

So, how are all of you doing? Has it been worth your time to be gathered together for this hour?

[Audience agreement]

I am afraid that I must report to you that it has not been worth mine—I have none! I can only hope that it has been worth my brother's time for allowing me to use both mind and body.

Know then, as we bring this brief time to a close, please know this: I love you. I love you in a preciousness and to a depth that it is not possible to understand until your consciousness is so fully established in the desire for Holy Instances, that those moments are woven together like beads tightly on a string, so much so that time itself dissolves and there is only one continuous Holy Instant. For in that moment you will have become so fully established in the Christ Mind that you will know me perfectly, for you will have known yourself; and together we will have known the Father and we will have been known of the Father; and our journey into dreams will have been transformed into the celebration of the Kingdom of Heaven, knowing neither birth nor death nor limitation.

I am but your friend and your brother and rest assured, please, I am *not* apart from where you are. And in the quiet of your heart and mind you can join with me whenever you want, for you will have no difficulty in convincing me to utilize relationship for creating the Holy Instant. I am always willing to play! This can only mean that it is not possible for you to be alone. It is not possible for you to have nowhere to go in which you are not seen and heard and recognized and restored to the gift and power of Love. Please, then, remember that I am but friend and brother to the world, calling all that would but listen to the glorious celebration of the Mass of Christ.

And with that then indeed, merry Christmas to each and everyone of you.

Amen.

JOY I
October 1992

Jeshua

Now we begin.

Indeed, greetings unto you, beloved and holy and precious friends. Indeed, greetings unto you, holy children of Light divine. I come forth with great joy to abide with you because I love you, and the joy comes from the simple fact that when I look upon you, I see naught but Light. I see naught but the face of Christ. I see unlimited potential, unlimited compassion, unlimited love, unlimited peace. These things are the characteristics of your only reality.

Indeed, I look beyond the body and I look beyond the history of your perceptions and constructs that you have created about yourself and what the world is for, and I see the Light that shines forever radiantly transcending this world and all worlds, and I see the Light you are that is already together with me from before the foundation of all worlds, and I see the Light that participates with me in the atonement of the momentary dream of separation between the Holy Father and His precious and only creation: you.

Now, if you are listening carefully, that should strike you as a little odd that indeed you are participating with me from that place of perfect union with God in the very process of atoning your own perception that you are separate from God. And that is why I have said you will awaken to your own call—not mine and not another teacher's, not another master's. You always awaken to your own call.

But because the call comes from the place in you that is of Truth, and it is a place that you have perhaps repressed and can no longer believe abides within you, what you do, you see, is that you reach your left hand out and you give a little telegram to me and you say,

> *Jeshua, deliver this telegram to me and make sure I get the message. And then indeed I will begin to awaken from my own dream.*

And since I don't have much else to do these days, I take the telegram and I look at it and I notice the date and the hour; and because I love you, indeed I come to you in that hour and I whisper to you in the quiet of your heart,

Precious friend, the time for awakening is now.

And there comes then a stirring in the depth of your heart and the depth of your soul, and a new journey begins. Not a journey deeper into dreams but a journey that begins to lift you from all dreams.

And in part of that process you will believe that someone has come a-knocking upon your heart and perhaps they have forced their way upon you just a little bit, but indeed it is not true. For *awakening can only come from absolute freedom.* Therefore, indeed, if you can acknowledge that you have begun the process of awakening, give yourself credit because you have heard your own call.

Does all of that make sense to you?

It is very, very important. And why? Because the small part of the mind that you have mistakenly become identified with, that I have called the ego, would lead you to believe that you are powerless and therefore need the constructs born of the ego, born of the very perception of separation from God, to find your way in life, indeed to keep you safe. And the ego would tell you that you are the body, that you are subject to birth and suffering and death.

The ego would cleverly lead you to believe that there might be some other masters that have somehow 'managed' ascension and no longer participate in this realm, and the ego will tell you it's okay to wish that you could accomplish that, and at the very same time it will whisper into your other ear,

> *But you know you really can't because you are weak and you are frail. You are far too busy and, after all, you've been a wretched, sinful creature.*

That somehow, somewhere, you have failed; and because of that you know that you cannot awaken.

But it's okay; go ahead, struggle to do so if you want. And each time you seem to come close, the voice of the ego rears its head and says,

No, no, no. It's not okay to receive that much joy.

And so you begin to contract the heart yet again because it is a pattern learned in the mind, and, if you would receive it, you have been operating under the guise of an illusion in which you have struggled to free the heart, and as it opens up you then contracted; and when you contract, it feels like you because you are used to it. And that is how dreams become comfortable—but it does not change them into reality. They remain eternally an illusion.

And the Truth of your being is that Light that I see shining in you radiantly at all times, the Light in which the Truth of your being resides in perfect safety—perfect safety and perfect peace—and unto you is given all power under Heaven and Earth to allow that Light you are to *descend*, to become incarnated, if you will, to shine out through even the cells of the body, to radiate your Light out into this world.

And why is that important? Because you have believed that you were something other than that Light. You will not learn the Truth of your beingness until you are willing to allow that Light to shine through you so that you can see the miracles it begins to create in your life, so that it will shine upon your brothers and sisters and show you the reality of their being, not what the ego would have you believe of them. And as you see those miracles pop up in front of your eyes, you then must acknowledge that the Light is in you now—the Light that heals your perception and shows you not time, but eternity; not an unsafe world but a world that is perfectly safe, and it is safe because *your Light* is in it.

When I look upon you, I see a great ray of Light that has no beginning and cannot know an end. I see a great ray of Light. Its strands shine out, embracing and touching the furthest stars, embracing and touching all the multifarious planes of creation, and there are many of them. I see a Light that embraces the whole of all things that have ever arisen and will ever pass away. I see a Light that shines forth from the Mind of my Holy Father, made in His image and, therefore, one with Him eternally. I see a Light comprised of compassion and grace and ease and power and creativity.

For indeed you are created to create like God, and that is why every loving creation is eternal and every loving thought is true. And why? Because God is but Love and His only creation is you. And Love can only beget that which is lovely. That is the one and simple fact that you must come to re-member, to re-cognize: that if you exist at all, you must be the presence of Love. And if you are that Love, right now, here in this room, you are free to begin the process of releasing—or perhaps even ending—the dream in which a host of thoughts have arisen that have mistakenly distracted you into believing that you are something less than the holy Son of God.

I have said to you many times that the greatest of keys to the Kingdom is the key of allowing. For allowing requires trust. Allowing requires vulnerability. Allowing requires that you let the Holy Spirit bring correction to your mind and you no longer strive to make that happen, and as you begin to rest into the key of allowing, peace begins to descend even into the cells of the body, and you find that you react differently. You smile even in the midst of situations that used to create such havoc within the mind. And you will look upon your brother or your sister and even if they are casting stones at you, you will marvel at the great Light that shines just beneath their awareness of themselves. And indeed you *will* know the great liberation that comes when suddenly the shutters are thrown open and you realize

> *My God, it's true. I am that Light. I am that Light I have been seeking for countless lifetimes. I am that Light and I am that Light, now.*

And then, you see, the body itself begins to be freed up a bit, for you will no longer be trying to stuff your emotions into the little pockets of cells, saying,

> *Hold on to this stuff. I don't want to look at it.*

Instead, you will say,

Okay, open the hatch and let it out.

And it will begin to bubble up, for, you see, when Light comes to shine upon shadows, it stirs them up and they will run like crazy, trying to find a corner to hide in; but there is no longer a corner, for even the body becomes filled with Light and the shadows of past memories and old emotions begin to be released. But instead of fearing them, you embrace them. You embrace them, knowing—*knowing*—that as you love what you have feared, you embrace it and you therefore transcend it.

That is why ultimately, you see, healing occurs only in the mind. And what is healed? *The perception that fear must be feared.* Fear itself is an illusion. It doesn't mean you don't experience it. Much of what you call your dreams, when you awaken in the morning you would say,

Well, that was unreal. It was just a dream.

Fear is no different, and if you would well receive it, *fear is the foundation of all dreams—all dreams of time, all dreams of separation, all dreams of anguish find themselves rooted in fear.*

But when you allow, when you truly are willing to allow the Light you are to shine upon all shadows born of illusion, you know that in you there is a power to say,

I am open. Bring them forth. Throw open the hatches.

And you will look at the memories that you may carry of times you have failed, of times you have hurt and been hurt, and you will say,

Oh, look at that. Yes, I can feel that. I remember that one—boy was I ever into it then.

And you'll shine your Light on it and you will extend forgiveness to yourself, and the shadow itself becomes dissolved into the Light that shines upon it.

Light added to Light only increases your radiance. And after a while the momentum gets going so fast that you can't stop the process. There is no weekend off. And at any time when things begin to flood up—and many of you know what I am talking about—always continue to shine your Light on whatever arises within you. Do not become identified with the thoughts of fear and the thoughts of limitation and the thoughts of loss. That is the voice of the ego saying,

> *No, no, no. Don't identify yourself with Light just yet. I fear my own demise of power.*

Just there, just there is the greatest of blessings given to you, given to you of the Father who loves you: *The freedom that can never be taken from you, the freedom of your choice—the freedom of your choice to look upon all things that arise with the Love of Christ.*

All loving thoughts are true. Everything else is an appeal for help and healing. Even within yourself. And so, when that voice within you—some of you occasionally know what this is like—rears its head and says,

> *No, no, you can't do it. Don't leap off the cliff,*

love it and realize that voice is not yours. If you need to, you can imagine that a stranger has slipped in, in the middle of the night, and is sitting in your living room, believing now that that home belongs to the stranger. And that stranger is the voice that would have you believe that you are other than what you are created to be: The thought of perfect Love in form.

Love cannot be accomplished. It cannot be gained. It cannot even truly be fashioned. Love cannot be found because it is not an object outside of yourself. It cannot be created for it has always been. Love waits in certainty. Love waits in patience for the holy Son of God, who has but dreamed the dream of separation, to rest for just a moment and to be willing to choose anew, to turn from the roar and the din of the world—and the world is not outside of your own mind—to choose again to touch the place of perfect peace and of grace. And there Love shines. And to look upon the face of Love is to see and know your Self.

And in the end of all seeking and in the end of all striving, the awakened Son rejoices and laughs uproariously and says,

> *My goodness, what a good dream I've had. But now the time of wakefulness is upon me.*

And for a little while you seem to find yourself yet in space and time, and you look down at the hands of "the" body formerly called "your" body and you marvel. You look at the body anew. For what seemed to be something that was always filled with conflict between a place that imprisoned you and a place you hoped to find safety, the thing that you don't even understand what it is, has been translated—translated into a beautiful and holy temple, translated into nothing more, nothing less, than a simple means through which the awakened Mind of Christ extends love to the parts of himself formerly perceived as strangers and friends, brothers and sisters, so that the wholeness, the whole Mind of Christ might awaken and merge back together into its own reality.

Now that happens to you more often than you give yourself credit for.

When you set aside every fear, when you set aside every need, when you set aside believing that you know what your needs are, when you are willing to just stop judging your brother and for a moment you look into someone's eyes and you embrace eternity—and everyone in this room knows what that is like because you've done it a million times; no matter how fleeting, you have done it a million times—and that moment of no thought and no time in which the two fragments that seem to be separated by bodies become one and the Light of Love shines through the eyes, for indeed the eyes are the window of the soul, and those sparks of Love meet. Not a love that craves. Not a love that needs attachment, but a Love that recognizes Love.

That is called the Holy Instant and it makes all things new. And that is why your relationship to your brother and sister is the most incredible blessing, the most precious possession you can ever have. Each moment of relationship provides you with the opportunity to choose holiness and not specialness. Love instead of fear. Forgiveness instead of judgment.

And because you look upon your brother and because you look upon your sister and you realize they are the means of your salvation, you will no longer tolerate error in yourself, and you will look upon them and see the face of Christ. You will learn to look past the body, to look past time and history. You will learn to discern that radiant Light which shines in them as it shines in you. And then you will learn the magic involved in the simplicity of this teaching: *You will learn what you choose to teach, and in teaching you must learn it for yourself.*

That is why there is no time to lose. Each moment is the opportunity for awakening. Each moment the opportunity for healing, that the things of time that have seemed to be a burden upon you and upon your brother can be placed aside and the mantle of peace, like a gentle dove, can descend upon you, wrapping you in the shawl of a perfect Love, bringing such joy to your being that you cannot find words to describe it and no way to contain it. And you finally realize,,

> *I don't have any choice. I have to give it away. My Father keeps pouring so much of it into me, it just keeps picking up the speed. I just have to keep giving it away.*

And then the miracle has occurred.

Gone is the seeker. Gone is the one who needs. Reborn is the finder. Reborn is the one who gives, who lets the Light of Christ shine so radiantly within them with every breath and within every thought and with every word and with every deed that they themselves marvel at the miracles that unfold. And you begin to dance through time, and you see that the Holy Spirit has translated it into a magical kingdom in which every day is filled with the grace of miracles. And every day is a little better than the one before, and the only thing you need to pay attention to is to simply watch so that you don't become a little contracted against the on-flowing tidal wave of joy that descends to light up your mind and your heart and even the cells of your body.

You have a saying in your language,

> *Let it rip.*

See, you must understand that when I walked upon this plane the language that I was given to use was rather serious for the most part—rather formalized—and so there were some limitations in how the Gospel could be expressed; at least when words were used, but not when there was dancing and laughter and singing and rejoicing and embracing.

Unto you it is given in this day and in this hour to truly look around you and see,

> *All that I need for my salvation, all that I need for my awakening is presented to me here. For here is my brother and my sister who has walked together with me since before time is, given to me of God. And as I love them, I love the One who has sent me forth. And as I love them, I honor them. And as I honor them, I learn to honor the Son that dwells within my own heart.*

And in honoring that Son, the Atonement is completed on Earth as it is already completed in Heaven. And Heaven is your home.

Delight—listen well—*delight in the blessings of time and see not a single moment as that which would imprison you.* For there is nothing outside of you, while within you is the absolute freedom of choice, given wholly and never earned, in which you can look upon the things of time, each event that time seems to require of you, and you can bring the blessing of Christ to it. You can choose to radiate instead of contract. You can choose unlimitedness instead of limitation. You can choose Love instead of fear. That is the great gift of time.

Because time was created in error, it is then translated into the means by which you awaken from time itself. Therefore, use it constructively.

Realize that you live in a domain in which avoidance of relationship is absolutely impossible. Therefore, embrace your relationships, even the ones that push your buttons. For, rest assured, they are the ones given unto you in that moment—and not a year before or a year after—they are the ones that provide the very stepping stones upon which you are asked to walk so that you can pass through an old ring of fear and realize that you've just awakened a little more fully. And the power of the radiance of that Light you are has penetrated, incarnated, a little more deeply into the mind, and even into the body.

So, next, when someone casts stones at you, rush up and give them a kiss on the cheek. Say,

> *Thank you so much. My goodness gracious, now I can heal this part of myself.*

Above all things, never let your vigilance slip.

[Jeshua chuckles]

I am sorry. Should I don the cloak of the savior of the world and kneel at your feet and beg forgiveness?

[Laughter]

Participant: Oh, no. That would be a funny picture.

It would indeed. It has always been a funny picture to me that others would put the mantle of the savior of the world upon my shoulders so as to avoid responsibility for awakening themselves. And I would scratch my head and wonder,

> *Why would they want to do that?*

When in the Truth deep within them they know that they must place the mantle upon themselves and see themselves as equal unto me, who has been sent to be only your brother and your friend.

If Christ dwells in me—and I assure you that Christ dwells in me—that same Light must dwell in you equally. For if it does not, it means that God has created a rather imbalanced creation. And whenever you have felt unbalanced, it is because you have denied the part of you that is true and real and whole and lovely—forgiven and loved wholly.

Listen well to what I have just shared with you, for there you will find the key that brings the mind gently back to peace each time you remember it ... each time you remember it. Each moment in time when you are not wholly joyous, it is because you have forgotten the Truth about yourself. When that really begins to sink in, you are going to feel a great weight lifted from your shoulders—the weight of perceiving that what has stolen your peace has come from somewhere outside your mind. It never has.

I have been working for five years with this my beloved brother to seek to teach him one thing: *there is no set of circumstances that can dictate the choice one makes between love and fear*—just as there are no special circumstances you must strive for and achieve before you have the power to choose between love and fear. The choice and that power abides in you now. It is equally in a newborn child as it is within you. And the process of life, the meaning of time, is merely to create a field in which you can reawaken to the power of your own choice.

At first as you recognize it, it may not feel too good because you will look upon some of your creations and go,

Whoa.

That which is called "being in hell", what some of your psychologists might call being psychotic, neurotic and all of the rest is simply because a part of the mind has looked upon its creations in which it has created unlike God out of fear, and it has taken upon itself the mantle of guilt. And guilt creates a block, so you spin in the same circle over and over again. That is what hell is: it is being in a rut.

But when you look upon your creations that seem to elicit unpleasant feelings—because perhaps you see how your creations involve manipulation or control or what have you—when you look upon those things and remember the Truth that they do not leave a single trace upon the holy Mind of Christ, and when you look upon them and realize that *your Father doesn't even see them*, you are free to be reborn in this moment and to allow your life to be made anew.

Oh, beloved friends, carry not the weight of the past upon you for it is gone already. It is gone already! And the heavy bag that you have been carrying upon your shoulders was removed, before you experienced it, by the Love that created you; and you have been weighed down only by illusion.

Would you not choose to join with me in casting off the bag that is no longer there? You can make a ritual of it if you would like. Indeed, go to one of your intersections, and underneath the thing that hangs from the wires that tells you when you should go and when you should stop, create a circle of precious crystals. Heap up dried branches. And in the middle of what is called the rush hour, walk as though you are burdened by a heavy bag. Drop it off of your shoulder, and then kick it into the circle and light a match. And then dance freely about your circle of precious crystals. Knock on the hoods of the automobiles of those that are honking at you and say,

> *Come, watch my bag burn. Come dance with me.*

[Laughter]

You might be surprised: a few will get out and do a jig with you.

In short, don't make the process of awakening so serious.

Is it not rather interesting that seriousness is what creates the world of confusion, of pain, and it's an illusion? Therefore, you bring the bag of seriousness to the very process whereby you think you are going to wake up, and you do your techniques, you read your texts, you memorize all of the lines, but still the bag is on your shoulder and you can't quite figure out why it's still there. The bag is filled with the weight of seriousness—and joy, you see, is made of Light. Isn't she?

And that is why whenever you are not wholly joyous, you have identified yourself with an illusion, a bag that was already removed from your shoulders in the very first moment that the holy Son of God began to fall asleep and to create the dreams of creations that are unlike God's. And the Holy Father reached into your dreams and took the tiny bag from your shoulders and dropped it into the fires of purification, if you will, and throughout every incarnation you have ever lived the bag has not been there, but you have perceived that it is still with you.

And now we come to the point of what I would share with you in this hour: The *Way*, the way in life that speaks of perfect peace is not a way of striving. It is the way of allowing. The way in life that demonstrates the Truth of your being is not the way that the world has taught you because in it there can be no seeking. The way in life that allows the Light of Christ to incarnate right where you thought you were requires only that you put into practice the acknowledgement that you are that Light, the Word being made flesh in this moment.

That is the shift that must come to the mind. I don't care if you practice complex spiritual techniques for ten thousand lifetimes. I don't care if you learn how to walk on water and heal the sick. After all is said and done, there is yet one step that must be taken: your willingness to put to sleep the dream of the seeker and to be the presence of one who has found. And the trick of the course, is that the ego will say,

> *Well, I can't do that because I haven't found it yet.*

And what I am saying to you is that in your choice, held in the mind, to simply say,

> *I and my Father are one. I am the one who has found, and that Light begins to live through me now,*

that is the way that you find it—by acknowledging that you possess what you have believed you do not. Seems rather paradoxical.

I have said many times that

> *The Truth of the Kingdom is diametrically opposed to the truth of the world.*

If your world says that you must struggle, then the way of the Kingdom must be the way of ease.

If the world says you must seek, the way of the Kingdom must be that you have already found.

If the world says you are guilty, the way of the Kingdom must say there is no guilt.

If the way of the world teaches you that you are born to suffer and die, the way of the Kingdom must say that you are eternal and do not abide within the space and volume of a body.

If the way of the world says that your mind is your brain, the way of the Kingdom will say the Mind of Christ is that which radiates, animating the brain and the body so that it can serve as a means of communicating the Love of God.

If the way of the world says you are frail, the way of the Kingdom says you are the presence of eternal strength.

And if the way of the world says it's not good to have too much fun, what do you think the Kingdom says?

[Laughter]

Participant: Fun! Party!

That is a good phrase, "Party".

Abide in that infinite Light of joy. Bring it down and express it to the world so that the world sees the demonstration of the Truth. So, you see, the theme of this hour is this—it is a three letter word: JOY. Joy is the theme of this hour. Joy is the theme of every moment. Joy is the reality of your being. Joy is that which infuses the cells of your body. Joy is that which seeks to radiate from the great ray of Light that you are and to descend through the crown of the head and to explode out through the very fingertips—rays of Light exploding in all directions.

Joy is that which will create laughter and smiles. Joy is that which seeks to bring lightness to the heart. Joy is that which heals. Joy is that which brings forth unlimited power to create like God. Joy— joy is the sign of an awakened heart and a corrected mind. Indeed.

And the greatest of blessings, the greatest of recognitions, is this: You cannot create the means in this world to become joyous, but you can bring the joyousness you are to the circumstances of this world; and when you do that, you are the savior of the world. You are the one sent forth of God, enlisted in what seems to be the Foreign Legion, indeed.

Can you come to touch that place of reality in you?

I want to share with you right now that part of the work that I seek to do in this world, not only through this my beloved brother but through countless others, is a correction: the healing of a deeply held perception that somebody else must be the one that the Bible is talking about. Somebody else must be the one who is the Word of God made flesh. Somebody else must be the one who is to be the Messiah ... If you know that you exist, rest assured you are that one.

Who? Me?

Yes, you. Rest assured I, too, said, "Who? Me?" And then I realized if somebody didn't do it, nobody would ever get it. I was the first, if you would well receive it, to complete the Atonement as a man: completely, irrevocably. And because of that, my Father has put me in charge, if you will, of the Atonement. And I come to give you the

Love that you are.

You may think that somehow I give you strength, but actually I'm rather good at sleight of hand and while I am talking to you, I reach into your hip pocket and grab your strength and your love, and I bring it up and I put it back to your face and you believe,

> *Wow. How did this one named Jeshua do that?*

Those of you that have tasted miracles because of our interaction in this form, is it not time to give yourself equal credit? For the strength and the Light that is brought forth, whatever degree of miracles of healing that have come and have been given to you, has come because you have chosen to awaken to your own call. I am just your delivery boy.

Ah. Joy.

Can you feel it? Can you feel it now? Are you willing to throw off the shackles of the mind and heart right now in this moment? Whether you are sitting or lying down, it makes no difference. Are you willing, indeed, to let joy radiate through the cells of the body? Are you doing it? Can you feel it?

Turn the attention of your mind as if you could look and see every cell. Just go in there and turn the knob and open the door and pour Light. Imagine, right now, you are looking down upon a body that has never been yours, and you are deciding to fill it with Light. Go ahead and do it. There is no great secret. No great technique. It's not going to take you six months of workshops to learn how to do it.

[Laughter]

Hmm. That's why they call them "work-shops". Why not have "gatherings of celebration of the Truth"? Are you doing it? Don't sit there passively. Do it. Bring the joy in. Enlighten the cells. Let them get lighter and lighter and lighter and filled with joy. Feel how it brings the breath more deeply into the body. Feel it down to the tips of the toes.

Yes, Light. Let there be Light. Say goodbye to the shadows of the past. They are with you no longer. Light. Let there be Light. Radiate it down deeper and deeper. Feel the heart beat a little bit faster. It's called passion for joy. Feel it. Yes! Have what you call an orgasm with joy. Bring Light and laughter and play to every moment.

[Singing] Where has all the seriousness gone? Has it been a long time in passing?

Who cares? Once it's gone, it's gone.

We abide together now. We are the great rays of Light that shine forth through the Mind of God, and we bring a new vision indeed to this planet and to this Earth. We are the joy. We are the Light. We are the bringers of the Gospel. We live it. We are the Truth. Look at us. Yes. We're the ones that have burned our bags in the intersections.

If you want to keep yours...

[Loud laughter]

... go right ahead. Indeed.

That is what it's all about. There isn't anything you need that you do not already possess. And when you throw open the shutters of the heart and allow desire born of a pure heart to lead your way, what you thought you must fear, called passion, what you thought you must fear, called your dreams and aspirations, what you thought you must fear because it might make you stick out in the crowd will no longer be a bit of concern. Trust me. I know about sticking out in crowds.

[Laughter]

Some of you in this room did not want me to stick out in the crowd because you feared that the world could take me from you. Surprise!

The world just freed me to be with you always, beyond all of your perceptions of birth and death, beyond your perceptions of suffering and doubt and struggle, beyond your perceptions of separation born of time. The world served my intention well, and the drama was played out and the resurrection was completed. And if you believe in me, you believe in the reflection given to the world of who you are. For the life of Jeshua ben Joseph is your own—as yours is mine. That is how intimately united we are. We share one Heart and one Mind when we rest in the Truth of the infinite and eternal joy that is the presence of the Love of God in us.

And when others say,

> *Lo, the Kingdom is here,*

and another says,

> *No, the Kingdom is there,*

look them in the eye and say,

> *No dice. The Kingdom of Heaven is within me because I am the one who chooses to be wholly joyous. I let that joy overflow so much that I cannot help but give it to the world.*

And if there are those that fear joy, give it anyway. And if they can't bear it, rest assured they will drop out of your life.

But it's only fear that causes that to happen. But no one can flee *from* Light who does not turn and flee *to* Light. For Light surrounds them wherever they are on the path they choose to walk. If that is true—and I assure you that it is—it means that you are safe to release your hold upon your brothers and your sisters, whatever the form of relationship may have been. You are free to give them to me, and I will keep them safe and I will whisper to them in their dreams until *they* make the same choice that *I* made in time: to release the dream of the dreamer and to acknowledge,

I and my Father are one.

Rest assured that I will leave no one that you entrust to me. Unshackle from your heart, unshackle from yourself the weight you have carried for so long. The awakening of another is the Holy Spirit's responsibility. Your only function, your only purpose, your only task, if you will, is to be the presence of one who has allowed correction to come to the mind so that you are forevermore the Thought of perfect and joyous Love in form. That is all that is ever asked of you. The rest is being taken care of. It's a bit of a release, isn't it?

[Addressing a member of the audience]. It's about time you gave that to me. Thank you.

Participant: Wish I'd thought of it sooner.

Beloved friend, whenever you think about that Truth, you have immediately moved into what is real and eternal, and it no longer matters if you didn't think about it earlier because in this moment all things are made new. It is called rebirth.

That little sigh that you felt released more than you know. Now, be ready for miracles.

Participant: Oh, I am. Bring them on.

Ah, yes. What then are your true dreams? For while you abide for a little while in time it is given unto you to allow unhappy dreams to be translated into happy dreams. And you will know the course that the Holy Spirit will take you on by the things that come into your life without effort. And you will know the course given to you to walk to bring you wholly to a dream of joy, as you become willing once again to become as a little child who celebrates the incredible creativity—the dreams that seem to course up through the heart.

For a child goes to what you would call a sandbox, and some image comes of an incredible castle and they are filled with such joy,

> *Ah, this is going to be so much fun.*

They don't go and ask somebody if it's okay. They don't ask somebody,

> *Well, do castles really exist? Is it true that I can build a foundation to sustain it?*

They don't ask for authorization of what you call building codes—they just build it. And they rejoice in every moment of the game; the game, the play. Allow yourself from this day forward to truly get in touch with your heart's desires. Don't fear them any longer.

Now, if you think a desire is coming up in the heart that says,

> *Boy, I've always wanted to murder that so-and-so...*

[Laughter]

I am not asking you to create chaos here. That is not your heart.

Participant: A clue.

It is a clue, indeed.

But if you dream of wealth, if you dream of service, if you dream of travel, if you dream of a new house, if you dream of a new cloak, if it feels really good and it keeps pressing, not from the mind downward but from the heart outward, why not let it flow?

The river of life lies within you. It sustains you and it carries you, and it will bring you home to the Father wholly—but only if you let it flow. Only if you let it flow. And that river is a river of joy. Indeed, with great sincerity I say unto you, "Let it rip!"

[Laughter]

Indeed. So, how are you all doing?

Participant: Great. Yes.

Indeed.

Participant: Jeshua?

Just a moment. Stand up. Now, you that just said, "Yes," I want you to become the leader here and lead them in at least three resounding "yeses". And don't let them hesitate or hold back. It must be at the top of the lungs. Feel it from the toes all the way up to the crown of the head. Those of you that were lying down have a little further to go but…

Participant: YES! More, more. YES! One more. YEEESSS!

Okay.

Participant: That was energizing.

Energizing? Why would you want to be energized? Isn't death and sluggishness much, much better?

Participant: No thanks.

Now, I have indeed watched certain minds begin to awaken to—and I believe they will enjoy this—their, I believe the word is the "piggy" nature.

[Laughter and oinking]

Now you have all seen what are called the pigs as they roll around, and the farmer says,

> *My God, there they are rolling around in that mud again.*

A true pig realizes and perceives that they are rolling in the river and the mud of *joy*.

And what if you were to go to your friends tomorrow and say,

> *I have just gone to a great teacher who gave me the last meditation that I need to master,*

and your friend says,

> *What is it?*

and you say,

> *Come, come. Come to my backyard and I'll show you.*

[Loud laughter]

You can roll in the river and the mud of joy whenever you want to because this world has no power whatsoever over the Holy Son of God; and that is Truth, indeed.

And all it took was the willingness of one person to say, "Yes", and to lead brothers and sisters in joining in that one place where the mind is one, to say "Yes", and you felt energy and passion and joy course through the cells of your beingness. And that means wherever you are—wherever you are—that power is at the tip of your choice. Who cares where and when you decide to roll in the river of joy? The world is a lie. Do not let it dictate to you.

Thank you, that was nicely led.

[Personal dialogue here – excluded in this transcript]

Many teachers in many ways are beginning to bring back the recognition: what it's really all about is living from the heart. And in my language I would say that to live from your heart is to live the life of the arisen Christ. These two are one and the same.

Where, then, is the pathway that leads you from this world to the Kingdom? Look no further than your heart. What has been your secret desire? What has been your passion and your vision? The journey is what awakens the mind and joins the heart as one, so that the mind becomes the servant of the awakened heart.

Therefore, I say again, in closing—for I want you to have some time to mingle together, and when you do so be willing to share your heart's desires with each other. Have some fun with it and do what you call the "oinking" of your dreams, yes . . .

Be, therefore, that which you *are*; and you are the Light that has come to this world; and you are the one who is the Prince of Peace; or Princess, if you insist.

In short, lighten up and get on with it.

[Laughter]

I love you, but not in seriousness. When you are wholly joyous, rest assured I am with you. When you are not, rest assured I am with you. When you doubt yourself, rest assured I do not. And when you rest in certainty, I celebrate. And if you have ever believed that you have loved me, then truly choose to acknowledge and love the Son that dwells within your own heart and let your Light shine. For only by so doing can you in Truth honor and love me—not as someone above you, but as your brother and as your eternal playmate.

Peace be unto the wholly joyous and awakened and arisen and resurrected Christ, who blossoms forth and brings such beauty to this world that your brothers and sisters, perhaps yet sleeping, won't be able to help but recognize that the Light is in them, too. Indeed. And Heaven comes to Earth because you choose to make the time now.

Have a good time mingling. Come up to somebody, give them a hug and say,

> *You know what I've always really wanted to manifest in my life?*

And let them know. What the Son decrees begins to move into

manifestation. What the Son hides is held as a light under a bushel. Decree and manifest Heaven on Earth. It's really all you've ever wanted anyway. Why settle for less?

Peace be unto you whom I love from before the foundations of the world. Peace be unto you whom I walk with and celebrate with, even when you don't notice and forget.

Peace be unto you always.

Amen.

JOY II
October 1992

Jeshua

Now we begin.

And yet once again I say unto you that it is with great joy that I come forth to abide with you—and often I have said that. And yet, have you truly sought to comprehend what those words mean: "that it is in joy that I come forth to abide with you?" And if I come in this rather particular way to abide with you so that your body can sit there and this body, temporarily borrowed, can sit here, and I can come and abide with you in this manner, rest assured that I come always with joy to abide with you where you really are. You do not abide within a body. The body, again, arises within a field that can be called your consciousness. It is born out of your desire, your expectations, your perceptions that have been built up and built up and built up. And one of those perceptions is indeed that you are within the body. But you are not.

Therefore, I come not to abide with the body, but I come forth to abide with that great ray of Light that you are, that shines forever beyond the body and beyond all worlds. It is to that great ray of Light that I speak and with that great ray of Light that I commune. And the process of awakening, the process of the atonement, is not just some mental gymnastics in which you try to exercise certain statements in which you say,

> *Well, good. I'm one with God. It doesn't quite feel that way but I'll believe it anyway.*

That is where it begins. But the atonement is indeed completed when the whole sense of identity that you carry is no longer in any way, shape or form limited to the space and volume of the body. There isn't even a trace of identification with it save that you acknowledge that you have allowed it to arise within the field of the Light you are. And it serves no other purpose save to be a means by which you communicate the Light that you are into this plane of density and to this world of yours.

If this were not true, it would mean that you are not as God, our Holy Father, has created you to be. And I have said many times, in many ways, that God has but one creation—His holy and precious child; His Son, if you will; that which is the offspring of the Mind of God. And that which is an offspring of Light, that is made in the image of Light, can only be Light, filled with wisdom, filled with creativity, filled with . . . joy.

Therefore, I come forth in joy because joy is that in which I abide eternally, and I come forth to abide with you. Not the body that you think you are. Not the body that you think you are in, but I come forth to abide with that great ray of Light that outshines all worlds and is forever one with me since before the foundation of all worlds.

And the miracle, the miracle that allows the atonement to be born on Earth—which means in the body—even as it is already completed in Heaven, the miracle that allows that is the simplicity of your willingness to set aside, constantly, everything about what you believe that you are, so that you can relearn the Truth.

And if I were to come to you and speak to you as though you were a body and if I were to acquiesce to your insistence that you are just this form, that you are just your hurts, that you are just your limitations, if I were to come and abide with that, there could be no such thing as a miracle. For it would mean that both of us have gotten caught up in the insanity of an illusion.

Precious friends, I abide only with—and speak only to—the great ray of Light that you are, that outshines every limitation that you believe exists in and as your life. And it is to that ray of Light that I gently whisper:

> *Awaken. Awaken from sleep and put away the things of dreams. Put away fears and put away doubts, and begin instead to focus the whole of your attention on Light and on joy.*

And why?

If this world has been made in error—and I assure you that it has—and if the world is diametrically opposed to the Truth of the Kingdom of Heaven, it must then follow that the perceptions and beliefs that have made this world are indeed the opposite of a knowledge that you can find in the Kingdom of Heaven.

The world is made of fear. The world is made of limitation. That is the world that you have taken to be real and, therefore, have allowed it to dictate to you what choices you will make in your life: where you will live, the friends you will attract to yourself. *Every last aspect of your life has come forth out of the perception that you are a body, separate from everyone else, that you live in this world and that this world is real.*

This world is constructed in separation, fear and guilt. Therefore, if you perceive it as the real world, you must then attract to yourself that which mirrors what you are insisting on believing in. And yet, I say, week in and week out: I come forth in joy to abide with you. Not with your illusions, not your dreams, but the real you, the real you that is filled with power and Light and goodness and love and capability and creativity; and you name it, you are it.

If you name it, you will be it. What you decree you become.

So, if I come forth in joy and I come forth from the Kingdom of Heaven, the Kingdom of Heaven itself must be a state, if you will—a quality, if you will—in which nothing can sneak in through the back door unless it is more joy. Does that make sense to you?

If a limited thought emerges and comes and sneaks into the Kingdom of Heaven, Heaven is no longer Heaven, so who would want to be there anyway? Not I. If there is a trace of shadow in the Kingdom of Heaven, it's no longer Heaven. If there is a doubt or feeling of psychological weakness, if that abides in Heaven, then it is beneath who you are and you might as well throw it away; it's no good to you.

The Kingdom of Heaven is a state and a quality of such joyousness that what takes place is that the Light that you are begins to vibrate at a higher and higher frequency until the things that arise in your world that seem to be limiting you don't even matter any longer. And that is extremely important, and that's what I want to speak with you about this evening.

If when what you would perceive as a limitation pops up in your life, rest assured it is coming forth to reveal to you that there is a shadow of perception, of thought, of feeling that is less than whole joyousness, if you will, that yet needs to be, shall we say, corrected within you.

Now, the mind, through its habits, will look at the limitation that arises and believe that the limitation is real and, therefore will, in a sense, step the vibration down to match the vibration of the limitation so that you can do battle with it. Do you know what that feels like? It is called "beating the head against a brick wall". Now, who is the builder? Who is the bricklayer? You are.

Enlightenment, empowerment, whole joyousness, if you will, cannot begin until you are willing to accept total and complete responsibility for everything you see, everything you think, everything you say and everything you do—but, above all, everything you feel, because the causative factor of what you feel and what you perceive is never outside of you.

> *Well, surely that must be wrong. When the landlord raises the rent and I don't feel good, surely it is the act of the rent being raised that causes the feeling that I am having?*

That is what the world will teach you and what it would ask you to believe, but remember, the perceptions of the world are just the opposite of the Truth of the Kingdom.

Can you begin, then, to allow yourself to admit, to consider, that every feeling and every perception has no cause outside of you? Each time you believe that it does you have chosen, you have decreed like a judge with the gavel, you have judged that the world outside of you is real and contains a power over you. That choice occurs nowhere save within yourself, within the mind that you are, and it requires something quite fundamental: it requires that in that very moment you have set aside the remembrance of yourself as a great ray of Light. You have given back your God-given power and have chosen an illusion to be your authority.

So then, can you understand the great blessing of each moment? The Holy Spirit has already translated the world that has been brought forth in error, that you've gotten a little caught up with, into the very means whereby you can awaken from the dream of separation, re-identify with the Light that you are and, therefore, outshine everything that has represented the world to you. Every anger, every hurt, every fear, every limitation, every empty wallet; whatever it is, you can outshine it. You can actually change the whole picture because you are using your Light to create the world that you see and have believed in.

And what is the key that unlocks that? Joy.

Joy is not just a word. It is not just a temporary feeling. Joy is something that you have complete control over twenty-four hours a day. It is a vibration. It is a frequency. And if you were to go into one of your laboratories and say to one of your scientists,

> *Well, show me the frequency and color of sadness,*

you could guess that it might be dark gray. And the frequency of love carries a quality of, shall we say, pinks and light violets to it. The frequency of joy vibrates at a very high color, if you will, of vibrant, radiant golden light that you can't even really tell if it's gold or white.

It is a vibration. It is a frequency. It is a tangible reality. It is a real doodad, if you will, that floats with all the other doodads in this universe, and you can claim it as yours every time you choose to remember the Truth. You can choose to open up the body even and literally draw that joy down through the crown of the head. You can draw it up through the soles of the feet. You can draw it in from the sides. It doesn't matter, that's just ritual.

The point is, you are enacting your choice to remember the Truth that you were born in joy, that you were created in joy, that you are sustained in joy, that joy is who and what you are. And out of joy comes the power to do all things, manifest all things, impact all things, change all things, heal all things—and to dance through all things.

Joy. Joy is the key that unlocks the door. When you have indeed desired first the Kingdom; and when your intention has been unwavering; and when you have learned to master the key of allowing in which you learn to forgive the world, to forgive yourself, to trust all things that arise so that you can begin to look at them with new eyes and learn how you are the creator of all that you have experienced; as you rest then into the safety of surrender, the Holy Spirit comes by with a little golden key and says,

> *Here is what you have been looking for. I couldn't give it to you earlier because you were too busy running around in small circles in the mind. But now that the mind of the world has been set aside, I can speak to you clearly, and I deliver to you the key whereby you begin to translate the unhappy dream that you may have created, or aspects of it, into a happy dream.*

A wholly happy dream in which perhaps relationships that have actually been what you would call in your language "dysfunctional"—quite an apt word, by the way—or harmful or limiting, you've finally learned that it's okay to set them aside, that it's okay for you to choose joy. It's okay for you to be happy. It's okay for you to be wealthy. It doesn't matter what it is. It's okay. And the key that unlocks it all is Joy.

So, all you have to do when next you are feeling a little down is sit here and say,

> *I am wholly joyous now.*

Then open your eyes, and if everything's the same, you can rest assured that the key of joy doesn't work. Some do that. They make a meager attempt. They make it from a mind that has become depressed, a body filled with toxins that has become tight and depressed. They make it from the foundation of the perceptions of the world. They give a thought to joy. Nothing changes overnight.

> *So, Jeshua must not know what he's talking about. And not only him but I understand there have been a lot of masters around that have talked about joy, and they have all been wrong because I just proved it.*

If you have learned to not punch your joy button constantly, if it's at best become an intermittent thing, so that at times you choose to be joyous if the situation looks okay and other times decide to hold on to judgment and thoughts of limitation and lack—if you have learned to do it that way, must it not follow that to re-identify with yourself as joy will also require the process of learning?

We have talked about how the Holy Spirit translates the things of time into the very means by which you may awaken. Therefore, be thankful for the time that is given to you for it is the means by which you will relearn how to not only press, but to hold your joy button until it holds itself. It is the means whereby the translation of an unhappy dream occurs so that a happy one replaces it. And as the dream becomes happy, what happens? Something that everybody knows. Anytime you feel relatively happy, you relax. You expand. You open. You become more creative. You feel more in tune, more alive. The cells of the body sing. That's why everybody likes being happy.

The problem is that you have learned to believe that happiness is a conditional expression. That is, it depends on external circumstances.

> *I will be happy, when...*

And, of course, "when" never comes. And if it arrives, because you haven't learned how to be happy, you feel uncomfortable. And many of you know what that's like.

> *Now that I have what I have been seeking, I can't quite be happy yet.*

Why? Because you forgot to practice being happy.

Now, joy, then—and that is why we began last week with *feeling* joy—as you practice becoming the frequency of joy, something begins to happen. And all of you know this to some degree. It's just a matter of making it constant. When you choose to, shall we say, abide and to vibrate in the frequency of the Light of the joy that you are, no matter what is coming up around you, when you choose joy, when you draw the Light in through the toes, through the fingernails . . . it doesn't matter, just do it, let the body begin to vibrate. It will feel like the body is vibrating at any rate. Feel the Light, feel the joy . . . it actually begins to blow the cobwebs out, out of the cells of the body and out of the mind, the Mind in which you are already connected with me and with God and with every mind that has ever awakened. Every master that has ever been is no further than a phone call away from within your mind.

Many have said,

> *Gee, I have been trying but I just can't hear you, Jeshua. I just . . . meditation doesn't go well. What's going on?*

It's because there is static in the mind—like a cloudy day that blocks the sun.

The sun that truly shines, dwells within your heart—now. Not one thing separates you from your right and your power to choose to dwell in the joy that is the presence of the Light of the Son of God that dwells within your heart.

As you choose that frequency and vibration, miracles accelerate. The picture that you have created, called your life, begins to vibrate a little, you see, because it always responds to the frequency that you are living in. You could say that the world is your perfect servant, and it will always show you exactly where your frequency is.

As you choose that vibration, you could say that you begin to vibrate the molecules of matter. You begin to break up the old picture so that that which does not resonate with the frequency of joy that you are choosing to live within, those things begin to have a few earthquakes. And if you are willing to allow them, they will drop out of your life.

Now this is a big stumbling block, you see, because part of the mind is still attached to believing that its identity, its reality, is made up of the things outside of it; so that as you choose awakening, as you choose joy, all the little fears that you've been carrying begin to float to the surface and you have a choice to make. Love or fear? Ever heard that before?

The way is easy and without effort, and yet it takes you through the eye of the needle. The way *is* the way of love and love is the expression of joy—a joy that must spill over into every dimension of your experience until every dimension of it mirrors to you the happy dream of your constant union with God. And then the world itself fades away; you transcend the world.

There is a process to go through. It is a process that will take you from where you think you are to where you long to be. And the process requires that willingness *to trust love*, to trust love to carry you beyond every fear that has ever limited you and ever made you believe that you can only be who you are now.

Fear can arise when the things that you have constructed out of misperceptions, whether they be relationships, careers, whatever it is, if you have made it from the perspective of the ego rest assured its foundation is a house built on sand and it is going to crumble sooner or later. Your world, you see, is one in which you are taught to strive, to struggle, to feel anxiety, to try to keep your creations on solid ground.

You have many people, by the way, that are locked up in mental institutions for no other reason than they see through the game of the ego and they realize any such construction is made on a foundation of sand, so what's the point? And they don't want to participate. Unfortunately, your world isn't quite ready to go to them and teach them another way; and so they are caught in what is called hell.

Beloved friends, be of good courage:

When you have truly relinquished every attempt to make and control your world, fear will arise, rest assured. But it is just to show you where you've been living; and just beyond it is the peace that you seek.

And each time you choose joy, no matter what, you, shall we say, pass an initiation would be one way to put it. You step to the next highest level and a strength begins to come into you, a strength that shall indeed become like a mighty river and the things of this world will not deter you from the path that would be set before you and that you would choose to walk.

The Holy Spirit requires enlightened and therefore empowered minds to join with It, with Him, in the translation of the whole of this world into a happy dream. Does it require strength? Indeed it does. Is it going to feel uncomfortable at times? Yes—to the degree that you try to hold on to old habits, whether they be habits of diet, habits of thought, habits of relationship, habits of career. If you believe those things are keeping you safe, you are going to go through quite a struggle because once you choose to awaken, that is like you have taken your finger out of the hole in the dam and the water begins to pour forth—first as trickle, but eventually the power and the force of that water of joy, of Truth and of Light will break down the dam completely. If you resist that, you are going to feel fearful and believe that everything is crumbling to dust; and it is. And yet, what crumbles is only an illusion, only something that has limited the holy Son of God.

If I walk with you, your way is certain and fear need not master you.

And the situations that are presented to you in your life are there so that you can recognize what you are now, as a soul, choosing to overcome, to grow beyond. Stop trying to keep the things that limit you in place and give yourself wholly to the force of the water that is the joy of the soul that would break the dam down so that the river can flow. The river of creativity. The river of joy. The river of eternal life that flows from the Mind of God to and through the Son of God, to be demonstrated and spilled over into this world.

I can never make that choice for you. Never. I can only whisper to you. I can only come to you. I can only abide with you, the Truth in you. And I can tell you that it's safe. It's safe to let the false constructs dissolve from your mind. It is safe and it is necessary, and if you would receive it, contemplate what this means: it is *inevitable.*

I have said many times that freedom does not mean—free will does not mean—that you can choose whether or not to take a certain curriculum. You are only free to decide *when* you are going to take it. And the reluctance of the mind to truly take the course, live it and master it (the curriculum), is that part of the mind that wishes summer vacation could at least last a little bit longer. But all the time you think you are enjoying your summer vacation, you are not really getting anywhere, and it takes a resolve—desire and intention—in which, whatever it takes, you finally voice within yourself:

> *No, I'm not going to tolerate error in myself any longer under any circumstances. I am the holy Son of God, and joy is my birthright and my Kingdom and I am going to be that. And if it kills me, good.*

There is a strength in you, a strength you haven't even begun to touch, a strength that when embraced will indeed dismantle every limitation that you believed exists in your life. And the right use of that strength rests on your willingness and your determination to choose joy always.

You see, when you get in your automobile and you leave your humble abode, and you are about to go off to what you call a job...

Hmm. Interesting concept. You are not going to a job at all. You are only choosing to go to what you have chosen to construct out of the infinite freedom of the molecules of physicality. You are an artist and you have painted a picture for yourself to abide within. What you are really doing is getting into your automobile that is a temple, a temple in which you have ten minutes, twenty minutes, an hour, whatever it is that you've painted for yourself, in which to practice being the presence of joy. That's the curriculum. And it's presented to you in every moment.

Every moment that you step forward into is a precious and holy temple in which you have the opportunity to choose fear or love.

And you will know if you have chosen the door labeled "fear" because you might feel tired, sad, confused, depressed. And you will know if you have chosen the door marked "joy" that comes from choosing love because, you see, if you are in your automobile, if you are making breakfast, if you are paying bills, it doesn't matter what you are doing—it's not going to matter because it, itself, is part of the dream that is being translated, and it is your willingness to abide in joy that will allow you to heal every limited thought that you have ever had. And each limited thought has been made manifest as the nemesis of problems that come to your life. It's all the result of a lack of joy.

Can it be that simple? Yes, it is. Yes, it is.

Joy is an incredible thing. An incredible blessing. Every time you choose to be wholly joyous, rest assured you have decided not to identify with the ego. And remember, you are asked to do only one thing: to live as though you are not an ego. Every time a judgment slips through the mind and is projected onto someone,

> *Oops, I misidentified.*

Take it back. Burn it up. Laugh and get on with joy.

Joy is like a light, like a fire that purifies the mind, that purifies the body. And why is that necessary? Because your Father longs to have you join Him as a co-creator and an awakened, healed mind. Such a mind's creations are always loving, always expansive, always healing. The creations of an awakened mind seem to attract other minds to it like moths to a light bulb. And that is exactly what is happening.

Your Father longs to pour forth the fullness of His power and creativity through you. But if you've closed yourself off so tight that only a trickle comes through, just enough to keep the body alive, is there any wonder that there is lack mirrored to you in your life?

Now, some will say,

> *I'm a pretty happy guy. I live in a high state of joy most of the time.*

Notice the word "most". And understand that if there is anything in the world that you are still judging, still fearful of, still condemning, whether it be your monetary system, your government, your schools, your mass transit systems, garbage strikes—whatever it is, if you are judging it, you are blocking off the flow of joy that would transform the whole of your life.

I have said often to you: become wholly outrageous. And outrageousness requires . . . joy. Joy! Has anybody dropped the bag off their shoulder underneath one of your lights at the intersection this week? [ref the previous gathering: Joy I]

[Laughter]

Why not?

Participant: I didn't have the courage.

Beloved friend, when you can say to me, "I didn't have the bag…" Indeed.

What I am seeking to share with you is that the world you have dreamed into being—with all of its complexities, including the body—is really no big deal. It's quite harmless and holds no power over you. Each time you see something that seems to be a limitation, realize you are just looking at the boundary of your mind that you have chosen for yourself. Now, there is a great power in that because if you recognize the boundary of your mind but you know that what you really want is joy, you can choose to walk through that ring of fear, whatever it is. And just like stretching a muscle, the boundary expands. And as the boundary expands, more joy flows from the Mind of God through you. More creative ideas—and more responsibility.

> *Damn. I was hoping to get rid of that.*

Do you see how the world would teach you to fantasize about winning a lottery so that you could be irresponsible? Isn't that true? So you won't have any 'worries'. *Worries are only the refusal to assume responsibility.* And yet, paradoxically when you join with me in being willing to assume responsibility for the atonement for the whole of creation—whew, now there is an eighty-hour-a-week job—paradoxically, your joy becomes full and you rest in what is eternal.

For when you have expanded the boundaries of your mind to allow joy to be the fountain in which you swim always, and when that deep part of the mind within you that is the Mind of Christ says,

> *All of creation is arising within me. This is my doing. Therefore, I'm going to heal it and I'm going to correct it and I assume responsibility for the whole of the world*

without jumping ahead to how you are going to take care of that—then the Father pours forth into you the power and the wisdom and the Light and the life to achieve your goal of healing the whole of creation and completing the atonement.

First things first.

This temple, the body, is the means whereby it is given unto you to extend love; and love can only radiate from a mind that is wholly joyous. Now, you all know that when you are in the presence of somebody that is not wholly joyous, you are not quite as attracted to them. Isn't that true?

The body deserves your love. Not because it's your home but because it is your tool. And when you abide with only loving thoughts, you will find that such things as diet, all of those habits that you have, begin to naturally correct themselves. As you come to love the body by resting in the joy that is within you, you will indeed find miracles, for you will be attracted to new ways of being in and with the body itself. And that's a very important step, not one to be rationalized away by saying,

> *Well, all I need to do is zap myself with a little Light and nothing really hurts it.*

Are you sure?

If you are not sure, be honest with yourself and take steps to correct what you are putting into it. The body, this thing that starts here [pointing to head] and ends at your toes, is like a transmitter and receiver. As you choose to tune it up, it becomes capable of radiating higher frequencies of joy. As you choose the frequency of joy, the desire to tune up the tool naturally grows.

That's Step One. And Step Two is to realize that no one is responsible for your thoughts save you. No one can change them. No one can heal them. No one is responsible for causing them but you. At first that seems to be a bit of a bummer because it means indeed accepting total responsibility, complete responsibility without an excuse, without claiming victimhood. And yet, claiming that responsibility is what empowers you. It empowers you to be willing, finally, to be able to choose to be wholly joyous.

And as you begin to tune into that frequency and you get a little bit of a shockwave going,

> *Whew, that was nice. Should I try it again? Oh, why not,*

and you open up and you say,

> *Father, I'm ready. Just pour it down through me. I dare You to overwhelm me.*

He'll try. He loves to try to do that. And then next the little shockwave goes,

> *Whoops. Well, that was nice, too, and I didn't even need another body to get it. I didn't need to go to the movies. I didn't need to win the lottery. What caused it? My God, I did. No causative factor outside my desire, my willingness, to feel joy.*

And the more and more and more that you tune to that frequency, you will find that your Father's cup overflows and never stops flowing. And every moment can become more joyful than the one before, and who cares what the circumstances are.

As you tune into that frequency, the life that you have been living will begin to shift and change. Just remember that you are like a painter who takes a look at the color and says,

> *That's not quite right. I'm going to erase it.*

And a new color will come, and with that new color might be new friends, might be a new career. You might find yourself getting up at 3am for prayer and meditation. You might find a desire to discipline yourself just a little bit more.

> *Oh, God. Jeshua is talking about responsibility and discipline tonight. I knew I should have gone to the movies.*

[Laughter]

Responsibility is what makes your joy full! Please remember that. Responsibility for the whole of creation is what will make your joy full.

Discipline? The terrible art of loving yourself. You have a statement regarding the improper use of some substances that seem to change the biochemistry of the body: drugs. The statement is "just say no". Discipline is the art of loving yourself, truly loving yourself, and saying "no" when you can tell that to say "yes" will be to compromise your frequency of joy. Sounds simple, doesn't it? Rest assured, if you practice that simple little test of never saying "yes" to something that compromises your frequency of joy, you will be in for a surprise because what will be revealed to you is how many times in each day you do compromise your joy.

Know you that which is called 'the rat-race'? Know you that which feels like conflict? Like you keep trying to get out of it but your feet keep getting stuck more in it? It comes because, to some degree, you compromise your joy and then the soul within you becomes sad. And when you become sad, your frequency drops and you find yourself butting the head against the wall because you yet believe that that wall keeps you safe somehow. It stops you from growing. It stops you from becoming more. It stops you from stepping into the arenas you thought you could never perform well in. The brick wall is your limitation and it keeps you in hell, pure and simple. It keeps you from . . . Heaven. It keeps you from . . . the power to effectively deal, with complete responsibility.

Joy. For those of you that were with us last week, do you remember what that felt like last week? Joy. Did you practice evoking that in yourself in the week that followed? Or did you only think of it as a memory and go,

Well, that was nice. I hope we can do that again.

Ah. Hmm. Do you see how that pattern in the mind is the very pattern that must become disciplined? If you truly loved yourself, your desire to drink in joy would become constant and primary, and you simply would not tolerate in yourself any willingness to make any other choice, no matter what. Talk about an addictive drug. Don't say "no" to it, say "yes" . . . say "yes".

I want you so badly to come to where I am. I want you so badly to give up your dreams of suffering and pain and lack. I want you so much to realize the Love the Father has for you, that is poured forth and shaken down around you so thoroughly that you can't even comprehend it. The mind could never comprehend the Love of God—but the heart can become an open valve through which it can flow.

Your life is worthy of reconstruction if that is what you desire. And I say this unto you, and those of you that have perhaps studied my *Course in Miracles*, rest assured that if you are truly getting it, if the atonement is beginning to stir within you, you are going to eventually have to come to face the fact that peace isn't just mental gymnastics. The healing of the mind must necessarily affect the healing of how you are in the world, that changes how you are in the world; it must. And if that is occurring within you, certain things that you may have constructed in your life are going to start to feel like a prison to you.

Now, what happens is that the mind says,

> *Well, it's reality so I'll conform myself to it,*

instead of letting your joy and your peace and your love burst the walls of it, so that you can grow into something higher, more radiant; so that more and more Light can be entrusted to you to flow through you.

In short, what I am talking about here is, don't fool yourself. Don't rationalize it away. Face it head on and admit it. If there is some aspect of your life that is not working, get straight with yourself. Nobody is doing it but you. And all around you is the power to effect change, because the power is within you.

What is one of the simplest ways of knowing whether or not you are allowing yourself to flow with joy, your heart's desires—not the ego's desires—the heart's desires?

If you feel frustration or limitation in any aspect of your life, it means that there is something yet within your perceptions that you have been fearful of turning to look at head on. And until you do so, you will never heal it. Never.

The same limitation will be made manifest to you in another thousand lifetimes. That's just the way it is.

Of course, the mind says,

> *Who thought up this game? That doesn't sound like fun to me. Can't there be another way out?*

No, *you* created the game. You are the Milton Bradleys of creation. Life is one great big Monopoly game. You designed it. You bought and constructed the house in which you live, and that house is your mind. And its foundation is the amount of joy you are willing to open yourself up to and the degree to which you are willing to let that joy pour forth through your life to burst out through the limitations that you might experience—until your joy so far outshines the world that finally the perception is healed. The light goes on and you realize,

> *Wait a minute. This Monopoly game can't contain my Light.*

And you will put away every last trace of need to try to conform yourself to the physical world And then you will come to where I am and abide in the unlimitedness given unto you in the very moment that our Holy Father thought you into being, as a perfect image of Himself.

Become unlimited. Choose to become powerful and it will look differently to everybody. It doesn't mean that you are all going to become billionaires and run for President on the Independent Party ticket. But it does mean that you'll get straight with yourself and realize that there is some friction causing unhappiness in your life. Then you know there is a limit there, a limitation. You will turn and face it head on and declare that you are no longer willing to tolerate it because it does not befit the holy Son of God.

Honesty begets responsibility. The choice of responsibility begets discipline, and discipline begets the return to joy. And joy completes the atonement in you. Indeed.

So I hope that in this brief hour so far I have perhaps been able to shed light on a few things, to give you a few thoughts to chew upon.

I mean what I said when I said that my way is easy and without effort. The willingness to live an unlimited life filled with power and grace and beauty and creativity and effectiveness, the willingness to learn, to change whatever habits of perception and thought and behavior you are carrying that are limiting you—the choice to live that kind of life really doesn't require any effort. What requires effort is the resistance to that life because it is a resistance to the overwhelming river of joy that longs to pour forth through you, to rebirth you. Being in the world is what takes effort. The mind has simply gotten it confused.

So, cut loose and go for it. Cut loose and be willing to use each day to face your limitations head on—to love them, to embrace them and to transcend them. And you will know when you have transcended them because they won't emerge any longer; a simple law of creation. And remember, it's a law written on a card resting on a Monopoly board that you created in your office and that you have sold to yourself—you've made up all the rules. Even the rules of mastery, and the mind has conveniently laid them aside.

I call you this evening to join with me in, shall we say, a bit of a new direction in our time together. I call you to join with me in learning how to express the mastery that you are. All that has transpired and all that we've done to this point is to shake things up a bit and find out who really wants to get on with it.

While I extend my love to everyone, I cannot force myself on any mind and I cannot give what gifts I would bring to anybody who chooses not to put them into action. And if you happen to have some friends who love to talk about unlimitedness and mastery, ask them if they are really ready for it.

For what we are going to begin in this evening is, if you will, a progressive experience of bringing mastery into manifestation. But it will require your diligence and your complete commitment. It will require that you support one another and love one another. It will require that you set aside the whole of the world wherever you happen to be and choose joy.

So, right now, in your own way go inside your own heart. Let the body relax and just breathe into the heart, and when you are ready, ask yourself with complete honesty,

> *Am I really willing to take the curriculum, now?*

And if as you seek to answer that question you see fears come up, you see questions come up that say,

> *Well, if I could only look ahead I might be able to make a decision,*

rest assured that part of you really isn't quite ready. And that's okay.

The atonement requires finders and not seekers. The healing of mankind requires finders and not seekers. It requires masters. Not those who say,

> *Well, gee, I'd like to master it all, but, gosh, I have so many other things to do.*

Those other things are there because you have resisted your own mastery to some degree and in some way.

To borrow a phrase that recently came into the mind of my beloved brother: *When you are willing to learn what you know you don't yet know, mastery is only a blink away.*

Interesting thought, don't you think?

And take it another step further: when you are willing to learn what you couldn't even possibly learn that you don't know . . . that is called willingness.

Now in your language that sounds a little funny, but the same thing was posed to me by the one who was my father. He put his hand on my shoulder and said.

> *Son, you've picked an interesting one. Quite a drama that you have scripted.*

And I looked at him and said,

> *What are you talking about?*

And he said,

> *Oh, I think you'll discover what I'm talking about. All in good time.*

And in his own way he asked me the same question,

> *Are you willing to admit that there just might be something that you don't know and you don't even know that you don't know it? Are you willing to learn?*

And something in me, God only knows what, said,

> *Yes I am.*

And that made all the difference in my own life and the completion of the atonement within me. And I like to think it's made some difference in the world. Just as your choice will make all the difference in the completion of your own atonement and, therefore, will also make a difference in the world. Hmm.

Well, that was fun. How are you all doing?

Participant: Fine. Great.

Has any of this made a bit of sense?

Participant: Yes.

Look around you for a moment . . . fellow travelers, desirous of mastering the only curriculum that needs to be learned. There are many ways to approach it, but until you accept that to learn that curriculum *must mean that the structure of your life around you becomes wholly and radically changed*—and that will mean something different to each of you even now—you really haven't quite yet been willing to learn the curriculum, no matter how many texts you've read. No matter how many verses you've memorized. No matter how many prayers you've said. Some part of you has not quite been willing to become vulnerable. And yes, I would tell the Pope the same thing. Hmm.

Participant: Jeshua, how do you make yourself vulnerable?

How do you make yourself vulnerable?

Participant: Choosing joy?

But remember, Firewalker, it's not just thought. It is a feeling of power that literally wells up, vibrates the cells of the body so you can't contain it. It's not quite the same thing as what you experience as ecstatic happiness that seems to take you to a crescendo and then you're burned out afterward. That's not quite what I am talking about. This joy is a frequency that you can feel vibrating, and it can become constant and you can learn to master it so that you walk around, albeit a few inches off the ground, and you'll find that you will be able to function even in that frequency. Certain things begin to emerge within that frequency. Your ability, for instance, to be in this world and yet be totally with me, in total communication with me or any master you want to be, becomes available—no separation between you and myself whatsoever. The ability to tune in to see how your friends are doing on the other side of the planet and to know what they are doing—all becomes very natural. Where to go, who to talk to; it all becomes an effortless flow.

Joy is like a fire and a frequency that burns off all of the cobwebs, gets rid of all of the static, clarifies the Mind of Christ. And if you don't feel it down to the cells of your body, you don't know yet what it is. Does that help a little bit?

Participant: It helps... So at first the idea comes to the mind, "I choose joy" or "I choose to come from Love". But the body isn't healing yet, or whatever is going on is a heaviness. My mind will actually makes that statement, "I and my Father are one." Then, what's the next step after the statement is made? The desire is there but the body is feeling heavy, whatever the reason.

What is the reason?

Participant: The only thing I can think of is because I don't want it. For some reason I don't want it and I'm blocking it. I am scared of it at some level.

And that's what I was talking about earlier. That fear gets projected outside of yourself. You become fragmented, thinking the thing you fear is something outside of you. The fear is what is within you.

The next step beyond the words—and I've given you many, many cues—is to become outrageous; play and sing and dance. Get a new motion going in the body. Get a little crazy. Do things you've never done before. Interrupt the patterns of the mind. Ask the Holy Father to overwhelm you. It is fine and well and good to begin by saying,

> *I and my Father are one. Isn't that a great thought? But I'm depressed.*

Now the next stage, Firewalker, is to learn to find ways to evoke joy even in the body. You know some ways, but I am talking about some others here in which you truly begin to create a frequency, and we are going to do a little bit of that in a few moments. But it must be *felt*. It must get to the point where you can turn the frequency on, no matter what.

Know you that which is Reiki or the hands-on healing? It's just a dimension of letting some rays of joy enter the field of another's mind. They think it's entering their body. It just enters the mind. The body follows suit. You've already allowed it to enter the field of the mind, but you are keeping the trapdoor closed if it doesn't pour forth into the cells of the body. Eventually, no matter what, you can turn it on and you won't turn it off.

That's the next stage. And there is indeed, as you well know, a part of you that's a little reluctant to be overwhelmed with joy. A part of you yet carries the sadness that you unwittingly yet identify with. Not as much as in the past. It's lessening, but it's there. And so, when you speak joyous words,

> *I and my Father are one. I choose love and not fear,*

it's almost like you tune into it up here [pointing to head] but there is a heaviness down here [pointing to heart] and there seems to be a gap between the two. What we are talking about now is really being willing to close that gap. To erase what is down here that blocks that downward descent of joy.

Indeed. So, Firewalker, are you ready to give it a shot?

Participant: Ready to go for it.

Fine. Come here. [The man comes in front of Jeshua]

Why did you get out of your chair so slowly?

Participant: I have a sore back.

Ah. Now, what I want you to do is clap your hands three times as loudly as you can.

[He claps]

Get into it.

Now, pick what an old friend of mine would call a goddess. Pick a goddess.

Now, dance. Get into it. Let's go.

Participant: I'm not a dancer.

Yes, you are. That's a perception. [Addressing the others] Clap for them. Let's go. Come on.

[Audience claps, and the two dance in the front of the room]

Shout your joy, Firewalker. I don't hear you. Shout your joy.

Participant: Joy! Joy! Joy! Yes. Yes.

[Clapping, dancing and shouting continue]

Okay, all right. Now, thank your goddess.

Participant: Thank you, goddess.

You are welcome.

Now Firewalker, how did that feel?

Participant: A little spooky at first. A little fear came up. "Am I doing it right?"

Ah.

Participant: And then I got more response from people I felt saying "yes" with me in joy. It felt better and more at one with the group.

In other words, you felt safer.

Participant: I felt safer, yes. That's a good way to put it.

Yes, it is a good way to put it. Now, listen. When I first asked you to dance, what did you say?

Participant: In my mind? I don't know.

Give him a moment here.

Participant: What?

I am asking them to give you a moment so that you can just rest and ask yourself to look back to that moment, and what statement did you make?

Participant: To myself I said, "No", or something like that. Some block came up. An embarrassment or something.

What did he say?

Participant: "I am not a dancer."

You said, "I am not a dancer."

Participant: Did I say that?

Oh my goodness where did that come from! That is what you said.

Participant: I didn't even know I said that.

Now, this is very, very, very important, and once again this man, Firewalker, has earned his nickname. Firewalker, do you see how I created a set of circumstances that evoked an old perception that expressed itself for this moment in the statement, "I am not a dancer"? What the Son decrees is. You see, I pulled a little bit of a fast one on you. You didn't know what was coming so you couldn't prepare, and the Truth came up: the perception you hold, "I am not a dancer."

Now, dancing isn't just a god and a goddess shaking their bags of dust around. Dancing is what life requires, you see. When you say, "I am not a dancer", it doesn't have anything to do with how you move your feet and all of that. Nobody is holding a placard with the little numbers up on them. Besides, God has a placard and He always gives you a ten. Do you see what I am saying here?

Participant: I do.

It means that that perception, that's the sadness inside. For you, Firewalker, have carried that belief, "I am not a dancer". And you are a dancer. You just proved it. I thought he did rather well.

Participant: Yes. [Clapping]

Indeed. Now, the dancing goddess. Did you enjoy it?

Participant: I fell a little self-conscious at first, but I got over it.

Exactly. Could you feel how his energy state changed? That is, as *he* began to get into it, you also began to get into it.

Participant: Yes, it helped me.

Ah, there's the key. Firewalker, you just extended love. You chose to begin to set aside a perception that said, "I am not a dancer", and yes, it required the support of those who love you to give you the safety to begin to relearn a different perception of yourself, and as you extended that out, your frequency raised and it affected the frequency of the goddess. That's how love is extended, and that is what brings healing to the world. Do you see?

Participant: Yes.

Firewalker, are you willing to become a dancer?

Participant: Very much so.

Ah. It wasn't so bad, was it? Now, I know some of you are going,

Boy, I'm glad he didn't pick on me.

[Laughter]

When you can't wait to get picked on, the end of the journey comes much more quickly.

What I want to give unto you—now I'm not necessarily done for the evening here, but I want to give unto you what you might call a bit of homework.

Contemplate what just took place with Firewalker, and allow yourself freedom, total safety, imagine that this group of friends is with you all week long. Imagine yourself to rest in that safety just like Firewalker did, and let yourself take a look within at the ways in your own life at which you might be making the same statement to yourself, the ways in any given day in which you refuse to be a dancer: the things that seem to evoke fear, that depress you and conform you and close your Light down. Allow yourself just to look at them. Not to make a judgment, that's not what it's about. The Holy Son of God is far beyond judgment. But just look at it, and then choose one of those ways—and you'll find more than just one that will pop up.

Within the next week's time create a situation that seems to evoke that, and make a different choice. Find a way to become a dancer in that circumstance. It doesn't mean that you have to necessarily stand at a street corner and dance—although that's a good one. Become creative at looking at your life. It may be the way in which you try to communicate to your spouse. It may be the way in which you refuse to take care of yourself.And find a way to dance, a way that evokes the feeling of,

> *Yes, this is rather nice. I'm loving myself.*

Because that is what Firewalker really just did. He loved himself enough to dance. He said

> *The heck with the perception that seems to block me. I am going to dance.*

And the day will come, you see, when Firewalker dances all the time and he won't really care if we are all around to support him in safety. He'll dance no matter what the world says. And that is mastery and freedom.

So, fair enough? Do you understand the assignment? Does it make sense to everyone?

Participant: Yes.

Indeed. So, Firewalker?

Participant: Yes?

Thank you.

Participant: Thank you for all your love and your teaching and your support.

Teaching and love and support are totally meaningless unless someone receives it.

Participant: It is received.

Thank you, I know. Indeed.

Ah. So, you see, we are going to be having some assignments as we go down the path. Some will seem to challenge you as you've never been challenged before—but not until you are ready for them. That's all you need to do this week: become willing to look at the

ways in your own life that you are refusing to dance and find a way to make a different choice.
It could be as simple as how you feel when you walk in the door of your place of employment. You might choose to skip through the door, kiss your little time card, smile at the supervisor and say,

What an incredible day.

It may be something that simple, but you begin to interrupt what has become a chronic and unwitting and unaware pattern in the mind, because that unaware pattern is what has been telling you that the world out there is really real. And it's not. It's an illusion—it's all done with mirrors.

[Personal dialogue here – excluded in this transcript]

So. I indeed love you, and in you is the worthiness of the holy Son of God to choose anew, to choose empowerment, to choose awakening—to find the small and little ways, that perhaps seem big, in which you are yet blocking that Light from flowing through your life. Will it feel like dying? Oh, yes. Thank God for that. Death is the most incredibly beautiful creation you have ever come up with. The death of the ego. The death of the small self. The death of all illusion. Oh, my God, what a beautiful and glorious sight. So go ahead and die a little this week that the joy in you might become full and the life in you might shine forth, and that life and that Light will be the means by which the atonement is completed on Earth as it is in Heaven.

Be at peace in all things, and know . . . it's not serious. Sing, laugh, dance, play. Indeed.

Peace be unto you.

Amen.

THE LIGHT THAT YOU ARE

November 1992

Jeshua

Now, we begin.

I have come unto you many times. I have sought to express unto you my deep and unfathomable and, in Truth, eternal love for all that you are. I have spoken unto you that I see not so much the body but I see the great ray of Light that seemingly animates the body and cries out to be allowed to express itself in its fullness through the guise of the body. Not in order to prove itself, not in order to gain Heaven, but out of compassion to be allowed by the small part of the mind that you have thought you are, to be allowed from the base of compassion to bring itself and give itself unto the world; to allow every moment and every thought and every deed and every vision and every dream—every moment of existence—to be imbued with a clarity of thought, a clarity of purpose, knowledge, and no longer false perceptions; to be imbued with the presence of the Love that God is; to joyously be expressed and to be given.

That Light is who you are. And that Light is the Light that I see. That Light is the Light to which I have come for a thousand lifetimes. I have knocked upon the door of that Light and said,

> *Yes, it is okay. Just press a little harder. Eventually they will let you in.*

And indeed that small part of the mind that you have restricted yourself to, must eventually be dissolved. And how? By your willingness. Your willingness to ask the Holy Spirit that the Bridge between you as the Holy Son of God and God Himself open that window, open that door and allow that Light to flood your being, to bring Light into every dark corner and every shadow that you have tried to hold back, so that you can keep yourself believing that you are unworthy of being the presence of Love and living above all fear and all limitation and all doubt.

And I have watched you through a thousand lifetimes come unto the threshold of the Kingdom, so close, so close, only to allow one thought to again steal across the mind:

No, no, no. I can't possibly be the Son of God. That was left up to Jeshua. Somehow I know, no matter what is said, no matter what is done or how many miracles come into my life, no matter how often I feel the descent of grace upon me, I know there is yet some place within me that is guilty of some sort of unpardonable sin, and therefore I must hold back a small part of myself and become identified with it.

And so you oscillate constantly between your dreams and your prayers of opening and your fear of that opening, which leads you to constrict into but a small point of the Light you truly are. And all the angels of Heaven, if you would well receive it, feel a tinge of sadness. The Earth feels the sadness and, if you would well receive it, the brothers and sisters who even now are with you also feel the tinge of sadness, because they need you as much as you have ever needed them. They need you to be the one who says,

No longer will I lie down in the bed of crucifixion, but I choose in this hour to stand in the resurrection.

Do you know what it means to exist? It means to stand up out of nothingness. Out of nothingness. To stand up and say,

Okay. I might as well be here. And where am I if I am not in the Holy Mind of God, embraced by a warm and fuzzy blanket called Love? What am I if I am not choosing to be the presence of Love? What is the purpose and function of my being if I am not allowing myself to open to unfathomable vision? To serve the rebirth of Light upon this plane? To bring Heaven to Earth?

Not to escape the Earth. Not to find some magical means by which you can flit about, become so light that you ascend the body and laugh at everybody left behind. But to choose to see that indeed you walk in a very magical kingdom. You walk in a kingdom that is a construct made from the energy of thought itself, and you are sharing in this great construct with your brothers and sisters who have created it with you. And your only purpose and function is to be happy.

To realize that where you are is not in the body at all. But where you are has *never* tasted birth and cannot know death. That the body is exactly that: it is the body. Not *my* body, not *your* body—*the* body. And through you, through the body, through its personality, a great Light can shine forth at any time you decide to allow it.

I have come unto you for so long now and said, I'm sorry, but there are no magical techniques. There is only a simple choice to be made: To sit down in the quietness of your own beingness, your own existence, and to realize the simplicity of the Truth that must be:

> *I and my Father are one. I have never been who I thought I was. I'm not this body at all. The small part of my mind that has thrown up the smokescreens of fear, in Truth, has no part in me.*

I have come unto you. I have cried out unto you as you stood at the threshold of the Kingdom and reached out my hand in a million ways—not just through this communication, but in your dreams, while you drive your automobiles, in the midst of your relationships. In every moment you can conceive I have extended my hand to you and said:

> *Come. Come to where I am. It's not far. It's not far at all.*

Heaven must exist right here in this room or it exists nowhere. It is where I abide, and the whole gist of my Gospel has been eternally that it is where *you* abide also— even when you believe you don't. That, you see, is the great trick. That is the paradox that brings illumination back to the mind. When you are willing to concede your needless sense of struggle, when you are ready to embrace the Truth that where you are now, Heaven is, because you are the one who chooses to be awake, now, in whatever moment the world throws at you:

> *I choose to be awake. Therefore, I will teach only Love because that is what I am. I will not choose to look upon strife. I will not draw it to myself.*

And that does not mean that while you are in the world you never see strife. It just means that you don't identify with it.

> *And I will choose to walk this world a little lighter because I am Light. And I will allow the Holy Spirit to use each moment of my life as a way through which there can be communicated the remembrance of Truth.*

What if . . . What if you were willing to acknowledge that there is absolutely nothing for you to do save to allow Love to be extended through you? What if you were to accept that there is absolutely nowhere to go, nothing to achieve save to be willing to join with me in serving the atonement, the awakening of the mind of the Son of God? What if right now—*right now*— as you look upon your life, you were to acknowledge that it has been fueled by a kind of searching, a searching that has become so habitual that you have convinced yourself that surely Heaven must be just around the corner.

> *And when I have squeezed out every last piece of emotional baggage of my being, then God will smile on me.*

What if you were to acknowledge that the Truth about you cannot be dimmed by the body, by space and time, by any trauma you have ever experienced? And that indeed to stand at the threshold of the Kingdom of Heaven—which is merely the remembrance of where you are always—requires only that you abandon fear and choose love?

To stand up, to exist, means to acknowledge that somebody on this plane has to stand up for a new vision and to live it. To be willing to be the presence of Love and to never need to cower before anyone. To look even a perfect stranger—and we all know that there is no such thing—in the eyes, and when they complain, when they lament, when they say,

> *No, it's impossible. I can't change my life's conditions. I'm too weak. I'm too poor.*

—there's this excuse and that excuse—look them in the eye and say,

> *That's a bunch of nonsense.*

Not because you are judging them, but because you see the Light of Christ that is just behind the limited set of beliefs that they have chosen to be identified with. And if you have to nudge them just a little bit and perhaps they hate you for it, so what?

Would you conform yourself so that an illusion can love you, or would you choose to love the Light of Christ that lies just behind every appearance of lack and incapability and doubt?

I have said to you a thousand times that what you teach will teach you. And if you choose to be a miracle-worker, miracles will necessarily transform your life. That means you don't have to get there before you begin. That by choosing to begin now, in this day and in every hour, to be the presence of Christ, you will learn what it means to be that presence. There is no other way. There is absolutely no other way that works. There is not a single set of skills you can master that will ever enlighten you. But you can bring your Light to whatever skills the Holy Spirit would ask you to learn and use in this world by acknowledging first,

> *I and my Father are One.*

And the perception of struggle, the perception of doubt, indeed the experience of fear is wholly unreal and touches not the Holy Son of God.

Now, I know that that brings up fear. Does it not? Can you feel it?

> *Gulp. If I accept what Jeshua is saying, I have no choice but to give up the game of separation and acknowledge right here, in front of God and everybody, that I am awake, that I simply will not tolerate error in myself again.*

That is the eye of the needle. That is the crack between two worlds.

That is the quantum leap that brings you home again. That is the simple choice that takes you from just on that side of the threshold of Heaven and brings you fully into the midst of the Kingdom, and you realize you haven't had to fix a thing. But you have indeed become humble because the holy Son of God *always knows*—and listen to this carefully— the holy Son of God *always knows* that of himself he does nothing, but the Father through him, does all these things.

Gone is the dream of the dreamer. Gone the hope of being the doer. All things are given back to God, and in the place of the dreamer there arises the perfect servant of Love and of Light. It doesn't even really know how it all happens. It is just willing to be the presence of Love and to become available. You never know what you might find yourself doing once you have truly made that choice.

Are you willing to risk it? Is that not what it's really all about? Are you willing to risk truly releasing every last trace of your hold, your grip on the ego, which *is* the thought of separation from God?

> *Oh, my God, what would happen in my life if I were to sit down, look at myself in the mirror and say "I am awake?" I couldn't possibly be anything but awake. And if I am awake, I know that all minds are joined in love. And because I love Jeshua, I can certainly talk to him without having to borrow Marc's "carcass."*

. . . but you can join with me to celebrate the Truth.

So, I know that was a rather interesting greeting. Good evening to you. But there were some who desperately needed just to get the little laser shot of Truth because, you see, the mind—the ego— constantly wants to play games. Constantly. That's what the ego is—it *is* a game. It's like turning on your television set and instead of watching a comedy, you watch a drama with sickness and disease and death and fear and egos beating up on one another because they believe they live in lack and if they give all they have received, they won't have anything:

So I'd better hoard it and store it all up.

When just the opposite is true.

And, indeed, if you do not find avenues through which you can give the grace and love that you have received, if you cannot choose to find the avenues and find the ways to give away all you have received, what you have is taken from you. Not by an evil God that sits outside of you and goes, "Tsk, tsk." But you relinquish it. And the tree of life within you withers and dies, and the mind will project the cause of that outside of itself—outside of itself.

Surely it was a set of circumstances. If only my maid hadn't left me. It was inflation; that's what did it. Why did they let those Democrats get in again?

Hmm. There's always something, isn't there? Another excuse to delay existing. Think about it. There's always an excuse to delay existing. And the only way to exist is to be real. And the only way to be real is to accept that you are the holy Son of God, here and now, and everything else is a fantasy, a delusion, based on a habit of fear. Everything.

All power is given unto you to attract to yourself the means whereby you can extend the Love of God into the world. They are all around you in every moment. And that is the turning about in the seat of the soul. The Greeks used to call it "metanoia." That is, the turning about that has to be chosen, simply chosen:

I choose to be awake.

And that is what will make all the difference in the world—because you and you and you and all of you, and me, together, choose to be awake. That's all. Then, you see, what happens is that I no longer have to walk with you, trying to shout in your ear. We can lock arms and skip down the path together.

Ah, love, sweet love. Love! Indeed, it rides on every breath you breathe and desires to be heard with every spoken word. Love is indeed the alpha and omega of all things. Love is the essence of all that is real, and the only thing that is real is you. Therefore, you are that Love that was there in the beginning with me, is now and ever shall be, a Love that wholly outshines the body and the frailties of this wholly insane world, that cries out to see the demonstration, the demonstration that it is possible to do things in a different way.

One of the habits of the ego is to turn a deaf ear toward the cries of your brothers and sisters. Yes, the cries when they are hungry physically, the cries when they feel abused and rejected; yes, all of those levels of insanity. But the cry that I am addressing here is the cry that comes up in every soul and is constantly going on. It's like a siren, and it's been going on for so long you become a little deaf to it. It's the cry that says,

> *Will somebody please tell me it's okay to be awake? Will somebody tell me it's okay to feel safe? Will somebody teach me that only by being vulnerable, by choosing to be the presence of Love, can I find my safety?*

I've said unto you that I need to hire you, in a way. You see, so many of your brothers and sisters have been so programmed to believe that only the body is real and what is outside its boundaries must not exist. And so I come to them and oh, my God, how I come to them. I come to them in their dreams. I whisper to them. If you want to know the Truth of it—and I haven't shared this with you yet—I have materialized a form in which to talk to someone more times that you could possibly ever count if you sat down for a hundred years and did nothing but count. I have come to so many, and they have seen visions of me and in the very next moment they said,

> *No, it had to be my imagination.*

Some of you know what that's like.

So, I've taken out a classified ad and I said,

Wanted: Servants of Light. Those who have become willing to be my eyes. To be my hands. To be my heart. To be my physical appearance in this world.

And I have asked only one thing:

Just be willing to join with me and to trust me. I know what your brother and sister needs all the time.

And I have explained to you how I know that. It's not because I'm smart. It's because I finally figured out two thousand years ago that if I go to the Holy Spirit and ask, the Holy Spirit will tell me. And I have said to you, rather metaphorically and jokingly— but it's much closer to the Truth than you know—when I ask what someone needs, the Holy Spirit races around and sneaks in the back door of their heart, pulls out what they need and brings it back to me; and then I show it to them. And they go,

Oh Jeshua, what a miracle. What a miracle. How did you know that?

And the Truth is, I didn't until it was asked.

Now, if the Holy Spirit can do that for me, it can certainly do it for you. I indeed need you to answer my classified ad and to come to work—which is really play, by the way—and to sit down with me and to look out upon all of this world, indeed to look out upon every world you have ever constructed and tried to wrap around yourself, to look upon all of them and go,

Oh, that's just a harmless sideshow going on. What was I ever frightened of?

Even the body isn't real. It's a hologram. It doesn't even have existence apart from the value you place upon it. And yet, for a little while, because it has been constructed out of infinite possibility, I can indeed teach you how to use the body anew so that it becomes the perfect means through which love is extended and taught—

and therefore received by the mind and heart that is willing to be re-taught.

It is so simple. So incredibly simple. And, of course, that's what makes it difficult. Because the world believes in struggle. Because the world teaches you—and the part of the mind called the ego *is* the world mind—teaches you that it must take effort and it must be complex. It must be very difficult indeed to ever become so purified that the grace of God would descend upon you like a dove and a voice from Heaven would shout, "This is my beloved Son in whom I am eternally well pleased."

> *Boy, that may happen to very special beings, but it will never happen to me.*

So what happens is this: your Father's been shouting that through all of eternity as He looks at you and the Holy Spirit says,

> *Dad, this one isn't quite willing to get it yet. What should we do?*

And the Father knows the answer and tells the Holy Spirit,

> *Weave a tapestry with everything that they create—every thought, every action, every deed. Let them pretend that they are running around getting somewhere in all of their seeking, in all of their striving, in all of their lamenting; and secretly weave a tapestry out of everything they construct so that without their even knowing it they will be brought back to the Holy of Holies, the place of peace within, in which they can again relearn that the only choice that must be made is the choice between Love and fear.*

And, rest assured, when the tapestry has been woven, when the Holy Spirit has brought you back face to face with God, He will take the last step for you. You don't even have to do that—He will do it for you.

Now listen very carefully. I have said unto you that time is given unto you so that you might use it constructively. And the only constructive use of time is the practice of being the presence of one who is awake to their reality as Love. That means that from the moment you realize you are awake until the moment you think you've fallen asleep—only the body does that, by the way— every single tick of your clock is the greatest of blessings you could ever receive. And why? Time has been constructed as a device to separate you from eternity but it has been translated for you into the tapestry that returns you to all that *is* eternal. And when you really get that, when you really truly get it, something wells up within you called gratitude. Do you know that feeling?

I know what it means to feel gratitude when you have enough golden coins to pay the bills. I know what it means to feel gratitude: I see it happening in your minds when the weather is just right. I know what it means for you to be willing to feel gratitude when you get the date you've always wanted. There are a thousand other times, special times, when you've allowed yourself to touch gratitude.

When you really understand the blessing of time—that it is not a prison at all—then every breath you breathe comes forth from an incredible gratitude because you've finally gotten it. It's just a game

> *All I'm asked to do is practice being the presence of Love. To be unlimited. To realize that I can't be limited. All I have to do is say, "Holy Spirit, what do you want me to do today?" And then set about to do it.*

And if a vision begins to be born in you, "Pack up your bags and move to this other place", why not go? Fear of loss?

> *What will I lose if I leave these things behind me, these roots that I believe have kept me safe?*

You will lose nothing.

> *Leave my friends? You mean, venture out into the big world? What will I lose?*

A limitation. A friend of the heart is never lost.

I learned that if I gave up the body, I wouldn't lose anything either. And, after all, is not the body the one thing that you continue to insist upon identifying with?

Has it ever kept you safe?

Has the body ever, ever, ever, ever brought you the perfect intimacy of a Holy Instant?

Have you ever experienced through the senses, through the use of the body, what we will call here eternal satisfaction?

Have you ever fed the body so that it's no longer hungry? Darn thing, you have to keep feeding it.

Has any adornment upon the body ever truly won the overwhelming approval of everyone you share this planet with?

Has the making of a muscle so that it is bigger than it was a year ago, has that ever given you the acceptance you would like?

You rise in the morning, you pamper it. You feed it. You clothe it. You construct an entire world around it, and then you busy yourself from nine to five, five days a week—and sometimes longer—so that you can feed it, clothe it, and house it and pamper it a little bit. Has the body ever presented you with the gift of grace?

They might be questions worth asking.

Now, of course, therefore, the conclusion is this: hate the body. Despise it. Beat it. Flog it. Some of you have done that before. Whip it into shape and keep hating it. Always see it as imperfect, so work on it a little harder. No, that's not the conclusion, but it is the conclusion some minds reach.

Since I'm not the body I'll just ignore the darned thing. Great error.

The great error in all of your spiritual traditions has been this: That the whole goal is to somehow find a means whereby you can escape the body; for the body is the symbol of the ego, it is the symbol of time itself. *The point is not to ascend; the point is to realize that ascension has already been completed, because the holy Son of God has never left the Kingdom of Heaven.*

The whole point of the game is ***descension***. To descend, to bring the Light and the Love that you are and to utilize the body as a means through which you communicate Light and Love. And that requires that you embrace the body just for what it is and not for anything else: as a means given unto you for a very short time whereby you can relearn how to radiate Light and Love into this world that believes that bodies are the final definition of reality. And if you shine enough Light and enough Love through it, other minds can begin to get the message that there is life after the body. There is life beyond the body even now. And there can then be a process of awakening.

The point I am trying to make right now is this: I have sought to find a thousand ways to get the idea across that you cannot transcend what you do not embrace and love. That does not mean that you try to add inches of muscle to body—unless, of course, you enjoy that. It means that you allow your perceptions of the body and of what the world is for to be corrected, and that requires your willingness to take all of your perceptions, lay them on a tray and give them back to the Holy Spirit, and just say,

> *You know, I haven't figured it out yet. Maybe I should read the directions.*

And indeed correction does come and you begin to look upon the body—*the* body, not *my* body—the body, and you sit back from a perspective in which you realize you are Light. You go,

> *Oh, what an interesting toy this is. If I press this button and do that, I can activate Light in the cells and they can actually shine from the body. If I do this and do that and do this, I can radiate so much*

> *Light through my eyes that people will actually stop and wonder what on earth hit them. Oooh, this sounds like fun.*

And the body begins to be something that no longer is seen as a prison, something that limits you.

And you can look at what it means to be in this world as if you have just come to a costume party. You see that everybody else seems to be playing the game of believing that the body is real, and you can look and see that so many minds are enshrouded with seriousness. They actually believe that life requires struggle and strain and lack and all of the rest of the things that represent limitation. And you can become so outrageous because you've thrown away all of your own perceptions and you are beginning to be re-taught. You can begin to be the one who lives just the opposite of the way the world would try to teach you to live.

You can become one who joins the ranks of those who have chosen to exist. And to exist does not mean to just get by. It means to be the radiant presence of outflowing Love and joy and dance and laughter and play and vision and contribution and service. Love, Love, Love.

That's what the world is waiting for. Gone is the time—and please hear what I am about to say—very quickly gone will be the time for me to come even in this way, because if I do not go away, the Comforter cannot come unto you. Therefore, cling not unto me for you do not know the day and the hour in which my Father will say unto me, "That's enough now. Either they live it or they don't."

> *Whew! But Jeshua, I thought you said that you would be with me always?*

Well, of course I will. But *you* are going to have to come to *where I am* to realize it. So now is as good a time as any. Right now. Right now. Are you willing right now just to take ten of your precious seconds and acknowledge in your own mind,

> *I am that one in whom my Father is eternally well pleased and all*

things are possible for me, because I am not the doer at all?

Now that means that, from this moment forward, you can never go to a single workshop unless you do so from the perspective, now healed, that you are the holy Son of God, and obviously the Holy Spirit wants you to be there or you wouldn't be there; and all you are there for is to polish up a few skills so that you can become like a laser and bring the Light of Christ and give it to the world—never again out of a perception that there is something you lack. And never again to believe, whether the friend you are with is me or some other teacher, that they are somehow other than who you are. And to honor them for being willing to play the role of teacher so that you get to play the role of what seems to be the student. And the whole purpose of teaching is that the student becomes as the teacher is. Otherwise, there is no point; there's just no point.

The time comes quickly now when this world is going to cry out for masters, not seekers. The time will indeed also come—and I am certainly not coming from fear when I say this—the time is also coming when this Earth, the vibration of it, simply won't be such that anything but masters will be able to be here at all.

So. I need you to answer my classified ad. Will you? Hmm. The great truth is that in accepting the job on faith, all things come to you.

Participant: *Jeshua, I need a new job.*

Why?

Participant: *Because I've outgrown the one I've had.*

If you have outgrown the one you have had, why does that mean you *need* another one?

Participant: *I think I'd like another one.*

Ah. What would you do with it?

Participant: Play.

That would be different than the last job.

Participant: For sure.

Would it then be a job?

Participant: I guess not, in the traditional sense of a job.

Hmm. What if the traditional sense was a wholly insane one?

Participant: Oh, I know that.

Indeed. We are talking about perception. The mind believes it must have a job in order to survive—that is, to keep the body in survival—so it accepts or receives impressions that says,

> *A job is a place of imprisonment. I can't possibly be happy here so I'll run and get another one.*

But, of course, you just take the same perceptions with you and nothing really changes.

Therefore, beloved friend, remember that what you decree is. Do not say that you *need* another job. But instead ask that the means might be brought to you so that you might be a servant of the atonement. Now, that doesn't mean a lot of serious stuff. It means indeed play—that you can allow yourself to, shall we say, abide in a different frequency than in the past, recognizing that while it pays the bills and all of that, your real purpose is to practice being the presence of Love, to nudge other minds to begin to think in an unlimited way. To be the one through whom the Holy Spirit brings gentle correction to your brothers and sisters, to their minds.

Say not that you need *another* job because that implies it must be like the one you had before—which means it implies the quality of beingness that you carried within the mind while you were there.

Ask instead for a field in which you can play at a higher frequency, if you will, with minds that are resonating with greater freedom within themselves. Do you see?

Participant: *That sounds really inviting. Higher frequencies.*

Indeed. Be careful how you wrap up the package of your desire.

Participant: *This constant vigilance is kind of exhausting, you know?*

Only because you bring effort into it. There is no need for effort. All that it requires is that,

> *This day I will be the witness of my thoughts. How am I thinking my thoughts? What words am I choosing when I speak?*

The word is very powerful indeed.

To be vigilant does not require effort as much as it asks the *relinquishment* of effort. It requires only that you watch. It's actually the easiest thing you could possibly do. But you've taught the mind to be sidetracked, and it becomes sidetracked—please listen to this very carefully—the mind becomes sidetracked every time you let yourself believe that what is occurring out there on the screen of your life is something that is real and independent of your own mind. Do you see?

It doesn't matter what the event is around you. What matters is, are you aware of how you are choosing to think about it? And when you come to see that there is nothing outside of *you*, that it really is all in your head—except that the mind is not in the head—then great power begins to be reborn in you; and you begin to realize that by reconstructing the foundation within the mind, what is projected out here must necessarily change. And when there are enough awakened minds that are doing just that, the world that you have been taught is real out there, the real world will be different.

If the mind can construct a world that reflects separation, it can indeed construct that which reflects union with God. Your philosophers call that being an idealist. Well, I should certainly hope so, since everything is the reflection of an idea. You might as well just admit it and begin indeed to turn the attention of the world from trying to conquer outer space, and turn it so that it begins to understand the power of mind itself. The further your scientists go out, the more they are returned to what is within. Your physicists in this century have indeed learned that the more they try to plumb the depths of matter, the more they run right into their own mind. Hmm. Talk about chasing your own tail!

Now, if it is true for the greatest minds within your realms of science, it is obviously true for you, too. You never see anything save that which you construct in your mind. The day comes when you begin to realize just how staggering a Truth that is because it includes the body itself. And to use time constructively is to be vigilant in observing how you are allowing the mind to work, to begin to see the patterns that create limitation and lack and fear and hurt and judgment and all of the rest, and begin to interrupt them at their inception and make other choices.

If I am feeling hurt, the correction is to extend love.

If I am feeling lack, the correction is to extend love.

If I am feeling rejected, the correction is to extend love.

Because to do so you must return to your right-mindedness in which you remember,

> *I am the holy Son of God. I cannot indeed be hurt. I cannot know pain and I cannot taste death. I am the Thought of Love in form and I am held perfect and safe now.*

Love indeed heals all things. Nothing else works. It's the cosmic salve.

And each time hurt seems to continue, you are only experiencing the choice you have made in the mind to insist that it continue. There is no other Truth. That's it. Your mind is perfectly healthy at all times—perfectly healthy. You may choose to use it in an unhealthy way but the power of choice is never taken from anyone at any time. Does that make sense to you?

Participant: *Yes, it does, But Jeshua, when I am vigilant and I see the pattern of negativity that I have allowed to run my life, it seems as though throughout my entire day I am constantly calling myself up short because I've gone back to that old habit, and I am saying to myself, "No, you don't need to think that way any more." And sometimes at the end of a day when I've had to do that a lot, I am really whipped. It's physically exhausting to me, and you sounds as though I can do it more quietly or something, and I am not quite getting that.*

Now, let's take a look at what you just said since what the Son decrees, the Son experiences. You have stated and therefore created a perception that when you are vigilant and you notice you've been allowing some negative perspective, some limited perspective to, in a sense, guide you, to own you—that when you notice it you are then constantly calling yourself up short. That is, you are berating and judging yourself, are you not?

Participant: *Yes.*

There is the source of the error. When you see whatever it is you happen to see in your perception, your perspective, that is limiting you, a strand of negativity— however you want to label that it doesn't matter—when you see it, there is only one cure: laugh your buns off at it.

[Laughter]

Because it is not part of the reality of who you are. You will never kill the ego. You will only love it to death, by withdrawing the value you place upon it.

> *Oh, my God, there I go again. What a jerk I am.*

Participant: Oh, that's me.

No, that's not you.

Participant: Or, that has been me.

No, that has not been you.

Participant: Okay. It just doesn't exist.

You are the presence of the Thought of Love in form. You are unbounded and eternal. There has never been a time that you have not existed as the Thought held lovingly in the Mind of God. Your reality knows no boundaries. It knows neither beginning nor end, and therefore you have never tasted birth or death. You cannot possibly have ever sinned against God. You are indeed loved wholly, and the Light shines in you as completely in this moment as it has ever shined in me. That Light you are. And to be vigilant means that in each moment when you watch the movie and the ego seems to creep in to the mind, you simply retrain the mind to notice that that's not a part of you and you have a very good laugh because the drama has become a comedy; and then you choose anew.

Don't make a transition by thinking you have to *beat yourself* into love. Just be love. The constructive use of time—which is the only use there is of it—is to choose to be the presence of Love. Each time the thought comes into the mind that

> *there I go again. I've blown it. What a jerk I am,*

that is part of the same voice that has created the strand of negativity trying to seduce you, trying to say,

> *No, no, don't let me die. I've been in control of you for so long.*

And all you need do is withdraw your value from it and choose anew. And have a good laugh while you are doing it.

Participant: *Jeshua, that really helps a lot. Thank you very much.*

I will send you a bill.

Participant: *Okay. More bills.*

Do you know what the bill will look like?

[Laughter]

The bill will have the names of brothers and sisters you may not have even met yet, and they will be sent to you so that *you* can be their teacher. For as you learn and as that awakening process deepens, your ability to be responsible also broadens, and then the Holy Spirit sends unto you those who need to receive what you have learned. And if you do not give all that has been given unto you, even that begins to be withdrawn because it dries up within you. And if you do not give all that you have received, you cannot know that your Redeemer lives, and that Redeemer is the face of Christ that dwells within you now. And that is why in giving, you receive; and to give all means that you receive all.

The only difference between us is that two thousand years ago I figured that one out:

> *If I give all that my Father has given me, I will receive it eternally.*

It's like—liking chocolate ice cream so much that you want to have it all the time. And you finally peer behind the scenes and realize that the way the universe works is that you keep giving it away and that's how more gets delivered to your door. Do you see? You give away a pint and they bring you a gallon. Your Father's going,

> *Oh, thank you so much for giving that away. Here, take more, because now I know you know what to do with it. You are finally understanding what it means, what you are supposed to be doing*

> *with love and with intelligence and with vision, with inspiration, with compassion. Oh, indeed, with all the power of Heaven and Earth. You are finally getting it. So here you are; I am going to give you more of it.*

And you turn around and you go,

> *Oh my goodness. Here comes more. What do I do with it? Oops, I'm not going to keep it. I am going to go give it away. Oops, here comes even more. Wow, what a fun game this is. The more I give away, the more I receive.*

You could call it, in your culture, being addicted to love. What do you think?

Participant: *I think it's a great idea...*

Just a moment. Now that's a very good word. It is an idea because *you* are an idea. Ideas are extended as you choose to receive them and be identified with them. *The only way to be awake is to choose to identify your self as one who is awake and no longer tolerates error within yourself. By choosing to draw the idea of being awake to yourself and identifying with it, you become the presence of that idea.*

It has well been said that everything in this dimension is channeled. It's a representation of an idea. So, you see, you can go to one of your malls tomorrow and just walk up to people and say,

> *What idea are you being today?*

Now, that sounds a little light-hearted, and it is because the heart is filled with Light. But it's also the Truth.

> *What idea am I being now? Am I being a Thought of Love in form or am I being a scum-bucket?*

Hmm. I do love that term. I don't know where my beloved brother found it. Beloved friend—and the rest of you know that obviously these questions asked are your very own—eventually then the last trace of ego vanishes from the mind. You don't even feel when that last trace leaves. You simply notice that it has been absent for a while and the Holy Spirit has crept into your dreams and stolen the cobwebs of shadows outgrown, and there is naught but the presence of a mind that is wholly corrected and a heart that rests at peace. And each time a thought seems to press against you,

> *Oh, gosh, the body is so beat. How am I ever going to get all these things done?*

without any effort at all you remember,

> *Oh, I'm not even in this world. I'm just the presence of Love. If I choose to take the day off, it'll be done tomorrow. And I'll take the day off because I've learned to ask the Holy Spirit's guidance in all things. And if I hear the thought, "Take the day off; go fishing," you will find me fishing.*

That is what it means when I said that the wind blows as it does and you cannot know where it comes from or where it's going; and so is everyone born of the Spirit, because they no longer mistrust the gentle voice of guidance given unto everyone wholly and without measure.

It feels rather nice just to be awake because nothing any longer obstructs your perception, and you look out upon a world that is indeed wholly safe; and you know that because the world is harmless you can live the fullness of the Light and Love that is longing to descend through you into the world. Gone are every last traces of fear. Gone, every doubt. Replaced by a perfect certainty and a constant state of laughter. Because the whole thing has taken but a moment, and you have become that mind that I once demonstrated to the world. You have learned what my old friend, Paul, learned when he tried to tell his friends,

> *Just let that mind be in you that was in our Lord, Christ Jesus.*

That's all. Let the whole-mindedness of Christ be in you—and that is all. And then indeed you walk much lighter in this world and you smile a lot, and even when you notice you are not smiling, a little bit of laughter comes up because you are just watching a little game called the ego and you are not even identified with it anymore. And you look upon your brothers and sisters and they sense a softness in you. They sense an acceptance. *They sense that there is nothing they have to do to earn your love.* You just accept them as they are because you see the Light that shines in them. And that is the Light that you embrace. That is the Light you talk to, though they think you are talking to their mind, their lower mind. That is the Light that you worship and give thanks for. That is the Light that you dance with. And they will know it, for they will walk around the corner and see you and something makes them turn and look at you twice.

> *I don't even know what it is, but something . . .*

The soul has recognized a reflection of its own Truth. And without raising a hand you will have brought the miracle of grace because you have chosen to throw off the shackles of the world and to be the living demonstration of one who is awake.

Does that require standing on a soapbox? There are no brass bands that have to play, because only the ego needs those things. There is just the presence of Love right where you thought *you* were. Indeed.

Now, in the last few moments have you not felt a peace descending upon you? Have some of you felt that? Seems to happen every time the Holy Spirit whispers to me,

> *Go and use the mind of your ancient friend and brother, and speak the Truth.*

And the peace comes not because I bring it, but because that part of you that knows the Truth recognizes it and acknowledges it within yourself. That is what brings peace to the world. And that is what it means to be gathered in my name.

You are the Thought of Love in form. You, right where you are.

You are free to change your lifestyle anytime you want. Free to give up struggle. Free to create unlimitedness if you want. Free to join with higher frequencies—if you want to use that kind of terminology—that are now descending into the minds of mankind. Free at anytime to take up your cross and follow me; and as you know, my cross is made of Light and it brings joy to the world.

Participant: *Jeshua, I have a problem, which I want to ask you for a little help with. There are three of us that go to a prison and there is a man there who keeps writing me these letters, and he evidently is projecting a lot onto me. I can't quite get it through to this man that we are just friends. I love him as a friend and I don't want to hurt him. How can I deal with this? Can you help me?*

No, but you can help yourself. Now, precious friend, can you see how this situation is mirroring what has been rather much a lifelong pattern? That is, when an energy is projected upon you, not just in this specific way, but in which other minds would perceive that there is something that they need from you, that it has always brought up within you the sense that you are responsible for somehow finding a way to fulfill what they need, and if you cannot, or if you feel that you cannot, it brings up within you a sense of guilt or failure?

Participant: *Yes.*

Well, that was a good guess.

Now, if that is true—and we both know it is—it means that this situation is also your blessing, to look at that pattern of perception. You need not try to find its source in some ancient childhood experience in which you were punished for eating your Cheerios with your left hand. But rather, in seeing that you are being presented with an opportunity to put into practice the Truth that when you abide in your integrity and in your Truth, you cannot possibly harm anyone. That you are not responsible for being the one who fulfills the needs projected upon you by fearful minds, by confused minds.

We are striking to the core here, aren't we?

Participant: Yes, we are.

That is what I meant when I said you can help yourself. I can't wave a magic wand and make that one disappear, and I wouldn't want to because it is really good for you. But you can stand in the integrity of your Truth and communicate to this one very, very clearly—and, quite frankly, I would suggest a bit strongly—that this is the way it is and this ceases *now*. Do you see?

Participant: Yes.

Now, does that not bring up a little "gulp?"

Participant: Yes.

And yet, do you realize just behind that old pattern lies a power waiting to be born in you?

To claim responsibility for your right in time to draw the boundaries, so that your Light can be like a laser and not be dissipated by the thought or perception that somehow you are responsible for being the salve on everybody's perceptions of wounds? Sometimes the greatest of gifts you can give to someone is to insist on absolute responsibility within them for what they think, what they feel, and what they do. That your friendship and love is never in question, but the form it takes requires impeccable integrity on that one's part because, you see, that has been part of that one's problem: this constant projection of fantasy that blurs the lines. Quite frankly, that's why that one is where that one is. Hmm?

Therefore, can you see then how every time an event takes place that confronts you with the need to grow, to be the strength of the one who is awake and realizes their own worthiness, what you teach also teaches your brother or your sister; and everything serves the awakening of the Sonship. It's healing. You are being given a grand, grand gift. Hold it in your hand. Don't lose this precious moment.

I am going to ask you indeed to write to this one in no uncertain terms, and when you do it, really let the feeling come up within you, not of anger—of power. Power of certainty and integrity.

> *This is who I am. This is what I offer you. Do not step on it because that will only show me that you are not willing to assume responsibility for true friendship and holy relationship, and therefore I will have no choice but to withdraw it and give it to somebody else.*

Let that one know that you are totally worthy of being absolutely respected at all times and in all ways, and that this is the last time that these words will need to be spoken. What do you think?

Participant: *That sounds right. It sounds good in my heart.*

Do you see how it will also heal what your culture would call part of a wounded little girl?

Participant: *Yes, I think I do.*

So, flex the muscles of the heart. With gratitude, by the way. Put PS: Thank you for being my teacher.

Now, once again, precious friend, you asked me a question and I raced over to the window and said, "Holy Spirit, you are not going off duty yet, are you?" He said, "No, no. I'll hang around if you want me to." I said, "Would you mind?" "No problem. I've got it." Out through the back door of the office, a little army crawl through the grasses, sneaking into the back door of your heart. "Ah, this is what she needs to do." Pulls it back out. Fills it out on a piece of paper and said, "Here's the prescription." So I took it and said, "Well, okay." And I spoke to this my beloved brother who, by the way, when we do this is, shall we say, elsewhere than where you might think he is. Because, you see, all that I do I always use as a teaching tool for him—that is, the mind, the Light that is him—so that he can someday learn to do these things on his own. I said, "Look, this is the prescription the Holy Spirit has given to me.

Now, I am just going to kick some ideas loose in that mind-field of yours, create a few sentences so that I can deliver the prescription to our friend."

That is why it strikes the chord deeply. The answer came from within you. And the only difference is that you already knew the answer but a part of you was fearful of receiving it and acting upon it. Is that not true?

Participant: *That's right. I had a dear friend share the same thing with me and . . . but I just really needed to have you share with me.*

I am your friend and I am your brother and I am your servant, as was your dear friend who told you basically the same thing. So happy letter-writing.

Participant: *Thank you so much.*

I really need to ask you something for my son and his girlfriend. I told him I would do it if there was an opportunity tonight. It seems that there is a little soul who insists on coming to them whether they are ready for it or not. And they've really been in an uproar for the last week or two.

And I told them what you said about their souls have an agreement before they are ever born, that their own souls agreed to have this child even if they don't remember it consciously, their souls agreed. And that even though this seems like the most inconvenient time, it's going to turn out to be a real blessing. And, Jeshua, even though sometimes they raise their eyebrows because I come here and I listen to you and I read the transcripts, they see that I am getting happier and lighter, and so even though they're still a little skeptical . . . I did laugh tonight because they asked me if I would ask you about this.

First, do you see how this represents what I prophesied for you?

Participant: *The teacher part?*

Yes. And you are beginning to see how it works

Participant: Yes.

As you become lighter, other souls begin to be attracted, though they may go kicking and screaming, they still find themselves drawn to asking you, in this case, to be one who goes and gets the message. Eventually they'll ask you for the message.

Participant: Oh boy.

Now, you will know that of yourself you can do nothing, and you'll slide over to the window and ask the Holy Spirit the way I do it. And then the student becomes the teacher. He who drinks from my mouth becomes as I am, and I become that one—a blending so deep. And why? Because the identification with the ego is relinquished and only the Mind of Christ shines.

That is what it is all about. I am not here to perpetuate the perception of separation between you or anyone and myself. I am here to eradicate it.

Now, about that little one. All souls are the same size.

[Laughter]

And yet the soul has no dimensions. It doesn't take up space at all. It cannot be measured. Now, the only thing within them that feels like this is the worst possible time is the part of them unwilling to acknowledge the Truth of who they are: that all power to deal with whatever situations may arise must necessarily be within them. They are just not yet at a point where they are really truly ready to own up to the fact of reality that nothing happens by accident, and everything brings a blessing and a teaching.

This, then, seeks to be made manifest because a part of them has been asking for something that will push them beyond the limits that they have become identified with. You could say an experience that is going to ask them to—how do you put it?—either you do, or you get off the pot.

It is not coming by accident. Now, they can lament. They can believe they are weak. They can believe they cannot find solutions. They can believe they cannot rise to the occasion. That doesn't change the Truth one iota. Tell them to stop lamenting and start celebrating. Time to start realizing that the power is in them. They have attracted it to themselves and, therefore, this "little soul" comes as a grand teacher.

What, you mean we have to heal our perceptions and become the powerful beings we were created to be?

Powerful, responsible, loving, kind, efficient.

> *You mean we have to grow up?*

Participant: *Oh. They're not going to like that!*

> Of course not. But that can't be helped. *I am not here to pamper egos. I am here to help everyone see that all power under Heaven and Earth is given to everyone, and there is no problem that is given to anyone without also the ability to find the solution.*

And that process is the process whereby each soul comes to realize the infinite strength and power that lies within it. *All problems are gifts*—when they are accepted and embraced.

Participant: *And I get the added pleasure of being a grandma. Thank you very much, Jeshua.*

Now, please do say unto them: I know they have all that they need because the Light and the Love with which the Father has created them are still within them. Please let them know that if only they choose to look upon this as a great blessing, if they only choose to look upon it as an opportunity to relinquish their fears and judgments of themselves, so much healing will come to each of them that even in a year's time they will look back and not even recognize who they think they are now.

Please tell them. Please tell them. That for the sake of that grand One Who loves them beyond all of creation, to seize this opportunity and awaken from the guilt and the self-judgment that has been the only thing that seems to be keeping a damper upon them. I know that the Light is in them and I long to see them accept it within themselves. Fair enough?

Participant: *Fair enough.*

I've got a little knot in my stomach of fear of even asking a question so I think I've got to do it to get over the whole step of feeling fear and inadequacy, because in listening to you and what you say, I know that there is no question that I can ask you that I don't know the answer to myself. So perhaps in formulating a question to put forth to you, it is just going to help me understand my own way of what's going on.

I realize from what you say that the dilemmas that are created in our lives are there to be blessed and to be thanked and to learn from, and I have in my living environment created such a perplexing, trying reality. I think this is part of what's pushed me off of the . . . I'll call it the diving board of the quantum leap, and I feel like I am staggering to the end and to where my soul wants to head first, go into that quantum dive totally trusting of Spirit. I kind of feel like I am slipping off feet first, and I've got a lot of fear and a lot of reservations of making that fall or making that jump. And a lot of it is concerned with the ego issue of making sure that as I am coming into awareness, that I am the living expression of the Love that I am. And I wondered if perhaps you could just share forth to me some things that might help me to understand that?

Please understand that everyone awakens to their own call. You are indeed awakening to that call. Beyond intellectual ideas, beyond the use of words and concepts there is a part of you that some months ago began to shift into a willingness to live the experience that the concepts point to. You are now undergoing what could be called a crucifixion. It's kind of fun, isn't it? Just kidding.

Now, you have described it rather well: a bit of slipping and sliding. You feel that if you could just dive head first, it would go much more gently, but something in you wants to throw your feet in the way. Now, please receive this then:

> *As you have made the belief that you are separate from God, so, too, have you constructed the drama, if you will, by which you will choose awakening*

Each soul does that. I cannot relieve that process from you but I can assure you that on just this side of the experience you are now undergoing—it need not last long— there lies the peace that passes all understanding and the rebirth of a strength carried by one who is well on his way to being nothing but a teacher of God.

You had a certain experience a very long time ago, and the experience was really an initiation and a test, if you will. But it got you. And there arose a sense of doubt and a feeling of guilt and of failure, and it began to turn you away. It began to turn you inside out a bit. And you have carried the weight of that perception for a while. And what you are undergoing now represents certain kinds of energies that were present in that experience where you made a mistaken choice.

Therefore, the way to complete the dive is to continue to hold all things that are unfolding with deep gratitude and—and this is very, very important—recognize that the choice you made a long time ago, in a sense is being presented to you as situations so that you can choose anew. And the choice requires your willingness to trust wholly that, indeed, all things could be taken from you, and all that does is free you. It will return you to the path that you were on once upon a time. For your mission and your purpose is indeed to be a teacher of God.

I ask you to trust the eye of the needle that is before you now. And if you are willing to step or to dive, to trust each day as it unfolds by remembering only to return love, to be at peace. And I can assure you that something quite beautiful will begin to blossom on just the other side of the eye of that needle.

Beloved friend, as I say this unto you, there is yet a bit of resistance within you at wholly accepting the profundity of what I am sharing. What you are undergoing is not unlike crucifixion. And if you are willing to look upon all things through the eyes of Love, and if you are willing indeed, just be willing to relinquish everything you have ever thought, believed or possessed, every friend you have ever thought you've had—if you are willing to relinquish the whole of the world, on just the other side of that choice is the completion of the dive.

Okay, so they'll only give you a three. So what? Let the dive be completed. Just the other side of that begins the rebirth of the purpose for which you have indeed chosen rebirth in this world. The time of your firing and of your final—shall we call it— purification is upon you. You cannot solve it. You cannot change it. You cannot fix it. You can only allow it. I know that it feels like the allowing of death to occur—and it is. But it is the death of everything that you have carried because of an ancient perception that somehow you had failed and, therefore, carried guilt upon yourself.

Participant: *Which I still feel very much from that past incarnation. And I know at least to love it, but yet there still is that fear that arises within that jump—because I felt like I let you down once before.*

I know.

Participant: *But it still comes up.*

Precious friend, rest assured, if you had let me down, I couldn't be here now.

Participant: *I understand that. It's how I feel right this moment.*

I know. And what I'm sharing with you is that dive requires that you *allow the fear to be there while you make a different choice.*

> *I am loved wholly and I have not sinned. There has been no judgment or condemnation. I have not failed my ancient friend.*

If you try to get rid of the fear first, the dive will not be completed. Dive into the midst of it and carry with you the jewel of Truth: I am with you always and, the appearances of your experiences notwithstanding, there can be no separation between us.

Participant: *Thank you.*

And if you think your strength is waning at any moment, remember what I taught you then: all you have to do is raise your hand and say,

> *Give me about a pound of your strength.*

And I will deliver it to you gift-wrapped. And indeed, precious friend, I love you. I am with you always and I will give you my strength until yours is once again as certain as mine. I have long waited for just this hour. Kind of like I had to say to the Holy Spirit, "Look, I know you're a good tapestry weaver but let's get on with it here."

Participant: *Thank you, brother.*

Jeshua, I've gone through a lot of changes lately and I am really grateful for them, most of them . . . but I can't seem to feel the Holy Spirit or anything. I feel sort of . . . I don't know, I don't know if it's resistance even. I know that things are going to be taken care of, I know that I am growing, but I can't feel the Holy Spirit. Do you know what I mean? I don't know if I should do something or if I'm resisting, or what it is that's going on. Does that make any sense?

Well, you've just been a bad girl and you are being punished by being sent to your room without dinner. And I'm afraid we are going to have to leave your glass empty for quite some time until you learn better! Beloved friend, what would it feel like to feel the presence of the Holy Spirit?

Participant: *It feels just perfect. I know where I am. I'm balanced. I know it just feels perfect. I don't know how to explain it more than that.*

Are you willing to acknowledge that right here in this moment you *are* balanced and you are whole and you are perfectly safe?

Participant: *Yes.*

How does that feel?

Participant: *I'm sort of trying to feel it. There is the problem. Trying?*

Beloved friend, do you not feel the volatility that is going on in the body right now?

Participant: *Yes.*

Do you notice how the breath has itself become a bit chaotic?

Participant: Uh-huh.

Breathe.

Participant: *I can't.*

If you don't choose to breathe, you die. So you might as well breathe.

Participant: *I feel like a part of me is dying.*

Good. Breathe anyway. Do you feel that welling-up that seems to be beginning about in the area of the solar plexus up through the chest?

Participant: *Uh-huh.*

It is a very ancient fear. I am with you and I am with you now. Do not think that because you look upon this physical form and you hear certain words coming out of it that I am somehow limited to it. I am just pulling the strings. I am with you and I am beside you, now. And I want you to be my breath. Give that body to me by breathing breath for me. You notice how the thought arises, "I can't?"

Participant: *Uh-huh.*

But is it not lessening?

Participant: *Yes, it is.*

Breathe, beloved friend. I need your breath. Breathe life for me. Feel that breath like a ray of Light. It gently begins to descend down the center of the body through the solar plexus. See it like a gentle ray of light that comes to dissolve the mists of the morning. Let the breath rise within you that its Light might descend through a very ancient fear.

Breathe for me. Be my breath. Let the body soften.

Precious friend, as you breathe, without needing to know the source of that ancient wound, give it to me. Within yourself just relinquish it. Give it to me. I love you and I need you. Breathe for me. Let the breath come now even more deeply and a little faster, as if you could just drink it in. And as you exhale, begin to create a little vibration as if you were just sighing within yourself. Hmmmm. Breathe for me. Hmmmmm. Hmmmmm.

Precious friend, as you breathe, without needing to know the source of that ancient wound, give it to me. Within yourself, just relinquish it. Give it to me.

I love you, and I need you. Breathe for me. Let the breath come now even more deeply and a little faster, as if you could just drink it in. And as you exhale begin to create a little vibration as if you were just sighing within yourself. Hmmmmmm. Breathe for me. Hmmmmmm.

And as the thought arises,

> *I don't know how to give this to you,*

remember that you don't have to know how. Just be willing to give it to me. I have a few friends who know how to take it from you. Hmmmmmm. You are loved so deeply. You are loved so deeply. I have not left you, and I will not. Please be my breath.

Those around you now are indeed your friends and there is not a thought of persecution, not a trace of judgment. Indeed. It is safe now to simply be loved.

There, do you feel that starting to change? Indeed. Trust the tears. Trust them and allow them. Each tear is a thousand ancient hurts, just welling up to be released from the place you've stored them. Breathe for me. Your breath gives me life, and I need you as much as you have ever needed me.

Radiant and beautiful soul, the past is taken from you and its weight need not accompany you any longer. Oh, indeed, you are so loved by those who surround you now, there is no place for hurt to enter in. There will not be persecution as you choose to live the Light and the power and the love that you are. The experiences of persecution are over now. Breathe. Hmmmmmm.

Each evening and each morning give yourself just five minutes in which you breathe in that way. And I meant what I said:

> *You are breathing for me and giving me life.*

Feel that Light descend to the very depth and core of your being and as you do so, remember you are loved wholly.

Your heart's desires are worthy of being manifested and lived, and by so doing, a thousand minds are going to be touched and healed. And I will never be further than the width of a thought away, because I love you as deeply as I know you have always loved me. Hmmmmm. Yes.

Tears are an extremely sweet blessing. Think not that your willingness to allow them has not also touched and healed and uplifted every mind, every brother and sister who is with you now. Nothing takes greater strength than to allow an old hurt to be released. And each time you choose to breathe and to remember how loved you are, you uplift the whole of the Sonship. And I give unto you my thanks for your willingness to breathe.

Though it seems a simple thing, rest assured, I speak not just to hear a voice with words. Each time that you do that, you *are* healing the Sonship. You are making it easier for your brother to complete his three-point dive. Indeed.

You have loved me for a long time, haven't you?

Participant: *Forever, I think.*

Know precious friend, forever you *know.*

This world no longer holds the power to ever create a veil between us. Rest assured that in this hour you have lifted your hand and our fingertips have touched. And mine are coated with a certain kind of glue and once you're stuck, you're stuck. Indeed.

There. There. If you can, tomorrow, be very gentle with yourself. The mind is going to tend to say,

> *Well, I have this to do and that to do.*

At least through a majority of the day, unto at least the early afternoon, as much as you can, just do nothing. Save breathe, of course. Just be gentle. Nurture yourself.

A bit of a rest after . . . what you call, post surgery. Indeed. Thank you for your courage. Quite frankly, right now, there are a lot of others who would like to say thank you, too. It's okay.

Participant: *Thank you, Jeshua from my heart.*

Some minds dream of what they think are grand and glorious things. A long time ago I learned there is no greater job than just to be a messenger of the Heart and to deliver my Father's Love to my friends. To some, well . . . it doesn't pay well. The hours are long and eternal, but the rewards are priceless—because you are priceless.

Love, sweet Love. The Love that heals all things cannot be created, it can only be allowed. Therefore, indeed, with allowance are all worlds transcended and all ancient hurts released. With Love, freedom is reborn. With Love, joy returns. With Love are all things made new again. With Love do you become indeed the Light that lights this world.

Oh, beloved and holy friends, in whom our Father has always remained eternally well pleased, you are His only creation. You *are* the Thought of Love in form.

Be you therefore, at peace in all things, and remember always you are the ones who are indeed allowing the things of Heaven to be wed with the things of Earth, that the Light of Christ might be extended as far as from the East to the West. Be you, therefore, the completion of the atonement and you are the Light that lights all worlds.

Amen.

WALK WITH ME

January 1993

Jeshua

Now we begin.

And once again, greetings unto you, beloved and holy friends, those that have journeyed with me since before time is and those who will *remain* with me after the purpose of time has been completed, and the things of space and time are needed no longer and dissolve away into the Source from which they have arisen, and the Holy Child of God remains eternally One with Its Creator. This cannot be described in the languages of your world and yet, by faith and with vision, the heart can see and sense and know that surely Creation holds a purpose, surely it will know an end . . . an end to the things that reflect Creation in time, but not an end to Creation itself. For Creation is but the unlimited extension of the Love of God, in perfect union with God's only Creation, His beloved Child—you, the one Heart of Christ, shared by all, beyond the body, beyond personality, beyond your dreams of a history that you think still is carried with you, for these things have been taken from you and you remain as you are created to be.

And yet within the dream of time and of space, even as you have known birth into this world, so too did I come and took birth within time itself. And I came as *you* have come. I came not as one who was already a master far above you. I came to *be as you are.*

I came forth, therefore, from the womb of a woman.

I came forth and, legend notwithstanding, indeed I screamed and cried, as every newborn babe does.

I came to learn hunger and cold.

I came to learn to feel the subtle energies of those around me. I came to wonder at the way a bird flies through the sky.

I came to marvel at the way the sunlight dances across the waters.

I came to marvel at the gift of song, and of dancing and of celebration that would seem to well up through the souls of those that I saw around me.

I became troubled, as I looked upon many and saw veils of pain, and of doubt and of guilt and wondered,

> *Where have these things arisen from?*

For indeed I came forth and chose, even as you have chosen, to be birthed into a timeframe, into a culture upon this Earth, in which the simple truth was always taught:

> **God is but One and God is Love.**

And yet the kernel of this simple message seemed to be veiled and veiled and veiled and veiled, complexity upon complexity upon complexity. Some would say that "The Lord thy God is a jealous God," and I could not understand this, for when I journeyed and sat beside the calm waters and watched the sunlight dancing across them, when I heard the song of a bird, when I heard the voice of my mother, I could not comprehend that God was jealous, that God could want anything but the expression of the Love that He is. And I looked upon my own people and indeed I was troubled. But he that searches *does* find, and when you find, you will be troubled, and that troubling creates an opening in which you ask more deeply than ever before,

> *Father, show me Thy Face, teach me* Thy Truth, *that* Thy Will *might be done through me, that Creation might be restored to you.*

Therefore in this hour I come to share gently with you the simplicity of the truth that you are as I am and have been, even in the field of time. I have felt the things that you have felt. I have questioned the things that you have questioned. I looked upon the political structures of my age and wondered,

> *Why this feeling of insanity? Why this fear, why the attraction of power that can never satisfy? Is it not enough to feed those who are hungry and to embrace those who are alone?*

Therefore, and because I chose birth into a family fully dedicated to discovering and expressing the Love of God, I was given many teachers and as a child I was taken to many teachers. There were many factions in the Jewish community of that day. One such group was what you would know as the Essenes and, unlike what many of your current scholars would say, the Essenes were not just merely a sect that separated themselves from the main population. Yes indeed, they had their monasteries, they had their communities apart—but there were many Essenes who lived *within* the Jewish population of that time, who lived in the cities and were carpenters and fishermen, who were merchants and teachers and yes, even rabbis. For the Essenes simply represented a core or an essence of a teaching that sought to restore the Jewish family to an ancient knowledge: that man is one with the Earth and that it is by honoring that connection that the soul reawakens to the truth of its dependence, not just on the Earth and things of time but on God as the Source and the Creator of all. The Essenes, therefore, taught me how to find attunement with the body itself, how to heal the body, how to balance the body, how to listen to its subtle messages, how to utilize the gifts of fasting and of prayer and of meditation to correct the subtle imbalances that come only truly from the mind, and from its fears and doubts.

By the age of five, I was already being taken to certain teachers, both within the monastic tradition of the Essenes and also to teachers that lived in Judaea and also in Jerusalem. One such teacher is one known as Joseph of Arimathea. This one also was a distant uncle, a part of my own family. He'd achieved what you would call great wealth in the merchant trades but was also a man of high standing within the Jewish community. Often I would spend time with him, my parents would simply leave me with him, and even at that age, he would begin to chant to me the heart and essence of Judaism:

God is but Love and you are fully dependent upon that Source of Creation. Therefore render *every decision* unto Him, trusting that Love will guide you.

Even as a child, these thoughts began to plant their seeds within me.

At the age of seven, I made my first journey with my mother, and the one who had come to be as my father, and my uncle. Because of his wealth, he arranged to take us by boat and we journeyed forth to that which you would now know as England. We went to study with certain groups, to begin to reveal to me the perceptions of various groups and their attempts to understand the Mystery of Creation, and their attempt to relink themselves with the Source of Creation—to study their ways, to feel their perceptions if you will, to *learn.*

Therefore, indeed, we journeyed forth and in my first experience in that land I was introduced to the priestly caste—you have heard of the term "the Druids." This energy, this basic strand of approaching the Creator and Creation goes back a very very long ways. As I spent time with them, having already learned to rest in innocence, making no judgment, but feeling and listening and learning through empathy, I came to see that there seemed to be a fundamental energy that pervaded their entire approach to the Mystery of God. They sought to align themselves with the energies of the Earth and yet, while this is perfectly okay, I began to detect that there was a subtle hope in gaining mastery or power *over* the subtle sources of energy in this creation. And as I began to feel that, I questioned more deeply,

> *Holy Spirit—given unto me of God—bring wisdom, that I might understand what I am feeling.*

And I began to sense and to see and to know that, while the intention of this strand had indeed been good at one time, the mind of man, the ego of man, can take anything and turn it for its own devices and therefore there was a subtle intention of seeking power *over* nature, accessing certain powers in order to gain power or control over others. It was not an overt or an evil thing, only in this perception. I stayed with them upon that journey for a period of nine months and then we journeyed back to Judaea. I brought with me many questions and the memories of all that had been shared with me.

I was guided then to spend much time journeying into the desert, to begin to learn the practice of resting in prayer and meditation—*alone.* And if any of you have ever tried it, you know that fear comes up when there you sit in the midst of a grand darkness, the things seen with the eyes by day have disappeared and certain sounds seem to come, and even the wind brings fear within you. And I was taught that these are but as demons, but you would not call them that today—psychological fears—arising within me that needed to be transmuted and healed, *to trust the Voice for God in all circumstances.* So even as a child, I was guided to begin this practice of leaving the roar and the din of the world, to seek a place of solitude, to re-establish my knowing connection with the Source of all of Creation that I came to call as Abba, Father. And Abba doesn't mean just "Father." It evokes and carries a sense that the Source of Creation holds an intimate and direct relationship with every aspect of Creation, that God was not just an abstract energy but a personal Being, through which there could be communication in the depth of the soul.

I studied much with the Essenes and learned much from them, but also I felt that often there was a subtle underlying energy of fear. There would be a tendency to make judgment of the Sadducees and the Pharisees, and indeed a subtle hatred of those that had come to our land: the Romans. And I could not reconcile this subtle underlying energy with the simplicity of the Truth that I found when I read the Torah:

God is but Love!

Therefore, I asked to seek further, and going then to my uncle once again—who was very much like a spiritual preceptor for me—as he began to see that my questioning was maturing, that I *needed* to seek out and understand, he made arrangements. And I went with, again, my family, my parents, to what you know as Egypt, and there were then at that time also groups, collectives of Essenes, who were aware of me (even though I was not aware that they were aware), that I had a mission to fulfill in this life, I was growing and evolving *into* that mission.

And so we journeyed forth, and there I was introduced to the priesthood at that time. And I asked them questions, and I watched their rites, and I listened to them, and I spoke deep into the night with their "philosophers" if you will, and here again—and even to a greater degree—I found what we'll call here a dependence on "magic." For the rites that had been passed from generation to generation in that strand, that culture, had come again to hold the greater power: that the rites themselves, the rituals themselves, held the power and that it was through the correct . . . hmmm . . . behavioral methods that you could unlock the powers, whether it be in stones, in crystals or staffs or chants. This did not feel appropriate for me. And yet, now that I was at the age of about eleven, as I questioned the priests, they would become greatly troubled and they went unto my uncle and said, "Take this one from us. This one is not quite ready to learn what *we* have to teach!"

[Laughter]

My uncle smiled. "We will journey back to our home." He knew that I was troubled on the journey, as still my mind and my heart sought to understand,

> *Why is there this difficulty? My Father is but Love!*

I was quiet and sullen on the journey home, and when I was received back at home I went back to my father's shop, the little carpenter's shop. I was never a very good carpenter, by the way . . .

[Laughter]

. . . I was somewhat preoccupied with other things and my father, unlike the tradition of that time, did not insist that I remain with him in the shop, and when he felt that I was being pulled to journey into the hills to meditate, to pray, to walk, to go and to speak with others, he would just let me go. And many of his friends would come to him and say, "That son of yours is never going to be a good carpenter. Discipline him a bit more." And he would smile and say, "He is called by a different Voice." There were some that understood that and supported me, but there were many who were greatly troubled by what they perceived to be my rebelliousness, my lack of discipline, my lack of a sense of duty to tradition.

I journeyed back, first to Egypt, and then back to Judaea, where I set about seeking out those who would support me and walk with me. You have known these as disciples; I prefer to call them friends. The abilities had been awakened within me and here we would speak for a moment of what many of you call chakras or subtle abilities, and as these energy centers open the mind, the heart can indeed access levels of knowingness that seem to have been previously veiled. As I sat in prayer, what you would call meditation, I merely asked,

Holy Spirit, what would you have me do this day?

And a picture would come and I would see one standing by the shores of the lake, a simple fisherman, and I knew immediately I was to make contact with that one. And so I arose, and I journeyed forth. It was a several hour walk through the heat of the day. And I arrived at the shores of what you would know as the Sea of Galilee, and there indeed was a fisherman: not a fisherman completely unknown to me, but one who was indeed a part of my family, a cousin. This one's name was John. And he arose from his work with his nets and he looked at me. He had not seen me since I had made my long journey. And yet as he looked into my eyes, he knew that much had changed and in our gaze, there was what you would call a communication in the depth of the soul, and he knew that the time was at hand. Something compelled him then to look upon me and say, "Well, what do we do now?" And I said, "Follow me."

Now in time, and to keep this story short, a certain group was gathered around me. You've been told that there were twelve disciples. Fundamentally this is true, but there were actually much closer to a few hundred and the vast majority of those numbers were women, not men, because it was through the feminine that the simplicity of the Gospel that I was to restore could be heard and understood and felt through the feminine nature; because my Gospel was the simplicity of Love, the simplicity that God and His

Creation remain as One and that *each simple act of Love is sacred*—for it is through the feminine, the woman that can understand what it means to prepare the simplicity of a meal and give it with love, without asking anything in return.

The men would often spend much time quibbling over the theological meaning of a simple parable, a simple story, while the women would smile and nod their heads and say, "Ah, this one's journey to ancient lands, to that which is called India, has served this young Jeshua well. His heart is opened, he feels the simplicity of the Truth." And yet they too knew that in that culture what they would teach would not be received. Therefore the simplicity of the Gospel of the Heart must yet come through a male form, a male teacher, one taught and raised within their rabbinic traditions, one looked upon as having some sense of authority and understanding of the sacred texts. Therefore, the women seemed to be in the background and yet in actuality held a very important role. Often it was to them that I would send my male disciples and simply asked, "Return to me when your heart is corrected and restored to the simplicity of Love, and you've given up questions, and because the heart is open you long only to give Love."

I was a man, born into a culture, like every other. I was a man who asked the questions you have asked. I was a soul who found the answers because I learned to *seek first the Kingdom of Heaven* and all things were restored to me. I came to see that I was as my Father had created me to be: that I was unlimited forever, that I was truly Spirit and not just body and that therefore the body itself could become but a vehicle for Love's expression and extension. I walked from village to village and simply taught, "God is Love, and you are with Him now." I taught the heart to celebrate. I taught my people to set aside the seriousness of the priestly caste and to spend their time playing, to set aside times of celebration and of dancing and of joy, not as a way to invoke the powers of God but to celebrate the Reality of God's presence: "I and my Father are One!" And indeed we danced often, we celebrated often.

Indeed, precious friends, there arose a bit of dissension: "Who is this one that teaches that the soul needs not intercession, that needs not the priestly vows, that need not come to the leaders of the Jewish culture at that time, but need only retire into the quiet of the Heart to be restored into the Love of God and then to seek out those to whom they can give service? For this one teaches even the farmers and the villagers that they have no need to pay homage to the tradition in which they are born but to honor that tradition by being the presence only of Love. This one makes great waves; what will we do about it?" Not all, only some in positions of power. And they went unto the political leaders, sent from Rome, and convinced them that I could cause much damage, create much dissension and because there had been the hope and the prayer for a Messiah—and many thought that that Messiah would come as a political leader to overthrow the enemies—I began to be feared as a political enemy. Even though I had participated in the healing of many, I came to be seen as one stirring up the pot. It was only then as I neared the latter days of my ministry that the full revelation returned to my soul that I had chosen to create a demonstration, a teaching of which could not be denied by anyone, that it is possible to suffer the slings and arrows of this world and overcome anything. I would teach that death is *unreal* and need not be feared.

I journeyed forth one last time into the desert, there to pray and, yes, to cry, and to feel the last vestiges of fear, of a moment's doubt and to give these things over to my Father and ask only that His Will be demonstrated through me. His Will is only Love.

There were at those times many travelers that would come from the East and in one such journey of certain teachers that came from what you know as India, they came and spent much time with a group of the Essenes that were living quite apart from the rest of society, and my uncle and my mother journeyed with me and went to this place in the desert, alone and isolated. And I sat at the feet of these strange men who spoke in a different language that seemed to hold a melody, that seemed to hold a resonance, as you would call it, deep within my soul and evoked the sense of peace that I felt when I myself read in my native language of Aramaic—as if they were sister tongues, singing the same notes from the same song.

I became greatly compelled to dive deeper into the philosophical strand that these teachers brought from this distant land. My uncle never once said, "You need to go here now." He waited for me to ask. And so early in my, what you would know as, teenage years, I went unto him and said, "I am called to go to their land. I need to understand their perceptions, their techniques; I need to study with them." And he said, "My friend, if you go, you may not return. It is a great distance and there is much to learn. Are you willing then to leave family and home?" Without hesitation, being young, I simply said, "Well, of course!"

[Laughter]

And he said, "Very well, we will make the journey, but first we will return to Egypt for a short while, to rest, spend time with friends, and then I will send you on with some of those who will journey with you."

Leaving then, Egypt, I traveled with a group of about seven that had been given unto me to protect me, to guide me, who had also been to this land. I did not know it then, but they knew where they were taking me. They seemed to know already who I was to meet, who I was to spend time with. And so we journeyed to what you call India, a very strange land indeed. And yet there seemed to be a pervasive knowledge, a knowledge of the eternality of God's presence. But there were many sects and many creeds even then, and some seemed very much to be attracted to "magic"—the attempt to invoke the Will of God, to attain power over it, to be seen with favour of God. This always troubled me, but I was taken into what you would know as northern India, and from there we journeyed to what you would call your Himalayan mountain ranges. Here I began to meet certain teachers who emanated a peace that I had seen but rarely, a peace that called to me and immediately brought my mind and emotions to silence. Here I knew there was a knowingness. I spent many, many months with a group of teachers at the foot of the Himalayas and I learned what you call commonly the ways of Yoga. I learned the way of the breath; I learned the way of the body: I learned to fast the body and to get by on very, very little. I was told that this was important. Only later did I know that it was simply a device for taming the restlessness of my adolescent mind that helped me think I was doing some arduous path. It was my entertainment.

As I spent time with these teachers, they taught me of the depths of consciousness, revealing to me—bit by bit, day by day—that the Heart and the Source of Creation was not outside me at all, but that the feeling I had had as a young child was accurate: that *God is but Love* and can be known by many names, and that which brings the mind to silence and allows the heart to freely and safely be opened by whatever means. This was a true path, a true teaching, a true gift that could be given to anyone.

I learned the subtle art of *listening*, of abiding with another in relationship, thinking not that I knew what my brother or sister needed, but learned to attune ever more deeply to the realization that there is the presence of one teacher that I have called the Holy Spirit, the Comforter, with me at all times, that would whisper unto me the simplicity of what was needed in each moment. I learned that the path of awakening was not one of gaining but of losing, not a path of striving but of allowing, not a path of the intellect but a path of the heart. And my practice became the simplicity of remembering,

God is with me now *and the only time that exists is* this *moment.*

And there in that land of very high mountains, yes, I experienced the cold of the snows, I experienced journeying into caves to be alone for weeks at a time. But in time, I saw through the limitations of these techniques. And of my own accord, I left those mountains and journeyed back down into the valleys and I found my teachers and simply said to them, "I think I'm getting it." And they smiled and then said, "It is time for you to leave, but before you do so, there is something that must be shared." Unbeknownst to me, they had already known that I was coming to the completion of all my learning that I could gain from them and had sent message. Had they had telephones it would have been much easier! My uncle, my father, returned for me and as I came down to meet with my group of teachers, I was surprised to find that they were with me. And there in a circle, my father shared with me that there was a purpose that awaited me, that there was the need to be like a light piercing the darkness of the culture in which I had been born; and that I was being asked to give, indeed, of my life—to minister unto my own Jewish family, to help remind them of the simplicity of the Truth that there need not be an intermediary between anyone and God . . . that the priestly caste, the rabbis, the temples, all of the complexities that had been created over a great period of time, were not truly necessary and yet could still be utilized to honor and celebrate the simplicity that "I and my Father are One." I did not know at that time that the plan for my life's mission would involve a rather unique demonstration. Therefore, indeed, I *allowed* the drama to unfold. It was not so much that I directed it; it was already set in motion. I simply allowed it.

And when I was asked, "Are you king of the Jews?" I simply replied, "Some say that I am." "Are you the Son of God?" "Do you say that I am?" And I answered every question with a question. For these things mattered not. This began to create much turbulence in my own followers, my friends, for they, just like you, knew their own fears. Some had become dependent upon me, some indeed hoped that I was the Messiah, the political Messiah that would come and overthrow the Romans through force. Some had come to doubt me and to begin to move away. There were many who loved me and they could not understand what was about to unfold, even though I taught them, "In three days I will raise this temple again. Therefore be of good cheer." And they were puzzled, "What does he mean? The temple took many years to build! Who is going to cast it down, who could put the stone upon stone in three days? What does he speak of?" And some of them began to understand that I spoke of the temple of the body.

Therefore, understand well that those that were with me were just like you. They were human beings struggling to understand within their own culture how to be at peace with God, how to extend Love, what does it mean to awaken? And in that day and in that hour that I was given over to the authorities, communication between me and my followers was broken, even though I had said unto them, "I am with you always."

Let no one say unto you that the crucifixion never occurred. If that is true, then my own experience was surely an illusion and perhaps I had gone mad. The body was crucified, dead and buried. And my followers and friends were scattered. Many of them took upon themselves a great sense of guilt and pain. They abandoned my mother, except for a few, and they fled to hide. Some stayed to be close to the action, but not too close, because they did not want to be identified. All of you know the feeling of guilt that comes if you feel you have abandoned someone. The guilt is always an illusion.

Understand well then, that upon the third day, the stone was rolled away and those that had been closest unto me—the women, who understood and were in communication with me—came forth to discover that something grand was happening. And I indeed appeared unto many. For when you understand that you are not the body, and when you want only Love and therefore see nothing else, you too will learn that you are Spirit, that you are Light Divine. You will come to understand that *in this very moment,* the only reason the body that seems to be yours is with you, is because you are choosing from the depth of your *compassion* to be present in this robe, and yet the truth of who you are has never changed. You remain Spirit and this alone. You are creating a façade through which you can extend Love into a world that needs it.

Precious friends, my journeys were not unlike your own. You too have traveled to distant cultures. You have studied every spiritual technique there is and has ever been created. You know the pathway of hoping for magic. You know the pathway of doing certain ritual acts to appease God, as if God has ever judged you. Each of you is awakening to the simplicity of the Truth that I too as a man learned,

> *I and my Father are One. Here and now, all power of Love can move through me by simply relinquishing every perception I have*

> *ever held, acknowledging only that Love is real and that what is real can never be threatened and what is unreal exists not.*

This Truth is diametrically opposed to everything the world would teach you but as you choose to practise it in *each moment*, correction comes to the depth of the mind and the heart opens. Laughter returns to the soul, for appearances no longer have the power to master *you*, for you see only Love and you have remembered that death, in all of its forms, is unreal. You remain as you are created to be and there *is no separation* between minds that are joined in Love.

Please understand, then, what is at hand, for you come to demonstrate in your own lives that there need no longer be reliance upon magical means to invoke the Power of God. *You are the presence of that Power!* Understand well, I come to *any heart* that prepares a place for me. This does not require lifetimes of purification, because guilt is *not* in you; perfection is the nature of your being. And the simplicity of abiding with me rests only in your willingness to relinquish the weight of the world, to turn from the roar and the din of what we have called now the voice of ego, which is the collective chaos of the worldly mind, and to abide in a simple acknowledgement:

> *I am as God created me to be. Because all minds are joined, I choose to rest in the presence of an ancient friend who has never left me.*

Only, of course, if you want to! It is not a requirement for awakening. Teach then this world, that I come only as a brother and a friend.

As a man, I completed my part in the Atonement and by teaching that death is unreal, I *learned it.* "What? Jeshua's saying that when he went to the cross, perhaps there was a doubt?" Oh yes. But if it was true that one receives what one gives, and that as one teaches one learns, because I knew what I wanted was unlimitedness forever, I allowed the demonstration to be *my* final lesson as well—to learn that it *is* true: *death is unreal.* And where death is unreal, there can be no thought of sacrifice and nothing can be lost. There is only all to be gained through remembrance,

> *I am indeed here to be truly helpful, wherever "here" is.*

For me it seems to be without a body, because it is not the Will of the Creator that I assume physical form, and you are coming in your own way to rest into that innocent simplicity of the meek that will come to inherit the earth:

> *Father, what would you have me do this day? Oh, take a nap? Okay!*

[Laughter]

It's very, very simple.

> *What can I do? How can I serve?*

By being the presence of Love! And your gifts will be activated through you, for there is one Teacher that knows how to weave the awakening of this world and is already actively involved in it. Hmm. Therefore seek not to be the supervisor, but the supervised, trusting the Voice for God, as I too learned to hear *only that Voice.*

You are the Light that lights this world, for if your brothers and sisters are to remember the Truth that lives within them, does it not ask that it be demonstrated to them? Therefore as you teach Love, you will receive Love. And as you allow yourself to simply be willing that Love be given through you, you will come to know that you cannot help but be in the right place at the right time and *here* is where you're asked to be, wherever "here" is. And as you allow that Love to be extended through you, you will remember Love and its attraction will grow evermore brighter for you, until not one trace of a thought could arise of ever wanting anything else. And then you will *see* nothing else! And as Creation is lifted with you, the veils that seem to show only separation will dissolve as mist before a rising sun and all of Creation will be restored as One and be lifted up unto the Heart of God.

Reflect then unto this world the simplicity of the Truth you have always known, and know that I am with you because I love you. Be you therefore that which you are with each breath, and already the Atonement is completed within you, and *you* are the Light that lights this world.

Be you therefore at peace this day. Enter the silent chamber of the Heart often, not to pray for union with God, but to acknowledge what *is* and cannot be taken from you. And then celebrate with every breath and with every thought, let every gentle deed become sacred for you, let every gentle touch and every smile that you would give unto the world—every action becomes the sacred means through which Love is expressed through you. Herein lies the end of all teaching. Herein lies the perfection of all Gospels. Now is the time come, and the Mind of Christ steals gently across the final veils and knowledge is restored to the Holy Mind of the Father's one Creation: you.

Peace be unto you always, you who have come to restore the Truth to the conscious- ness of mankind.

Amen.

THE BLESSING OF FORGIVENESS

March 1993

Jeshua

Now we begin.

And, indeed, greetings unto you, beloved holy friends. Indeed, greetings to you, beloved and holy great Rays of Light shining eternally in the mind of our Father, bringing forth that which is Love, bringing forth that which is Light, bringing forth that which is Wisdom and Peace and Simplicity—and Forgiveness.

For in Truth, the world waits upon your forgiveness. It waits to be anointed by the Mind of Christ that would look upon all created things and grant it forgiveness. For your world lives steeped in fear. Your world is filled with many brothers and sisters that are plagued by a deep sense of unworthiness and guilt. Having fallen asleep, they continue to dream an illusory dream. But much like any dream, it holds the power to enchant the mind and block the very cells of the body from exuding only that which is real: Light. And Light is Love. And, therefore, to begin this evening and to share this message with our many friends, we would indeed speak of forgiveness.

Beloved friends, forgiveness requires a graciousness; and graciousness is but the extension through form—through the body, through the emotions, through your touch, through your smile, through the glimmer in your eyes—of that which is the Grace *already* given unto *you*.

It is always wise, then, to remember that if you would know Grace, give grace. And each moment, then, as you walk through your world, as you would cry out unto me and to many of my friends,

> *Teach me what my purpose is, what is my function? What is my unique and special role?*

And your mind would teach you that it must be some form of service outside of your own being. I say unto you, your purpose and your function is the same as was, and is mine: To be that one through whom the Grace of a loving God is given unto those who yet dream the vicious and dark and awful dream of separation. For in that dream there cannot be anything but a deep inner anguish. And one who dreams thus acts in such a way that almost every thought and every action becomes a cry for help and healing—a cry that falls on the deaf ears of the world, for the world believes in judgment and not forgiveness, in condemnation and not healing.

Therefore, know well the power that dwells within *you*, for you have already awakened to your call. You have already begun to lift your eyes up from the dream of separation, and have begun to behold a great Light shining forever, that seems to shine forth from some place, from some source so far removed from all that you've known and all that you think you are. And yet the Light that you behold is *your* light, placed within you by God himself from the moment you first began to dream your own unique version of the dream of separation.

How, then, will you know that Light? Not by seeking it, but by allowing it. Therefore, as you walk through this world, when you cry out wondering what your purpose is, bring your attention back to the simple fact that *you are here to bless the world through the Forgiveness of Christ.* Look, therefore, gently upon all that you see. Learn to return the mind, the emotions and, as long as it lasts, even the body, to peace—that the graciousness of Christ can flow forth through you unimpeded, unlimited, *shining in its joy.* And let that Light fall upon whomever you see, whatever you see: a blade of grass, a leaf falling from a tree, a wisp of cloud passing through the sky, a snowflake that falls. Bless these things, for they too have arisen from within *your* Holy Mind. And they are pervaded by that self-same Light that gives *you* your existence.

The world cries out for forgiveness, and the soul cries out for union with God, and seeks in a thousand convoluted ways and technologies to find a way to merge created and creator, beloved and lover. For, indeed, you are the lovers of God, and in truth cannot help but be that. For God does not create that which opposes Himself. Because you are a great Ray of Light shining in that one mind, while you are the created, *you are the lover of God.* And your peace and fulfillment will come to you fully when you have retrained the mind to settle for *no other thought* than that which expresses the joyful, heart-centered devotion to your Creator—not as a stern master apart from you, but as the presence of Love itself, that ignites the very creative process whereby you have come into being. Not to suffer the things of the world, not to dream the dream of separation—it was never necessary, it was just a momentary choice—but, rather, to extend all that God *is*.

Therefore, if you would know your freedom and peace, use each moment to bring the attention of the mind back to the graciousness and the blessing of forgiveness. For, as you forgive, you will learn that you have already been forgiven. And as you bless the world, you will know how blessed you truly are. And the day will come when you no longer fear the unlimited blessing of your Father, for you will know that all things are created for *you*, out of Love—that you never need to limit yourself in any moment, within your consciousness, whatever world you might be playing and dancing within. Take, then, upon your shoulders my cloak. Take upon your head my crown of Light. For it is given unto you to be the embodiment of all that Christ is.

And, in truth, because only Christ is the creation of God, it is the only thing that you can be in Reality. Now that means that if there is even one moment in your day when the thought in your mind would pull you to the perception that you are *other* than what you are created to be, it means that you, in that moment, have chosen to become identified with pure and utter insanity. Hm! I have said often that there is a choice between but two emotions, Love and fear. And two other words that could be used would be sanity and insanity. There is no gray area. You're either in one or the other. You might fool yourself and say,

> *Well, I'm really moving toward Love, but I have to get through these certain things first and then I might get there.*

You are either home, or you're away from home. You are either One with God, or you are dreaming the dream of separation. One brings the reality of Peace, one brings what seems to be insane to this upside-down world of yours: the recognition that you are as you're created to be. And in *this* moment you hold all power under Heaven and

Earth to *choose* for peace. To *extend* only love. To *forgive* instead of judge. To be *open* instead of contracted.

The way, then, is easy and without effort. It requires only that you make a deliberate choice: to surrender the perceptions and ideas you've ever held about anyone or anything (including yourself) that is anything other than the preciousness of the Reality of Christ. And to allow the Holy Spirit, then, to bring forth those circumstances that can show you where you had once failed and chosen insanity, so that you can simply correct it.

And that is why, as you dance through your many incarnations, you keep bumping into the same folks. And the energies that each soul presents to you will continue to be presented ad nauseum until you have embraced that energy and owned it within your own being; and then through the reflection or the mirror of forgiving that energy, you begin the process of dismantling or dissolving that energy in your own being. For they are one and the same. You have never truly looked upon another at all. Your eyes would show you bodies that seem not to reside in the same place that your body does, but that's an illusion, because *you* don't have a body. There are *bodies*, but *you* do not have one. You do not dwell within it; it dwells within the holy expansiveness of the One Mind, the One Mind that is incarnate upon your earth. Forgiveness is the bridge to healing.

Two thousand years ago, as you understand time, I came with a very simple message. And the message *was* the message of forgiveness. I have come yet again in many ways giving the same simple technology, *for it alone works.* And yet the mind would have you believe that you must constantly make it more difficult.

> *Surely there is something else to acquire, some great power, some great mystical experience. If only I could get all my outer affairs in order,* then *I'll remember to forgive the world because I'll be comfortable.*

Rest assured that what you want to see reflected in the world around you is influenced by—is an extension of—the quality of awareness that *you* allow within your consciousness, moment to moment.

And if you seem, then, to know struggle, there is some corner yet remaining that has not been touched by your own forgiveness. Now, are you going to be able to search out that corner? Many of you might try.

But is it not easier to simply recognize that the Holy Spirit has *already created* the exact circumstances that you need to awaken? Therefore, if you would seek your path, open your eyes. Notice the place where you seem to be, physically upon this earth. Notice who you seem to be with. Take a very deep breath, and remember that all things are perfect, that that is your golden doorway, your eye of the needle. And if you would make the choice to simply be the Presence of Christ and extend the gracious blessing of forgiveness, you will feel your restlessness begin to dissolve.

And as it dissolves in the depths of your beingness, through your deliberate choice to use the power of your mind (which is all that you have) to extend forgiveness and thereby the dissolve patterns of perception within the depth of your mind, you will then come to see the world around you differently. And miracle-mindedness begins more and more to be that which carries you through this life. You meet just the right person. You get just the perfect job. And all of the rest. It rains when you want it to rain, and it's sunny when you want it to be sunny. And you will be mystified by it all.

In the end, *when the mind is completely purified*—which simply means that it's been corrected from any conflict between Love and fear, forgiveness and judgment—when the mind is completely purified you will know that you are *unlimited forever.* You will know that, if you are seemingly in the bodily experience—whether you're washing the dishes or taking out the garbage, whatever you're doing—you will know that you, as Christ incarnate, have deliberately chosen to allow your being this experience as yet another opportunity to bless the world with the forgiveness that it cries out for. And if the body seems to dissolve in light and you are no longer seen by other bodies in space and time, you will know that that, too, is the perfect choice of freedom.

Imagine, then ... imagine ... walking through this life you are living, in a world that seems to have forgotten the Reality of God, and feeling, from the crown of the head to the tips of the toes, not one trace of contraction or fear. Imagine the cells of the body feeling as spacious as the heavens. Imagine the Peace that passes all understanding to be pervading every organ of the body. A gentle smile upon the lips, barely perceptible to others. A gentleness in the area of the heart. A sense of bodily relaxation from what you call the solar plexus to the base of the spine. The mind calm and clear, missing nothing, yet holding onto nothing. Imagine being compelled by nothing, and yet not having a trace of judgment about anything arise.

Imagine walking through this life in which *nothing is unacceptable to you*, because you are so busy blessing the world with the Forgiveness of Christ, recognizing that the dream is a dream is a dream is a dream. And dreams hold *no effect* upon the dreamer when the dreamer awakens. Imagine living this life in Perfect Peace.

Is it a difficult road? No. It requires, first and foremost, the willingness *to completely embrace yourself as you are*. Even as you perceive yourself to be, though you may be perceiving insanely—you are indeed doing so if you think there's anything amiss; but that's okay—first embrace the dream, and love *yourself*. Love yourself for being right where you are, *as you are*. For there is a simple law of metaphysics, as you know this, and it is this: it is literally and always impossible to transcend and heal what is not fully embraced. And to embrace something means to *love* it to death.

Therefore, when you go through your day, ask yourself this at the end of each day for the next seven days:

> *How many times in this one 24-hour period did I stop what I was doing and love myself wholly? ... Well, I would have gotten around to it more than once, but I was awfully busy.*

Hm. No. You were deluded. And there is a big difference. You were in insanity whenever you contracted away from love of Self. So that's the first exercise we would offer you this evening: for the next seven days, before you fall asleep at night, count how many times in that day you truly and wholly loved *yourself.*

Now, as we pause here then, what we are viewing from our level, our perspective—that has nothing at all to do with bodies; so you see, you can't really hide, there's no such thing as privacy—what we are seeing is many minds contracting with guilt at the recognition that more often than not this day they've actually *loathed* themselves. They found something to judge themselves for.

> *I'm too tall, I'm too short, I'm too far, I'm too thin. I don't speak well enough, I don't have enough money,*

and on and on and on and on goes the list. Do you know that list? That list was made by a completely insane mind—and in Reality the list does not exist.

So, remember, then, to pay attention if you notice yourself being in judgment of yourself, that is the opposite of Love. So look upon the contraction in the mind that goes,

> *Oh my God, I didn't think about that once today: loving myself.*

Love yourself *right there and then—now!* And you've loved yourself. And then you can go to sleep, peacefully. Does that make sense to you?

[Audience agreeement]

I've said many times that the way is easy and without effort—for what comes of effort is of your world, and not of the Kingdom. I've said to you the world is diametrically opposed to the Truth of the Kingdom. The world is just the *exact opposite* of all that the Kingdom is. And if you're tightening the cells of the body and tightening the mind—fueled by fear and trying to make things happen, and they're not happening—that's a clear sign that somewhere you've forgotten to rest in the graciousness of self-love. Self-love opens the door to the spaciousness whereby you remember that *you are One with all minds everywhere.*

There is no lack. And those beings who are perfect for you at your stage of the journey will be sent to you, if you will but welcome them before they arrive. Hm. Interesting thought, isn't it? Your world will teach you: what's the point of welcoming somebody until they've rung the doorbell? Why not welcome them before you ever see them with your physical eyes? Can you imagine what would happen if you awakened in the morning, took five minutes to forgive the world and bless the world and love yourself, and then *welcomed* everyone who was going to come into your experience that day as an angel bringing you the opportunity to bless the world with forgiveness. You see, your peace would walk ahead of you. It would enter a room before your body even gets there. And before anything is said and done, you will have already created the space large enough to hold *whatever* comes into your experience. You will have *embraced* what must be embraced, and thereby the pathway to transcendence is set before you.

Hm! Now is this all getting too complicated?

[Laughter]

Remember this: when the mind seems stymied by what is said, there are actually two things going on. First of all, the attempt is to stop the mind. Only when the mind is stopped can space come to it. If you feel blocked in trying to grasp what is being shared at all, remember that that sense of being blocked is nothing more than an old, insane pattern. It is the culprit. If you notice that you're blocked, not quite putting the pieces together, simply stop and stop striving to do so. For the Soul hears the Truth. And when we come in this manner, or in many different manners, to speak with you, we come not to speak to your earthly mind, we come not to speak to the body and your emotional field. We come to speak directly to the essence of your Soul, which already knows the truth, which *is* the Truth, and is, in fact, the *very source from which these words are coming.*

Hm... By way of levity, if that is permitted...

[Laughter]

… I'm never quite sure when I look at your world whether it is or whether it isn't!

[Laughter]

How many times in each day do *you* vacillate? You know the pattern of laughing at the foibles of others, but taking your own very seriously?

[Laughter]]

You see, all that I do in this work with this my beloved brother, is this: I abide in a place and in a dimension where nothing is hidden, where all minds reside right where I am. And when anyone asks a question or even thinks a thought and doesn't speak it through the body, I merely am like one in what you call your racetracks—imagine me with a little green visor on the head—and when one comes and says, "Well, I wonder if I should bet on this one or this one, what is this truth or that truth?" I go, "Just a minute." And I close down the window with the little bars on it, and I race out the back door, and I run behind and I sneak up behind you and I examine your heart from behind, and I see what is written there, and I go, "Oh, yes, okay." And then I race back and come back, and open up the window, and I give you the answer!

[Laughter]

Now, many of you—it's rather an easy process because, you see, I keep records, and many of you ask the same things over and over.

[Laughter]

Hm. But rest assured, and understand this well: when I once said "Of myself I do nothing"—I meant it. My Father does these things *through* me. That requires the willingness to learn how to be *empty of self* with every breath. So those that would see me as someone filled with all of this great cosmic wisdom, please see me differently. I am empty and spacious, resting in quiet adoration and devotion of all that my Father is, witnessing *nothing but* miracles, and that which extends and radiates the Love of God through all Creation. And if in *your* mind you see it not, it only means that you have not yet been willing to train the mind to teach only Love; to give up all of your own ideas, moment to moment, breath to breath.

I am nothing special. I am merely *your equal*, your brother and your friend—created in the very same moment you were, with all the same attributes, all the same potential, all the same reality. And I marvel, just as you will when you truly ponder this, I marvel becausethroughout the expanse of my existence—which has been since before the beginning of time, just as yours—I have never been able to fathom the moment of my creation. Think about that one. Do you know the moment when you began? No. And you'll never find it. And that means there is, indeed, an unfathomable mystery that I have called Abba that is present at a place within me that is deeper than can ever be known, no matter how much the mind becomes enlightened. Knowing that, there can only be humility, devotion, appreciation, love. There can only be the fulfillment of the truly only meaningful relationship that you can ever have: Relationship with your Creator. For all of the rest of your relationships are merely reflections of you abiding with an aspect of yourself. And the only way *that* relationship can reflect Holiness is from the spillover from your devotion, and the purity of your relationship with your Creator. Does that make sense to you?

[Audience agreement]

Creation is grand. How could you ever comprehend it all? You can't. You can *only allow it* through your beingness without fear. For fear is a contraction, which is the opposite of Love. And when you know fear you are in the world and not in the Kingdom.

And so, beloved friends, I've revealed to you something about the nature of my own being. I am not a great master, as many would have me be, wanting to project onto me all manner of skills and abilities and powers because they are afraid of embracing these things for themselves. And *projection*, what you have tried to regurgitate out of your soul and get rid of, is what *makes your perceptions*. So if those that would come into a temple to worship me as the savior of the world would only stop and understand the truth that *projection makes perception*, they would see that they are *literally creating* the savior they believe must be there out of the denial of who they are.

That is why I have often said to those of you who would choose to build an altar, to have a room of prayer, whatever you call it: why do you have all of these pictures of saints and masters from all over the world? Where is *your* picture? Rest assured, try that for one hour. Get a picture of yourself and treat it like you would—pay homage to it like you would—a picture of your favorite master. Place it upon your altar and light your candles and your incense, sprinkle it with holy water, whatever you want to do, whatever your rituals are; and then do nothing but relax and contemplate your own image. And ask yourself this one question: From where has that being come? Can you see how that would be very opposite of what the world teaches you to do?

I'm not speaking here of the danger—and there is a danger—of slipping into an egoic identification of yourself as being so great and regal and special, and everybody else a peon. That's not what we're talking about, but to move through the temptation to let the ego grasp the insight that you are as God created you to be. For while you abide in space and time, vigilance and discipline are absolutely required. And the more you awaken, the more you will need them.

In my day and age we spoke often of the temptation of Satan. The story that many of you know of my forty days and nights in the desert, in which Satan himself came to tempt me, is a symbol, of course, that shows that the more Power and Light shines through you, the ego—the egoic energy that pervades your creation at this dimension, to a lesser degree other dimensions or planes—will *always* try to find a home in your mind ... *always*. Therefore, the more your Light shines, the more what is called these little specks of darkness want to rush in and clog up your drains. Hm. Never become lazy.

Never become satisfied. Keep wanting more and more of God, selfishly *demand it*, and learn to be vigilant over what thoughts you are allowing into the mind. And be very careful. For, as you awaken, and suddenly you have a vicious and evil thought, the temptation is,

Oh, my God, I've blown it!

That is a judgment, and that is the opposite of Love. And only Love can heal. You simply notice the thought, go,

Ha, yes, I've had those before.

Self-love. Love alone heals the mind. No other technology will work.

Forgiveness, self-love, the recognition that no one comes into your sphere by accident, and that in Reality each is an aspect of your own being, bringing treasures of gold and frankincense and myrrh, coming to see if you will *receive* those treasures and thereby recognize that each day is the Birth of Christ within you accomplished. Each time you accept those gifts, and the way you register your acceptance of their gifts—that do indeed come in some rather interesting packages!—the way you recognize it or pay recognition to it is through your willingness to return to your reality, your purpose and function, and to bless that being, that gift-bringer, with the Forgiveness of Christ.

And that forgiveness is not from a mind that thinks it is *above* the other, but recognizes not just the commonality but the *self-same identity*. Do you see the difference? It is very important.

Well, I'll forgive you, you poor simple creature.

No.

I forgive you and bless you because you are who I am, and in Reality there is only one of us present, and together we have the power to bring Heaven to Earth through our holiness—now!

Somebody's got to extend it to the other aspect of themselves. Why not you? What are *you* waiting for?

> *If only my mother would forgive me, if only my father would forgive me, and oh gosh that first wife I had and then the fourth husband, oh my goodness. If I could just get things straight with* them, *then I would get on with being Christ.*

So. The pause that was just created seemed to be in the midst of a thought or a direction, and your second exercise is this: Abide at peace and become your own conduit for completing the direction or momentum of the thought that was given just before the pause. Does that make sense to you all? If you will give yourself to that exercise, not just once but often, and in a relaxed mode, you will find that the process takes you to deeper and deeper levels. And those of you that sincerely engage in that process will embark on a series of what you call insights or revelation. And it will assist in refining the deep energies of your own mind. So would you be willing to do that?

[Audience agreement]

We will see. Remember, there is no privacy!

And, so, it will be appropriate to spend a short time and there will be questions asked by those who are seemingly seated here with bodies.

Therefore, in conclusion of that which has been shared with you this hour, remember: forgiveness, self-love, accepting the *perfection* of each moment in which you discover yourself—for because you have already asked for healing and awakening, the Holy Spirit already goes before you, setting straight your path. Remember, if you knew how to set your path straight, you would have been done a long time ago! So accept the fact that what is occurring is part of a pathway being set before you by an Intelligence or Wisdom that knows far better than your thinking mind how to find the way home. And the more you surrender to each moment's perfection, the more you discover that the eye of the needle is *always* before you, and it's actually a royal highway that carries you to peace.

And so, with that, if you would prepare the technology with the buttons and all of that, we can continue.

....

Participant: Jeshua, as we enter this very profound time of year, is there anything that you would recommend that we hold in our hearts?

A request for winning lottery numbers would be nice.

[Laughter]

Beloved friend, you asked a question that must be filled with levity, so therefore I answered the question with levity.

For listen well to your words: "as we enter this *profound time of year.*" What makes it any *more* profound than any other time of year? There's nothing special about your month of December. There are symbols written in the stars that indicate a process of consciousness that's going on in you all the time.

Therefore, rather than ask what should we hold in our hearts *now* as we enter this profound time of year, ask what you can hold in your mind to create the profundity *in every moment* of your experience, until there's no difference between any day of the year—so that every day is the Mass of Christ.

Hm. Got you!

[Laughter]

Participant: Always, always! But it makes a lot of room for other people to ask their questions.

A profound sacrifice you have made.

Participant: Thank you. I love being your bull's eye.

So does that answer help with you question?

Participant: Yes it does, of course. Thank you.

You see, the tendency of the mind that has become enamored with the thinking of the world will carry the egoic pattern of wanting to shift its frequency by making something more special than something else, even a time frame. And that attempt to create *specialness* is the attempt to create *inequality*. And inequality, as you obviously know, is the opposite of equality. *If you seek unity, give up the need for specialness.* Therefore, this Christmas season, ask not what you can do to bring a profound experience to this time, but reflect on what you must be doing in your consciousness the rest of the year to not experience the profound mystery of life.

That's a very good question. I wonder where it came from?

[Laughter]

Participant: The One of us, yes?

Indeed.

So the one of us on this side of the horse race window asked a question, and the one of us on the other side with the green visor (Hmm… I never did like the crown of thorns, I changed it for a green visor) simply raced about and plucked the answer out of the Heart that we all share and has given it to ourselves.

[Laughter]

[Inaudible, audience member speaking]

There are two forms of busyness. One is based in fear, the other is based in Love. Which energy is fueling your busyness? For the one generates the extension of the Kingdom, and the other denies it. Hmm.

Hmm. I believe we have done well with that one. So, any more questions?

Participant: In regard to the land we call Shanti Christo, there are many friends coming to this area to participate, and many of us have in our hearts the desire to live more closely to each other, in sharing our growth processes, our loving each other, our understanding of your teachings, and so on. There seem to be many unanswered questions and desires of people who want to come together more closely, quickly, and I wondered if you would address this?

Beloved friend, unanswered questions are *always* a form of *doubt.* Unanswered questions reflect the quality of mind birthed not in God but in the world. The attempt to *hope* that someone else will create the energies necessary in the third dimension to allow you (not necessarily 'you' but the general you) to get what it thinks it needs, closer proximity to other bodies in space, yet being in denial of stepping into the role of what you might call leadership to bring that about. Therefore, understand well, there are many that are being called, and some seem to have answered that call a little sooner than others.

The call to Shanti Christo is the call to awaken first from every obstacle to the presence of Power and Love and Light within their being. To no longer tolerate anything in your consciousness that creates the barriers to the manifestation of the vision that seems to be calling you, and the willingness to take complete responsibility for being the one that manifests it.

For you see, that vibration is a very refined vibration. There is no room for gamesmanship. There is no room for riding on the energies of others. There is no room for denying the power of Christ within yourself. This level of purity is absolutely necessary to bring forth in the field of time, patiently, with quality, the vibrational *field* into which even more can be called, who will experience what you call spontaneous healings of mind, emotion *and* body.

For if you would view that which is a communion or a coming

together of souls in the third dimension, and some are relying on others to carry the frequency, you have inequality; you have conflict; you have dissonance. Dissonance weakens the field of energy and the note that would come through the instrument does not carry the power you would wish to behold. That, then, creates resentment in the minds of those who are wanting others to *really* take responsibility, and resentment simply creates in-fighting and death. Therefore, mark these words well: Shanti Christo is the responsibility of everyone who genuinely feels called to its manifestation. Pure and simple. For it is a grand experiment to bring forth the unified field, which is the Christ Mind.

Does that make sense to you?

Participant: Yes it does.

Therefore, where there is impatience or unanswered questions, help those with that type of energy to remember that they are already looking outside of themselves. They need to come back to right where they are *in the moment*, and allow the process of purification of their own consciousness through forgiveness, through accepting the great power you hold to take care of anything you think looks like a problem around you, or a limitation or a lack—and to handle that *first*. That is, to seek the Kingdom first, from which all things can be added.

That was a rather good question. And, again, we must ponder its source.

Participant: Jeshua, I'm reminded of our conversation about co-creating Christs a few months ago, and I wonder if you would extend that conversation somewhat tonight?

Yes. Get - on - with - it.

Participant: Think you could make that any clearer?

[Laughter]

No.

[Loud laughter]

All that you need is given, right here, right now. All power under Heaven and Earth resides within the depth of *your* consciousness, which is that which literally is creating what you see around you and what you feel within you. Therefore, claim that power, own it, take it into your being, and *never, never* again allow yourself to deny that you are the One, *the One* Creation of God. And unto you nothing is impossible.

Does that help clarify?

[Laughter] Participant: You're wonderful!

I am only yourself. Hmm.

So, James, you have no question?

Participant: Yeah, I have a question. I'm not sure. Okay, I'll ask.

This one used to always want to take me aside and ask *privately*...

Participant: Okay, I'm wanting to ask about this 12/12 stuff. So I've already listened to all these other questions, you see, and then I decide what's the point of asking any questions? The answer is already given.

So what's the answer?

Participant: So I'm still curious, that "there's nothing special." I understand that, and yet the mind in me goes, there's this dimension that we operate on and many other dimensions, and energy coming forth in waves...

From where?

Participant: From within us.

And so then, what is this 12/12? Speak from the Truth that is within the depth of your being.

Participant: The desire for freedom to be made manifest upon the planet, that's coming forth, pouring forth, from a lot of our hearts.

From the One Heart. Indeed, beloved brother, beloved friend, well have you spoken—for in truth, that which is being called 12/12 symbolizes an expression of the desire of the One Mind to awaken from its dream. And have we not said that there are four Keys to the Kingdom? And is not the first Desire? Therefore, you see, you did get it, right from the very core of the deepest Truth. It is an expression of the desire of the Mind of Christ to give up the dream of the dreamer. So, you see, you knew after all.

Participant: Mmmm.

Beloved friend, there is only a small trace left of the deep pattern or tendency you've been dissolving through many lifetimes—the pattern and tendency not to trust yourself. And that, then, causes the mind to project onto others a better connection with God than your own. Always have I loved you, and always shall I. And the day comes quickly when you will look through the eyes of your heart upon me, and no longer see me as above you. You will see in me the shining radiance of *your perfect equality* with me. And then, indeed, the dance can begin.

Participant: Yay. Yay!

Yet another timely question. So, how are you all doing?

These (what you call) gatherings of the family will now commence; and will grow. And remember—with patience, without doubt, trusting and allowing the perfect unfoldment. And if you think it's not unfolding perfectly, don't look outside yourself—go back to the question:

> *Did I love myself today? How many times did I express forgiveness to the world? Am I, pardon the vernacular, cleaning up my own act?*

Because remember, this world is nothing more than a grand act.

So, with that, we can bring this time to a close. For what was needed to be shared has been shared; and the questions asked are the questions also, not necessarily the same words but the same essence, that are carried in many of your brothers and sisters. And, therefore, accept my blessings as my equal. Please take the cloak from my shoulders and the crown from my head, and adorn yourself. And, then, *go and do likewise* for your brother and your sister.

Be you therefore at peace in this moment and always. Be you therefore the Light that lights this world in simplicity and grace and a gentle smile. Be you therefore awakened in this moment to the Truth of your only Reality. Be you therefore of good courage, for I have overcome the world, and in that moment *so did you.* If it is completed in me, it must be completed in you because there is only One of us here. Can you, then, accept that you've already faced Crucifixion? You don't have to repeat the process. Can you accept that the Ascension is already done? Can you be—will you be–the embodiment of the Truth that sets all things free? Can there be any other use of time?

Blessings then be upon the One who shines brightly forever in the Mind of God, who has created us we know not when or how. And *that* truth is inescapable.

My love to each and every one of you, for in you I see the reflection of myself and know the Grandeur and the Radiance and Beauty and Love that my Father is. And I praise my Father without ceasing.

Amen.

DEATH AND EARTH CHANGES

May 1993

Jeshua

Now, we begin.

And indeed, greetings unto you, beloved and holy friends. I come forth to abide with you from a place that is not apart from where you are. I come forth to abide with you because I love you. I come forth to abide with you because you are already all that I am and all that I could possibly represent to the mind of mankind. I come forth as a promise kept that I am, indeed, with you always. I come forward because the time comes quickly. And I come forth to gather my friends to myself who have already chosen to join with me in this age, to bring forth that of the Christed Consciousness from the depth of their *own* being; to walk this earth *as* the arisen Christ; to be that one through whom the Love of God is extended unto the plants and to the animals, and to every brother and sister that walks with you and yet carries the veil of fear; that walks the light, the temple of their heart. I come forth because I am asked to come forth of my Father.

I am in charge of the Atonement. That is, I am in charge of the process whereby this planet, this human consciousness, this third-dimensional realm, will begin to move toward a transition of vibrational frequency. Hm? Therefore, I come forth to any mind that prepares a place for me by choosing to relinquish the burden of trying to be conformed to a thought system, to a way of life that does not work—a way of life and a thought system that must be reversed completely, so that the heart leads and the mind follows; so vision is the guide, and the body is used only to bring forth into manifest form that seed of holy vision which the Father would place within you.

I come forth because we are one. I come forth because we are friends. I come forth *for the simple joy* of abiding with *you*, the Holy Children of God. For from the beginning, which is before space and time, already were we together as One Mind. And in an ancient moment, a useless dream was dreamt, a dream of forgetting, a dream of separation. But even in that moment, already did your Creator, the one that I have called Abba, Father, set the bridge in place that would one day become activated in the depth of your soul, by which you would come from the world of your making into the truth of the Kingdom . . . that the very words I once explained to the world would become *your* words, that would become *your* truth, *your* reality, your *remembrance* . . . that after all dreams have been dreamt and the soul chooses to cross the bridge, it rests and reclines in the simple truth that *I and my Father are one.* And we create together only the good, the holy, and the beautiful.

Therefore, indeed, beloved friends, it is an honor and a joy to abide with you, to co-create with you, to walk with you on the way that you've chosen. For it is only through the innocence of a perfectly free will that the soul can return to the Kingdom. Love does not need to strive, Love does not need to reach out and hold onto, Love does not need to persuade. It merely abides in its own nature, waiting for the seeker of reality to turn from the roar and din of the world, in which peace cannot be found, in which fulfillment is forever lacking, and begins to hear the crystal-clear but very quiet song of the Creator, whispering eternally,

> *Beloved child, I love you. Come, remember me, and let us be as One.*

So, with all of that by way of greeting, I give thanks unto you, each of you, for your willingness to hear the call and to answer it, to step upon the bridge and allow its light, its intelligence—for the bridge is but the Holy Spirit, the link back to the Mind of God—to guide you in all things. And as you learn not to hear the thoughts born of the world, but to hear the whispers of Spirit that arise from a quiet mind and a peaceful heart and a decision to trust the voice for Spirit, you cannot fail but to complete this journey. The end, therefore, is certain, and each of you in your own way—and indeed, all of you collectively—are witnessing and experiencing within yourselves and in your relationships, the manner in which the Father, God, is calling creation back to Herself.

Therefore, *rejoice* with one another. *Be glad* with one another. *Celebrate* one another. *Love you,* one another. For the end was written in the stars before the stars were birthed. And that time comes quickly.

For long have I waited this age to be upon this plane, when enough momentum has been created in the consciousness of mankind so that a wave of awakening can no longer be shut out, that a wave of awakening can no longer be resisted, that a wave of awakening will melt away all fear . . . and once again the Kingdom of Heaven will be spread across the face of this Earth. But unlike the time when Man recognized it not, mankind *will know* that *the truth is true, always*—and that what is real cannot be threatened, and *only* what is real exists.

There, indeed, will come a moment when all dreams of fear are forgotten, when all strife and enmity between brothers and sisters is dissolved as but an echo of a thought—thought so long ago that it's hardly even imaginable. The Earth will radiate the light of Truth yet again, as she, too, prepares to make her transition, her ascension, her vibrational change; and the waters of this planet will run clearly, and the skies will radiate with colors that have not yet been seen by human eyes. There will be a harmony between all species and mankind. And the way of the world will be forgotten. And the way of peace restored. And the Earth will provide all that mankind could possibly need, simply by the asking.

And in that day and hour when all things have been set in place and the Atonement, the correction, has occurred, for a brief moment that state will be experienced. And then [snaps fingers] this whole plane of density will simply dissolve from view. Not gone, but *translated* into an entirely new domain.

There are many—indeed, we would say unto you that everyone living on your planet at this time is being pressed to make the decision: Are you going to stay and go for the ride? Or are you going to have to move to a different neighborhood? Everyone is being confronted by that decision, from the oldest to the youngest, even the brand- new, newborn child. By the way, many of those that are being new born have already made the decision, and that's why they're being birthed—to assist in setting the frequency. Many of the children being birthed in the world now are already light years ahead of where humanity has been stuck for a while. And they bring a new frequency of consciousness; they bring a new sense of unlimitedness.

And they will not settle for the limited fear-based ideas that have created the world into which you were birthed.

Each and every one has a role to play, a part that has been assigned. It has been with you since the moment your soul was birthed; and the hour and the day comes when each must turn within and finally *allow* that part to flower and be played through them. And in whatever way that you come to it, you will understand the words that I spoke, seemingly so long ago, when I was confronted with the finality of my drama, the finality of my own teaching—what some would the Crucifixion (I've never desired to emphasize *that* part of it; that was just stepping-stones to the Resurrection.) And those words are simply this: Nevertheless, not my will, not the will of the separate fearful ego, but Thine be done—the will of the One Mind *that is but Love.* And when Love guides the way, miracles sprout before you. And not one obstacle is left in front of you; it dissolves before you reach it.

So . . . here you are. In a little building in what you call your Santa Fe, gathering with brothers and sisters that you have known across space and time, because you've all answered the same call and are beginning to be called into a resonance that accelerates the growth of all of you. Just as many are being called together through different lineages, through different teachers—orchestrated, if you will, to gather together in their own ways, to learn the lessons they yet need to learn, to discover their way of service to the planet, to humanity, to the Kosmos, to the Heart of Christ and to the Creator. *An ancient dream begins now to end.* The circle is nearly completed, and the pendulum returns all things to the pristine and innocent truth that all things are but the extension of the radiance of God's presence. And fear can have no place in a mind that has awakened to the reality of God.

And what you are doing here, *even in this evening*, is a part of that very process. I've said many times that I come to call my friends to myself. Imagine that all of you have been given a script very, very long ago. And part of the script said that the day would arise when you would reconnect with an old friend—the one the world has called Jesus.

And that through that connection a vibration would be created that would accelerate the fulfillment of your own part, your own unique role to play, the stepping into the fullness of *your* Christed nature—just as once, as a man, I decided to take my Father's word at face value and stepped into my own Christed nature.

And while many beings sit before their televisions in this town of yours tonight and many more sit in what you call the rooms for unconsciousness, putting the liquid in the body (the bars), while many seek a lover to keep them warm through the night, the night never lasts forever. *You* have chosen to come *here* because you have heard an invitation for this one evening, and you have accepted. Therefore, celebrate and rejoice, for the day is at hand and there is no greater joy than the re-communion of ancient friends who, deep within themselves, *know* that *the time is now*. The dance has begun, the music has started . . . Hmmm . . . And the whole of creation *will come* to this party.

So. We want, then, in this evening to speak specifically to certain questions that have been generated, for they hold a purpose in helping to extend and to clarify a simple message about this time frame, about certain changes, about certain things that are now occurring within your governments, upon your planet, as this Armageddon boils to a crescendo in which all souls are being asked,

> *Well, are you going to join the dance, or are you going to have to leave the neighborhood?*

That is not a judgment, it is an *offering* being made to the soul of everyone: Use time constructively, you can heal your heart, you can practice forgiveness, you can awaken as Christ. You're going to have to, because the planet is doing the same thing; and if you don't come with her you won't be able to handle her light and her frequency, and you'll need to move to a different neighborhood. That's all. No judgment, no fear, no being struck dead by God—only a simple offering. You can awaken now, or you can awaken somewhere else, later. There have been far too many "laters".

So. We believe, then, that you have questions.

Participant: Well, Jeshua, it's not terribly fair for you to answer the questions before I pose them.

It's just a simple mistake that we occasionally make.

Participant: There seems to be a polarization going on now between people who are answering the call and people who would remain in fear. And those things look like wars and fights and racial tension. Is this part of that process?

No, it's because of what has been placed in the water.

[Laughter]

Participant: I'm glad you haven't lost your sense of humor.

Indeed. Too much of what you call your fast food.

[Laughter]

Beloved friend, you have heard it said that when you hear of wars and rumors of wars—no, the time is not quite yet but, boy, is it getting close. Hmm? Indeed. As we spoke a moment ago—and please understand this—*there is no such thing as punishment.* There is no condemnation or judgment in the mind of God, who is above, and seeks to give his Holy Child all good things, and would lead the child from dreams of strife and suffering and fear to dreams of freedom and peace and empowerment and Christedness. There is a vibration beginning to build in the depth of this dimension, this density you call your third—third dimension, third-dimensional reality. Although we would say, there's no reality here yet, but it's coming.

[Laughter]

This vibration is like a pebble dropped in a pond that is beginning to send ripples. It's been going on for some time, it's beginning to pick up pace, beginning to vibrate a little more, like water beginning to boil. You sense that it's happening, although you don't even see the bubbles rising yet. You *know* something's changing in the energy of the water. And as that occurs, it is literally rippling through every soul. Why? Because separation does not exist. And if God holds the thought,

> *Okay, time to nudge the child. I've let them dream long enough. Let's see if they can hear my voice over their dreams,*

that ripple must go through every created soul. And as it does so, it is stirring up all the old fears, all the old patterns, all the old habits, and the soul is being asked,

> *Are you ready to purify?*

which simply means to make a different choice. It's not . . . it doesn't require lying on a bed of nails. Hmm? Simply the recognition that something's coming up that no longer feels as comfortable as it once did. Are you willing to let go and allow a small period of disorientation until reality settles in? And what you thought could have never been, becomes your norm. And you walk the world awake.

There are many who are having their fears escalate. And why? Because they are committed to fear. They believe in fear; it is what keeps them safe. I know that sounds odd, but it's very true. As long as I can look out upon my neighbor and see you as the bad person, then I know who needs to be attacked. And all we have left to do is figure out how to attack you before you attack me. Very simple. And if I win, I get all the marbles. But in attack, no one *can* win. For when the attacker attacks, the attacker *is* attacked by the weight of the negativity of their own fear.

So, yes, what you're seeing on the planet *is* a polarization that is occurring because every soul is being confronted by the decision to heal and to forgive; or to hold onto the idols of their woundedness and to judge.

Once I said, "With what judgment that you put out, rest assured you will be judged in the same way." Why? Because you create your experience. So again, there will be many who will not be able to live on this planet. That is why there is also a creation of many odd and new dis-eases upon your plane. It is why there are very bizarre things being done by certain governments on your planet as the fear builds—in an attempt to remain in control of something that they don't even understand. And yet, *none of it* can affect the pure in heart, the meek who will inherit the Earth, those that choose to heal the gap in their own being between themselves and the mind of God. For they will be led in each moment. And nothing will befall them. A few lessons on the way, yes, but only by way of purification, only by way of a deeper wisdom, a deeper understanding. Where you extend to your Father a smidgen of willingness, the end is certain; and you are safe to trust what you feel in the depth of your heart, which is the temple of the soul, where Father and Child rest together: God and Christ.

Does that help you in regard to that question?

Participant: Yes, thank you. But everything you've said tonight can be taken either physically or metaphorically. Is this a physical change that will occur on the planet, or is this a metaphorical change and the planet itself remain unscathed?

Beloved friend, I am very glad that you have posed your question in just that way. Now, we both know that to put anything into language in the form of a question, you are forced to deal with the language structure you have. Your language structure lives in duality. Things are either on or off, white or black, they're metaphor or they're physical. But I say unto you, the whole of this physical dimension is a metaphor. It is a symbol of a vibration of thought. Does that make it less real? Not at all. For how can the Holy Child of God create unreality? Therefore, this *dream* will be played out and involve the whole of the created domain. And yet it's still just a metaphor, *part of a dream*. For this house you sit in, the town in which it resides, and the planet upon which this town resides all exist in a space no wider than the tip of a pin. And yet, where *you* abide, all of creation is contained within you, and you are vast beyond the reach of all solar systems. And when you get a feel for that, you will, indeed, marvel.

Yes, it will occur, and it is inappropriate and inaccurate for anyone to assume that this change is merely pictures or symbols, that it really only occurs in something called the mind that's somewhere tucked inside a body and has nothing at all to do with the planet, with the stars, with the comets, with the photon belts. 'Tis all one thing: Mind creating. Therefore, for Mind to awaken, all of Mind awakens and changes. Yes, it will involve the planet itself. I believe that should help make it clear.

Participant: Then the role of Shanti Christo must also be clear in this process. Is it a beacon?

Actually, beloved friend, we have merely beguiled you, and that which is called Shanti Christo is a distractive mechanism, being created by the Devil.

[Laughter]

Beloved friend, yes. Shanti Christo is an expression of a vibration of thought, like a pebble dropped in a pond, that is created to manifest specific vibrational patterns or ripples. It will be utilized by us to attract many minds and many beings who can step through the portal into awakened consciousness. There are many portals being created. And why do there need to be many portals? Because there are many levels of consciousness and there are many forms of experience that you've all created, everyone on the planet. I am not everyone's teacher, even though I am in charge of the Atonement. So, imagine that I'm merely sitting behind a small little desk out in the meadow, and I pick up the, what you call your cordless telephone. In this case it's even a non-physical phone. And I will call another teacher, another being, and say,

> *You know, this one over there had a very good connection with you back in Egypt four thousand years ago. Why don't you pop down and have a little chat with them?*

So there is an orchestration going on. There may seem to be many forms of the universal curriculum, many teachers, many methodologies. And yet, all of them are but portals through which the soul chooses to walk—to step from fear to love, from insanity to sanity, from dreams to reality. Shanti Christo, then, is one such portal through which I specifically can activate the call and create a gathering place, if you will—a gathering frequency—through which I can call those to myself who, because of past resonances, past experiences, have come to love me and have come to trust me as one who can carry them over the bridge. Hm?

Yes, Shanti Christo has a role to play, and rest assured there is a safety mechanism built into this vibration. This vibration cannot be manipulated or used for personal gain. It cannot be misdirected, for the mind that may be attracted to it and then sort of bounces off and goes to the left or right is one that merely realizes that this vibration requires (what is your phrase?) the "getting real". This is a vibration and a portal that helps souls step into the next vibration. You can't sneak anything past the ego- detector. Hmm.

Does that help in regard to that question?

Participant: Yes.

Are there any other questions in the group about Earth changes?

Participant: Yes. Are we going to experience a period of three days of darkness during this change upon the earth?

We would suggest here that it is very probable that this will occur. And yet, it will be a little longer than three days. This will eventuate, if it is necessary for the change of vibration, to require what would be called the changing of the axis of the planet. This will create a bit of a shake-up, as one can imagine, and there will be created a blackening-out, and the sun's rays will not touch the Earth. This sun itself is going nowhere.

Yes, but listen well to what I say, for there are many prophecies coming out, and there will be many more as we move closer and closer. Many are getting pictures that are the effect of the generation in their own minds of how they need to understand the ripples that are coming to them. We speak of probabilities because it is never certain what must eventuate for a change of vibration to occur. And you can liken this to your own lives. Sometimes you need to be hit with a broom handle to get your attention. At other times, a quiet whisper seems to be enough.

We would suggest that, because there is no separation, the more that souls choose to awaken and to heal, the less the need for shocking circumstances to get their attention. The more mankind awakens, the easier the transition of the Earth.

Does that make sense for you?

Participant: Yes.

Is there truly any difference between entities that describe themselves as Germaine, Jeshua, Michael, and who would bring their message through an individual? Is there really any difference among the messengers?

The answer is a resounding yes. And why? When you speak of difference, what you are alluding to is that is there an entity that is its own unique sphere of consciousness arising out of the One Mind. God is aware of God because of God's creation. You are God's creation. Therefore, the Father knows Himself because *you* exist to be aware of Him. Individuation, like the ripple arising out of the ocean, does not change the substance—it's still all made of one thing—and yet, there is individuation, uniqueness, just as there are several souls associated with the bodies that have gathered in this room, and you all have your own unique, cosmic social security number.

[Laughter]

Participant: Will it be bankrupt when we get there?

No, it is always, shall we say, overflowing. And you don't even have to pay into it!

So, understand, then, that when we speak of One Mind, we are not saying that individuality does not exist. We're merely saying that each being, each created being, has within them the power to operate from the One Mind that I have called Christed Consciousness. It can go by many names. And yet, individuation is eternal. There will never be a time, a moment, or a non-moment, when all of you simply dissolve into some amorphous blob of awareness. In other words, the more you settle into God, the more the desire there is to individuate, so that you can have relationship in which to celebrate the good, the holy, and the beautiful—to dance, eternally at play in the Father's Kingdom.

Does that help in that regard?

Participant: Most definitely.

Now, by the way, I would highly suggest that I would never listen to the Germaine fellow. And Michael sometimes is a little... Hmmm. Just kidding, of course.

Participant: And Mary shops at K-Mart.

Mmm... I've never been able to keep that one under control. Rest assured, we delight with one another, we play with one another, we *see* the Creator, we *see* the presence of God *as each of us,* and we respect our individuation, just as you respect yours. To see the oneness in diversity, to experience communion between two wholes—that is the great promise of the Kingdom. To be in holy relationship in which two Christs, as individuated beings, yet emerging from and operating from the same mind, the same values, the same love, the same compassion, the same wisdom, the same unlimited power to create the good, the holy, and the beautiful . . . Now *that is a dance worth attending.*

Therefore, seek not the death of the self, but seek the arisen Self. Hm? That should help.

Participant: Would you care to summarize this evening?

It has been... worthwhile. Beloved friend, as you well know, since the thought was dropped in the mind, that this short gathering of this evening was designed to bring forth some specific corrections that will be flowing out to many minds—many more minds than you're even aware of. For those first ones who receive it will be struck, a little chord is struck,

> *Oh, yes, that's right. Thank you for the nudge. I have to get on with it. I have to get on with it. I was beginning to fall into the hope that I could just dissolve away and not have to birth Christ.*

And then they will give that to many others.

There is much being taught in your world that is *not* correct. Anything based on fear is incorrect. Anything based on the *end of creation*, even in positive terms, is incorrect. For the Father extends himself *eternally*. How, then, can there be an end to creation? There is only ever-expanding fullness—fullness expanding into fullness, and into fullness, and into fullness, and into fullness. Higher and higher, and wider and wider, and brighter and brighter, and ever more blissful and ever more wise and loving.

And you all know exactly what that means, for every consciousness reciprocates or plays out the very journey of creation. You all know that you've made creations that were a little difficult, they were a little crude; and so you sought new ways, didn't you? And you keep birthing better and better creations. Guess what? That's it! That's the power of God, which is the soul, seeking to create the good, the holy, and the beautiful. And there reaches a point, of course, where you realize that you have to give up being identified with egoic consciousness, so that Spirit can truly use us all to create in a Christed realm. Hm? Like leaving the things of childhood behind and taking up your rightful place of a powerful, mature adult. To be an adult in the Kingdom is to *be* Christ.

Therefore, indeed, beloved friends, *allow* the good, the holy, and the beautiful to pour forth through *your soul*. For you are the ones sent in this age, with all power under Heaven and Earth, to reveal to your brothers and sisters the truth of a happy dream, the truth of perfect freedom, the end of fear, and the remembrance of Love.

Be you, therefore, with one another often, and remember always that you are the Light of this world. Why not get on with it? And with that, peace unto you always, from the heart of one who loves you and has reached across space and time to touch you and to whisper to you,

Beloved friend, come, take my hand. We are on the bridge already. Just step lightly. Come with me. I know the way.

From that one—who is me, and speaking on behalf of the many who gather with me each and every time this specific work is done—I love you and we love you. It is not possible for you to journey alone. And what you are asked to do in the depth of your vision and in your heart, rest assured, it would not be asked if you were not also given the power and the support to bring it about. Never think you need to be the maker and the doer. You need only be, as each of us is, a servant of the Mind of the Creator who is but Love and whom we serve with perfect freedom and joy and fulfillment.

Peace, then, be unto you always. Amen.

Participant: Jeshua...Don't run off.

Where could I go?

Participant: Thank you. Take two.

I'd like to discuss with you, pursuant to the book that we're working on, The Way Through Death, you brought to our attention this past December that there were many individuals who died in the explosion in Oklahoma City who were at that time unaware of their death situation. They were somehow hung up in that moment of time of the explosion, unable to extricate themselves from the collapsed building. We've all heard stories of ghosts still inhabiting the locations of their death. Why is this so, if what Emmanuel says, that death is "like taking off a tight shoe" is true?

Death *is* like taking off a tight shoe, but it does not, necessarily, bring enlightenment and freedom. The tight shoe is the density of the physical form. Yet, where a mind is not yet prepared, and where the mind carries attachment to what that mind had learned to value—other bodies in space and time—the energy of that soul cannot ascend to the Father, to use an old Biblical term. There can be no ascension to the Father, unless that soul has gotten over a very important hump: the hump of *at least* having *faith* that there is something beyond this world. Does that make sense for you?

So, in a very real way, a weight has been lifted. There is no cold, there is no heat, there is no need for fuel for the body. Experiences continue. The interesting thing is that without the physical density of the body, there is no experience of time as you know it. Therefore, a soul can remain stuck in a building that is collapsing for what you would perceive as thousands of years—if that mind remains attached to the belief that it is *only* the third-dimensional physicality, and that the only thing of value are other things of third-dimensional physicality.

Just as, many times, you would walk down a street and not even notice that a friend has passed you by because you're so fixated on where you're going, the soul at death can be so fixated on its perceptual values that it doesn't even notice angelic choirs singing in their ear: "Come, beloved friend, ascend!" Doesn't even notice it, until there is communication, till somehow there is discovered a way to create or to bring its attention to value something else—to realize that something has profoundly changed, and that its belief system had been limited.

Does that help you in regard to that question?

Participant: So, from what you're saying then, there is no set sequence that occurs at that moment called death. So a lot of people report on going through the tunnel and you're there and...

That is a very... The tunnel experience being spoken of in your cultures as the near- death experience is a very, very basic first stage of the dying process. Primarily, it entails the withdrawal of energy from the brain core—from the brain core to the stem of the body or toward the spine of the body. It creates the *perception* of the tunnel, in which there is a withdrawal from the senses of the body into this, what appears to be a tunnel. And it is a portal and a doorway. And yes, I appear to many, and others appear, as well. But the belief system is still functioning. That is only one of the first stages of the actual death process.

As it continues, and as the brain core literally dies—which simply means that life force is withdrawn and not returned to it, so it is dropped like old baggage—then the soul, the consciousness, experiences a vibrational leap, what you might call a quantum leap in vibrational states, into more and more subtle states of its own being. But there is a period in which there is a playing-out of the residual effects of all of its perceptions and beliefs. It is called the . . . in one stage, the life story is played back that fast. [Snaps fingers] Thoughts or fears of a Satan or beliefs in a Savior become the energy which attracts that experience to that individual.

So, in a general sense, there is something that occurs energetically. But what occurs within that energy is *entirely unique* to each individual. And what will matter is this: If time has been used constructively—that is, if you utilized time to let go of limiting beliefs and begin to foster first faith and then direct experience in tapping into other dimensions, into remembering the mind of God, if you practiced forgiveness and healing—then at death fear has no place to grip the mind.

Yes, the tunnel begins to happen because the energy is being withdrawn from the cellular structure of the body, from the brain itself toward the brain stem—what I call the stem or the interior of the spine. And since the mind has been cultivating devotion to God, the willingness to heal, the ability to *let go* without fear, then as these things come up and move through very, very quickly, they have no effect whatsoever, and the mind proceeds toward light—greater and greater dimensions of light. Hm? And it is possible for the soul, then, to remain in those dimensions without any need of incarnating again. It is always something left unhealed—a fear, a self-judgment, a resentment, an old anger—that creates a heaviness that draws the soul, using its infinite power, to re-create third-dimensional physicality yet again, to try to get it right. It is always much wiser to use the incarnation you have, to get it right! Don't think about the old ones; don't think about the ones that might come. Realize that right where you are, *right where you are,* everything is *perfect for your awakening.*

You can awaken *now*, by choosing to teach only Love. And that must include to yourself. To love the self is ultimately the final portal, for only when you truly love yourself can you serve another. Only when you love yourself so much you're no longer willing to tolerate anything but the presence of Christ in you. When you believe that you are so valuable that you should be treated like a priceless jewel. Then, indeed, Christ will arise. For the Holy Son of God, who is but Christ, will not come up and take his abode in a home unworthy of him. And what is that home? It's not the body; it's the Mind. Therefore, love yourself.

When I once said, "Love your neighbor as yourself," I thought it was obvious that that meant you had to love yourself before you could ever experience loving your neighbor. Therefore, to learn the way of love, practice with diligence forgiveness. Release expectation from anyone or anything. Create your vertical alignment in the mind of God. And seek not from the world what it does not possess: the eternal and perfect peace that birthed you and that you are seeking to recover. "Be you, therefore, whole and perfect," means just that. Wake up. Get it right while you're on the planet. Let the mind heal. Choose to be the presence of Love. Trust God above all things, and walk this world as the meek who will inherit it. Be you, therefore, the presence of Love.

And when the time comes, as it must, for that temporary density structure called the body to dissolve and be given back to the Earth from which it came, fear will have no place in you. And as the tunnel begins to appear and you *know*—this happens to every mind, by the way—there is a moment when *you know* something is occurring that's going to occur and you're not going to be able to interrupt it any more; you're not going to be able to avoid the portal. When you literally feel the energy withdraw from the cells of the body and move toward the stem, or what you call the spinal column, you will welcome it like a joyous ride. And you will turn your attention immediately upward—that is a metaphorical term—but upward to the higher teachings of the mind of God, rather than the teachings of a fearful world. And you will let these things go like toys that have been outgrown. And then the soul can *ascend* into its full remembrance.

"And in my Father's house are many mansions," which means that there are an infinite number of dimensions in which you can come to make a new home, based on the quality of vibration that you have brought yourself to in your understanding and in your consciousness, which is nothing more than your love. But the only thing you can ever truly regret is that perhaps you resisted giving that love away, even up to the moment of death. And therefore, love freely, love abundantly, and love without ceasing. And above all, love the Self that has been birthed in the mind of God, for no other reason than to *live in the consciousness of God.*

Participant: So, I'll be the gnat shouting at the universe.

Is God self-aware, or is it simply a benign metaphysical force?

Benign metaphysical force.

Participant: Don't pick at it, just answer it.

There is nothing more benign than Love. There is nothing more metaphysical, which mean beyond and permeating the physical, than God. There is nothing more forceful, if you mean by that infinite power that cannot be denied, than God. So if that is what you mean, I would say yes to the use of those terms. Is God self-aware? Are *you* aware?

Participant: Hmm.

Hmm.

Participant: Hmm, hmm. Got it.

Hmm. It won't be the last time.

[Laughter]

Participant: That, for me, begs the next question. Is there a force outside of God?

Just you. I well do understand the direction of your question. There can be nothing outside of God, and what is unreal does not and cannot exist. Yet, you have the power within the infinite freedom of God to *believe a perception* that there is a force outside of or other than God. Just as you have believed that you are separate from God. 'Tis is an optical delusion of consciousness. It is a dream of a child sleeping in a meadow, in whom no change has truly occurred. That which is called Satan cannot exist or have any power, save in that mind that allows it, and who *gives* that power *to* it. For did I not ask you to speak unto one, could the devil withstand your love? And did it not bring that one to silence? In other words, Love heals—because Love is real. And when you step from fear into Love, where did the boogeyman go?

Participant: Well, I'm through with my questions. If you have a summary...

Could I ask a question?

Yes.

Getting back to Shanti Christo, could you give us an idea when this will materialize?

Beloved friend, it already has. And in your third-dimensional plane of time, you are witnessing the process whereby that materialization occurs. In reality, it is already finished, because God does not think thoughts that arise incomplete. Hm? You are merely tuning in to what has already occurred. I know that's a bit of a leap but it's okay, let yourself take it. You are merely choosing to allow yourself to participate in what you've already done. For hear this: In reality, the dream and the process of awakening never occurred. For what has no effect has never happened. The dream, the awakening of the dream, is already done. You might say you are watching the film. Film at 11:00. Can you imagine a newscaster saying,

> *Mmm. All of creation has awakened today and returned to the Holy Mind of God. Film at 11:00.*

[Laughter]

And what you are experiencing is the watching of the film. Like being within a hologram. Yes, and when are the specific parts going to manifest it and love you? When would you *like* them to manifest?

Participant: Tomorrow.

Very well. Simply awaken tomorrow, and know: It is finished. Let no doubt arise in your mind, and simply allow the Comforter, the Holy Spirit, to reveal to you what has been finished. Imagine a... what you call a supervisor at a construction site, building a beautiful building, and you come by and you go,

How did this happen?

And he puts his arm around you and says,

Come. First I'll show you the foundation, I'll show you the blueprint plans...

And yet, the whole time you're in the building and your mind begins to tap in to the day they first brought the concrete to make the foundation, then the steel girders, and then later the interior decorators putting the final touches—as he describes for you the process whereby the very building in which you live was created. The buildings on that land are already there. You just don't see them yet. But they're settling in, and you will see them. And when you see them, you will know, just like hundreds of other beings will know,

I've seen those before.

Not in another place and time, but because you've already experienced the completion. Does that make sense?

Participant: Yes.

Indeed. And what can stand against the will of God? That is why those that are called to add to and create this vibration must always rest in certainty, in knowingness: It is finished. What a delightful way to spend the last afternoon of the dream of separation. Something to think about.

Participant: Thanks, my friend.

Mmmm. Indeed. So, may I be allowed to leave this time?

[Laughter] Where could you go?

Exactly. I merely recede, and what is called this communication process. And by agreement always, I merely nod to my brother who no longer, no more exists within the body than you exist within yours. Hm? You're just animating a temporary communication tool. I merely nod to him, and I say, "We're done now." And usually he goes, "Oh, so soon? Thank you." And he returns *his* attention to the body, as I *release* my attention from it. That's all. Kind of like two friends, and one night one of them sleeps in a certain bed in the house, and the next night it's the other person's turn. We just slide in and out of the bag of dust. Sometimes you never quite know who's there.

Participant: It's a chance to sleep around though, right?

Indeed. 'Tis good to choose loving cosmic bedfellows.

[Laughter]

Indeed. Therefore, again—and always—I leave, yet I leave not *you*, for I am closer to you than your own breath, and never further from you than the width of a thought.

Think well, then, and remember the truth that is true always.

Amen.

LOVE HEALS ALL THINGS

June 1993

Jeshua

Now we begin.

And indeed, greetings unto you, beloved and holy friends. I come forth to abide with you in this hour and in this day and in this way, not in order to *teach* you, for there is nothing which can be taught that you do not already know. I come forth not as one who is *above* you but as one who walks *with* you on the way that you have chosen. I come forth freely to communicate in this manner because I love you, and I come forth to abide with you because you are my Father's Creation. You *are* Christ. You *are* That One birthed eternally since before time is. You *are* my brother and my sister. And when I come forth to abide with you, I know my Father. When I come forth to abide with *you*, I see the reflection of who I am. When I come forth to abide with *you*, I *know* that only Love is Real.

Therefore, throughout eternity, and again since before time began, I am with you, even as you are with me. Though the journeys may seem many, in Truth there has been no journey. And you cannot journey to a reality from which you can never in Truth be separated.

Yes, you have heard it said that you create your own reality, but I say unto you, you can only create *from* your Reality—in the perfect freedom that the Father accorded to the Son, in that moment, that mysterious moment, in which the Father chose to create that which is like unto Himself: His *only* begotten Son, or offspring.

You *are* That One, and you have been therefore a Creator, ceaselessly, since that timeless moment. And even now, in this hour, you have chosen to create your experience. You have chosen to take what you call the body, which is really a temporary communication device, you've chosen to place it spatially at a certain location in order to attract to yourself a unique quality of experience. You are the one, even in this moment, who freely creates the perception through which you behold and experience this moment. In Reality, I cannot heal your perception. In Reality, I cannot persuade you to see things differently. In Reality, I cannot awaken you, but I *can* in my infinite freedom choose to love you.

Here, then, is the great secret of consciousness, here the great secret that so many would seek in so many magical ways. The world that you experience, the world *of* your experience, as with mine, is wholly uncaused by anything outside of yourself, and there is nothing outside of you. The freedom which *is* your existence, the unlimited freedom to create perception—to create, period—that unbridled freedom, the Essence and Truth of all that you are, is unchanging forever.

Therefore, in any moment of experience, cultivate the decision to not look for a cause outside of yourself, but merely ask:

> *What have I* chosen *to see? What have I* chosen *to experience?*

And if you look with the eyes of the heart, it will not be hidden from you. And to look with the eyes of the heart requires only a simple honesty.

> *What am I experiencing in* this very moment*? For this is the fruit of what I have chosen previously—what thoughts I have allowed to make a home in the mind, what perceptions I have attached a value to, so that they carry with me, like a filter, through which I color what is entirely a neutral event: Creation.*

All power under Heaven and Earth abides within *you*, each and every one of you, equally—all power under Heaven and Earth, through which *you* create your experience. Therefore, you are free at any moment to see yourself as one who is *seeking* God, or you are free to see yourself as one who has *found* God. The difference between the two is the difference between Heaven and the world, between Spirit and matter if you will, between Heaven and hell, between suffering and peace, between doubt and wisdom, between anxiety and a very subtle joy that never leaves.

If I come forth to abide with you in this hour, it is only because I recognize you as my equal. And I come forth only, again, because I love you. And I love you because I have learned to make the choice consistently to *teach only Love.*

Once, when I walked upon your plane, your planet, as a man, I too was confronted with the very choices that you are confronted with. And though they come disguised in many ways, ultimately the choice is simple: Love and fear. And as a man, temporarily, like you, identified with the perception of myself as a body-mind separate from all others, perhaps even separate from my Father, I too had to cultivate the decision to see differently—to *choose* what all of my teachers were telling me, what all of the scriptures that I studied were saying: that God and His Creation are never separate one from another, that I *was* that Light, that I *was* that Creation, that I *was* the Christ.

And a certain day arose, as it has already for many of you, and will arise for others of you, a day arose in which it suddenly occurred to me, that rather than seeking magical means for closing the gap between myself and my Father, that *perhaps* I should do something outlandish, something so outrageous as to be almost sacrilege in every spiritual tradition in which I studied. And that one outlandish thing was to simply take God at God's Word and to begin to live as though it were true that I was not separate from God. Now you have to admit, that's rather outlandish.

[Laughter]

So. I decided in that day and that hour, as I sat beneath a certain tree on a certain small hill in what you call Galilee, and as I looked out upon the last rays of the setting sun, in the depth of my mind I made a decision:

> *I will walk no more as a seeker for God, but I will give myself over to the Reality that Iand my Father are One. And then I'll see what happens.*

Hmm? It is not true that I came to this planet fully awake, popped into a womb without the help of what you call the—ah, shall we say—'normal' means. It is not true that I was sitting next to my Father and He said, "Look, would you mind going down?" and I said, "No problem."

If I did not walk this planet as a man, if I did not feel all that you have felt, if I did not perceive what you have perceived, if I did not know judgment, if I did not know fear, if I did not know sadness, if I did not know lust, if I did not know the cold of the skin if I did not know the doubt, the longing, the desire to search and to seek—then nothing I ever did and nothing I have ever said to you, whether then, whether since then, whether now in the many multitude of forms in which I'm seeking to communicate to your humanity, *none of it means anything and has no value unless I have been where you are.*

Does that make sense for you?

Therefore, please, please do me a huge favor. If you're going to insist on having a picture or some icon of me upon your altar, please put a picture of yourself next to mine. Hmm? Better yet, take mine down and put yours up and recognize that the same Truth that awakened me lives within *you*. It waits on your welcome, your welcome to make the decision to never again tolerate the insane thought that you could be separate from God, and bring that Truth and that commitment to each moment, remember that Truth, and then live from that Truth and see what your Father would have you do.

It's really not too complicated. What you will discover, after you hear the message a few thousand times is, "Oh! Teach only Love." Same message, many forms, same content. Teach only Love, for that is what you are. Teach only Love, for that is what you are.

Father, what should I do in this moment?

Teach only Love, for that is what you are.

Should I go here or there?

Listen to Love, let Love guide you.

Be you therefore the presence of the Truth that you are, and you are the Light that lights this world. And you cannot help but be in the right place at the right moment. And if you would know your

Father's will, open your eyes. Who are you with? Where are you? How can you bring Love to the spaciousness and the sacredness of this holy encounter?

And rest assured, whenever you meet anyone on this plane—in fact we'll go a little further now and say, in any moment of relationship, whether it be with a blade of grass or as you gaze upon a star—every moment of relationship is *a holy encounter.* For your Father creates only that which reflects the good, the holy, and the beautiful. And through you, Creation waits to be blessed, waits to be redeemed, waits to be saved as you choose to perceive through *only* the eyes of Love. And the decision to do so must necessarily correct the depth of the mind, heal the emotions, and yes, while the body lasts, even transform the way these tiny little cells that you call the body have been responding to you like a good servant.

Love heals all things. Love embraces all things, trusts all things, transcends all things, transforms all things, and returns Reality gently to where it has never left: the depth of your own being. Mmm.

Well that's enough of all of that Love stuff. I too as a man used to cry out to my Father,

> *But, but Father, it can't be that simple. Mmmm. I had this struggle with this person I know. They are* (what you would call in this day and age) *pushing of the buttons, pushing the buttons,* (what we called) *vexing the soul. And if only they would stop vexing, my soul would be just fine.*

[Laughter]

> *Surely the cause is outside of myself. Surely there must be some magical means whereby I can protect myself from the psychic onslaught of those poor unenlightened sinners who don't get it. Teach me the way, Father!*

And yes, I journeyed to a desert for forty days and forty nights (actually, it was about thirty-seven days and nights, give or take a few), struggling—with what? Struggling *only* with an incorrect perception of who I am and where I am *always.*

And as I began to live from that simple decision to accept my Father at His Word, the events of my life began to be organized not by me, but by the One that I have called the Comforter, the Holy Spirit, the Voice for perfect right-mindedness, a perfect sanity, the bridge between my personal consciousness and the Mind of God—just as *your* life begins to be reorganized (and many of you know what that sometimes feels like) as something beyond yourself as you have known it begins to reshape your destiny. And thank God, for if you follow your own, you'll walk off the edge of the Universe and disappear into an abyss. Hmmm.

But that which the Comforter is begins to organize the relationships, the meetings, the chance encounters, the books, the careers, the friends, and that which has been placed within you is slowly birthed, right up through the soil of everything you had mistakenly created which had been unlike Love, which had been an attempt to keep yourself safe, which had been an attempt to hold on to a judgment—which had been an attempt to view Creation other than the way it is, to see not the real world, but your replacement, your substitute, for it. Right through that very soil, the Comforter begins to work within your mind and your heart to correct your perceptions, to bring *exactly* that perfect learning situation in which you can choose again for Love.

And each time you make that simple choice to listen only to that Voice, you take what—if we might borrow words from your contemporary world—you take what is called a quantum jump, a quantum leap, in the process of healing, in the process of birthing Christ. Each decision for *Love* is more precious than all the gold and silver this planet could ever produce. It is worth more than all the adulation, all the successful careers, all the girlfriends and boyfriends that you could possibly ever amass. *Each decision for Love* outweighs *everything* that has ever been birthed upon this plane. That's how *powerful* you are. That's the *power* that waits within you and waits upon your welcome.

> *In this moment, though the body is shaking... in this moment, though the tears are flowing... in this moment, though I'm noticing fear of loss come up... I am going to choose Love anyway. And I will love the tears, and I'll love the shaking, and I'll love the fear, and I'll love the one before me, and I'll love the blade of grass upon which I may be standing, and I will love the lover of God within me that wants only to awaken.*

Love. It is the only power that exists in Creation. And *you*, right where you are, you are that one who can make the simple decision to bring Love into your environment. You can be the channel. You can be the cup that overflows. You are the one that can make the simple decision to allow healing to occur.

You are the one who walks upon this planet. You are the one that has what you call a body, which means you have a temporary device that everybody else on the planet can see. They often cannot see me because they look with the eyes of the physical body and not the eyes of the Awakened Heart. You are the one through whom Love, given as the Comforter, can guide your words, your gestures, your very being, so that Love comes into this world and can touch the heart of another in ways that your thinking mind could never possibly understand or comprehend. For the mind was never designed to be your master: it was designed to be the servant of the Awakened Heart.

And by 'heart' here, I simply mean the *depth* of the mind that is deeper than conscious viewing, so to speak, different than your ideas and your perceptions, just like the ocean from which all of the waves arise. I simply call it the heart to differentiate it from what you call the intellect or the thinking mind.

That mind never knows what anyone needs. And when you are in silence—which simply means to withdraw your valuation *of* those ideas—when you choose to withdraw into the sanctuary of your heart, into the depth of your Mind with a capital "M" and remember the Truth that is true always, that only Love heals, then you can be *in*spired, and that Mind can become a servant of the extension of Love. And in that moment, there is literally *no difference* between you and the lifetime I lived that has gotten so much press. Mmm? . . . You *are* Christ incarnate, you are the Word made flesh, you are the Only Begotten of the Father, you are the Redeemer, because you have chosen to be redeemed by choosing Love.

When you choose Love over fear, it does not mean that you will not experience fear as a movement or wave of energy, just like a ripple on a lake caused by a pebble that was dropped into your consciousness. When you choose Love *over* fear, it simply means that, no matter what is going on within you or around you, you've chosen to value *only* the Voice for Love.

And you begin to cultivate the ability to discern the Voice for Love amidst the roar and din of the world, which is the expression of fear. The world can exist within your mind, within your emotions, within the cellular structures of what looks like the solid mass called the body. The world can exist what seems to be around that body in other minds. But the world is always the symbol of the choice for fear. And in the midst of all of that, you can indeed cultivate the skill, the ability to hear ever more clearly the Voice for Love, and it begins by deciding to make the *decision* to hear it.

Imagine that you are at what is called the symphony, and as you sit in your chair surrounded by hundreds of other beings in what are called the, ah, tuxedos and the gowns, you make a decision in the depth of your being to hear the note of the flute, and you begin to learn how to temporarily set aside the sound of the violin, the beating of the drum, the sound of what is called the oboe. Hmm? You begin to cultivate the ability to discern the note of the solitary flute playing beautifully in the midst of the music of the orchestration of that symphony. That is very much like all that you need do to cultivate the ability to hear the Voice for Love.

But it does require a commitment. It does require that as you go through your day, though no one may know what you're doing, you are using time differently. Hmm? You're choosing to use it *constructively*, and there is no greater use of time than to cultivate the ability to hear *only* the Voice for Love, to act *only* from its inspiration, to give up the voice of the world, whether it seems to be coming from around you or from within you, and actually those are just terms that we have to use for your experience. There is no inner and outer; there is nothing outside of you.

This means that when a brother or a sister seems to be acting insanely, it is occurring within *you*, and you have the power to look upon that one and see them as yourself, to even transcend the perception of them as a brother or a sister, for that is still a language that is based on a perception that there is something outside of you. You can learn to look and see *only* yourself and make the decision whether you would bring Love to yourself, or fear.

For as you treat your brother, you have treated yourself. And as you have looked upon your sister, you have looked upon yourself. And in fact, the reason you are seeing your brother or sister in a certain, shall we say, unloving light, is because you have already first looked upon *yourself* in that manner, and you're merely experiencing the effect of that choice.

Now I know that means that if you want to cultivate Christ Consciousness, you're going to have to completely give up all hope of ever finding anyone or anything to blame.

[Laughter]

> *But I put so much time and energy into it. I've been looking everywhere, high and low, for lifetimes! And sometimes I'm quite convinced I truly did find someone or something to blame.*

And yet, beloved friends, consciousness is such a delightful game. Each time that you have withdrawn Love from another for any reason, you have hurt only yourself, and you have ensured that *you* will sense a lack of Love.

Forgiveness releases the world from the perception that *you* have placed upon it. You cannot forgive the world for what it's 'really done' because it has done nothing. You cannot forgive your brother or sister for their act against you, for you can experience nothing that you have not called to yourself as a result of the judgment with which you have already held yourself.

So the world would teach you that what you experience comes from outside; something called "accidents" can occur. The world would teach you that you can be a victim of the world. The world will also teach you, "Don't worry, you're not to blame," and actually that's quite true, but from a different level. The world then, and everything the world teaches, is diametrically opposed to the Truth of the Kingdom. And where on earth is the Kingdom? It's right here. It's wherever you are.

And the Truth, which *is* the Kingdom, *knows* that nothing is outside, that Consciousness is the Creator, and that therefore, in any moment, whether you are hearing the beautiful laughter of a newborn child, whether you feel the tiny feet of one that comes soon, touching and kicking the sides of the internal area of the woman's body. Hmm?
. . . or whether or not it's what you call April 15th and you're watching your money go out in the mailbox, *nothing* has come into the field of your experience except that you have *allowed* it.

Now that doesn't mean, and listen carefully, it doesn't mean that you sat down and made a blueprint and said that on April 19th, 1994, someone's going to run over my cat. That's not what that means. The event of someone running over the cat is a symbol, it is an expression of a certain vibrational quality of consciousness. Hmm? You have already dropped a pebble in the pond of your own mind that resonates, sends out a ripple, so that what you've dropped in here shows up out *here* as a reflection, not to punish you. God is not someone who drops you on the planet, makes you suffer, and then when you die tells you why He did this to you. Wouldn't it be nice? Then you'd have somebody to blame.

[Laughter]

Hmm. All events occur for one reason, and only one reason, not to punish you, not to make what you call the stress occur in the body, not to prove that the world is an evil place. Events occur in order to shock you if necessary into turning your attention toward the real world, toward the Kingdom, to force you if necessary to learn to think differently, to learn to choose differently, to place value on different goals: ultimately the goal to awaken, the goal to heal. The events that occur in themselves have no effect on you. None whatsoever. Trust me, if they did, you would not be here now; you would have disappeared 45,000 years ago. But here you are. And the world has not been able to kill you, has it? Just as it failed once to get rid of me.

[Laughter]

The event, no matter what it is that you are experiencing, is the result, the outcome of, how you have been choosing to think of yourself previously, and shows up to reflect to you what's really been going on so that you have an opportunity to choose anew—and thereby learn what Love is, how Love heals, what experience is, what Creation is, and what power dwells within you to co-create with God the good, the holy, and the beautiful. And that power is unlimited forever.

Therefore, look not with judgment upon the experience you're having. If you notice the mind say,

> *I feel so trapped. I feel so imprisoned. Oh, if I just didn't have this dumb body.*

Mmm? No, that's a judgment. And judgment only creates a certain vibration that must show up to reflect to you what you've been doing with the power of your mind.

But learn to look lovingly. Learn to look with sacredness upon each and every moment. Learn to look that even with this thing you call the body, you can have a holy encounter. You can look upon the body in a mirror. You can look at your face in the mirror. You can touch what are called the hands of the body. You can touch the shoulders and the arms. You can touch the area of the heart. And you can realize that right here and right now, wherever you are, *you* are the consciousness that can *love* this temporary creation. You can appreciate the incredible device it is through which you can call to yourself experiences in this certain domain of frequencies, all for the opportunity to choose differently than you did in the past: to choose Love, to teach only Love, to become so arrogant and outlandish that you make the same decision I did.

> *I think I'll walk around as though what my Father says to me is true.*

Hmmm! And when someone asks you what your birthday is, you can say, "It's December 25th. When is yours?"

[Laughter]

Actually I was born in what you call August, but never mind.

[Laughter]

Now, you have literally the power to have a whole lot of fun with birthing Christ. The ego, which is the insane thought that you could be other than what God created you to be, has one chief characteristic—seriousness. Rest assured, any time that you are praying with great seriousness, you're not praying. Mmmm. And loving seriously is a contradiction in terms.

So what would it be like if you made the decision to leave this place this evening, having decided to play your way into the Kingdom? Hmmm. To *play* your way into the Kingdom. To be light, to laugh, to be outrageous, to have fun, to tweak the minds of others. Hmmm?

[Laughter]

Imagine walking into one of your stores and giving them a five dollar bill for the gallon of milk and whatever else you've bought, and they give you a penny back because that's the way it goes these days, and you take the penny and you look at the clerk, and you put your finger in your little cheek and go, "What a good Christ am I!"

[Laughter]

. . . and walk away. Hmmm. And then you come back in and say, "And by the way, what a good Christ are you!" Rest assured that clerk will *never* forget you.

[Loud laughter]

And I want to share something that is very, very sacred, and very true. It is not serious, however, though it is sincere. Listen carefully. Whenever two minds have chosen to join in Love, *never* will those two minds ever be separate, one from another, again. That is, the dream of separation will never drop a veil between them. And Christ *longs* to be joined with Itself, showing up as every being.

Therefore, when you choose, and please listen carefully, when *you choose* to begin to teach only Love *as the Arisen Christ*—it doesn't mean you get an operation manual that tells you what to do, by the way, it just means you begin by deciding that that's what's true, and then the Holy Spirit fills in the gaps—when you've made that decision to look upon the clerk in the store, or your spouse, or your child, or a friend, or someone who just suddenly, mysteriously pops into your mind and your prayer, hmmm, when you decide to look with Love upon that one, and allow yourself to see that Christ dwells in them, *you* are linked to that being eternally.

And as you awaken, students are sent to you. And each of you has a multitude of beings waiting in the waiting room for you to decide to get on with who you really are. Most of them you haven't met yet. And the *majority* of them, you will *never* meet in physical form. But because all minds are joined—and what is mind but a point of Divine Light, a point of consciousness, a point of intelligence, hmm?—it doesn't matter what dimension they're in. Everything exists in a space which is no greater than the head of a pin anyway. And in fact, it exists in a space which is the measurement of the width of a thought. Hmmm. And if you can figure out what *that* is, please let me know.

[Laughter]

It means that even within this dream that occurred with the thinking of one insane idea, you are linked in relationship with all beings. And as you choose to heal, every decision to heal, every decision to extend only *Love*, uplifts the whole of Creation.

And as Christ is rebirthed in your remembrance, because it's already there, all of those beings with whom you've ever extended or exchanged Love immediately get it. And they start showing up in the most outlandish ways. Many of you know what I'm talking about. Suddenly you meet someone, and you *know*, you *know* you've known them forever. And there is an immediate teaching/learning relationship that is established, and you didn't have to do a thing. Didn't have to hire an advertising promotional person to get you known. They show up!

Every time you make a decision for Love and thereby allow the memory of Christ to come more and more into your mind, into your consciousness, into your beingness, you send a message to everyone waiting in the waiting room that has a connection with you, and they know class is starting. And as *they* awaken because you are awakening, those that have been assigned to *them* in *those* waiting rooms, so to speak, begin to get the message. And then the bottom line is: there's a huge network of relationship that exists within a temporary dream that never occurred, that's happening in a space no greater than the width of a thought, in which the Holy Son of God is remembering and awakening.

[Laughter]

And here we are.

I am part of that; I am not outside of it. As I chose to awaken, those assigned to me began to show up. I didn't run an ad in the paper that said "Looking for disciples."

[Laughter]

Mmmm. "Long hours, bad day. Must be able to handle projection."

[Laughter]

Hmm. They just showed up. And while I was in the body, I was guided, just as you have often been guided: "Turn left."

Why am I doing that?

And you end up having a chance encounter of the fourth kind, a connection of the heart, and of holiness, and of healing, and of sacredness, and of divinity, and of Christ; and Love touches Love, and Love is remembered. You've all had those moments.

And when I chose to allow circumstances to shape an event known as the Crucifixion as my final learning lesson that I held the power within myself to teach only Love, no matter what the circumstances are, and dissolved even the need or valuation for this kind of particular learning device [taps the body], I became freed to reach across time and space, if you will, to begin to extend and teach only Love to many beings. And many of you here in this hour have known what you call incarnations [taps teh body several times], hmm, in which you became aware of me. That's one good thing what you call Christianity did. At least it gave me an avenue to get to know you. I didn't create it, but I can *use* it.

[Laughter]

Many of you—and you know in your heart that you know perfectly well this one who was known as Jeshua ben Joseph, translated as Jesus—many of you *know* that you have known me somewhere in an ancient past. Many of you have very clear remembrances. Many of you simply feel a vibration that suddenly went *wham* in your heart, and you knew you were supposed to be here. You answered the call.

For my intention as a brother and as a friend, one who has chosen to assume responsibility for the Atonement, is to call my friends to my Self, to send out the invitation, to find the ways to reawaken the connection and the resonance that transcends all boundaries between my heart and those that I love and those whom my Father has sent unto me—not that I can *save* them, but that I can *love* them and give them my strength until theirs is as certain as mine.

And that's when the dance begins. That's when the dance of joyous co-creation between friends occurs, between you and me—you who *seems* temporarily and for a very short non-time to have a body, this body, this tremendous communication device, through which in space and time you get to be the embodiment of Love to the degree that you want to, and nobody can tell you you can't—between you and me, who *seems* not to have a body but is closer to you than your own breath, who knows you, who loves you, who longs to dance and play with you in the extension of the good, the holy and the beautiful: that which sends a signal out into the world and begins to touch other minds and hearts.

It can be as simple, as *simple*, as telling someone you love them. It could be creating what you call a group of people to study *A Course in Miracles*, which is really just a course in one's self. It seems to be different. "Well, there's a book. We're studying this, of course." And of course, those of you that study it know the more you study it, the closer to *this* you get [indicates the body], and you realize you've really just been studying yourself . . . Hmmm. And you are the book.

It could be so outrageous that you allow the Mind of God to drop, like tiny seeds, grand visions for a healed planet. In Truth, there is no difference between the tiny, quiet, unnoticed act of telling someone that you love them and you see Christ in them, and the grandest of visions that the Holy Spirit has ever dropped into any mind. Hm?

Love is always equal. And each expression of it holds an equal value. The tiniest extension of Love moves mountains because it heals fear. Never let that little chattering monkey called the ego say, "But you're not doing enough. But you're not doing enough. But you're not doing enough. But you're not doing enough." Hmm. Broken record, broken record, broken record.

It is *enough* to *Love*. It is enough now in this moment to take the hand of the one sitting next to you and hold the thought,

I sit next to Christ, and I love them.

That's enough, because Love heals. Love—precious Love, precious Love—heals all worlds.

And if you ever stand alone or sit alone beneath a tree on an early morning in which the first rays of light are beginning to caress this precious Earth of yours in which mystery, *untold mystery*, is all around you, you can never figure out how it got there. Hmm? If you ever sit quietly where no one knows you're there, and the heart opens, and you think a loving thought of someone you've known, and you take the time, that one moment, and use it constructively to bless that being . . . in as much as you have done it unto them, you have done it unto the whole of Creation as deeply and as powerfully as anything that I ever did. And more than that, you've done it as powerfully as a lot of things that were ascribed to me that I never did!

If you receive nothing else in our time together this evening, *please receive this:* There is no such thing as a small act of Love.

To hold a newborn child in your arms and set aside the perception of yourself and them as being two separate beings, as you hold that child and decide that Christ is in your arms and that therefore you're in perfect communication, to hold one quiet thought, "Beloved child, it's okay now to remember who you are," there will no longer be persecution and crucifixion in the world as Christ is birthed. That tiny little act is the greatest act that can ever occur. You have remembered Love. You have reclined in the Truth of who you are. You have recognized it in the one in front of you, and you have blessed the world through your loving communication.

And no greater Love hath anyone than that one that lays down their life for a friend. Now I know perfectly well that that's made a few people shudder because they thought that meant they had to die.

Think about it. "Your life" is your egoic state of being: the thing you think you possess that is separate and different from everything else, the thing you've got to keep going, no matter what. When you lay that life down, your Reality abides where once there was an insane thought. Christ lives. You'll have laid down your life for a friend. And a friend is one who looks upon another and chooses to see only Christ and commits themselves to holding that perception of them until they can hold it for themselves. That is what a friend is. So no greater Love hath anybody than those who would lay down their life for a friend. Does that make sense for you? Hmmm.

So. When next your UPS driver comes with a package to your door, look him in the eye and say, "I'm going to lay down my life for you today. Have a nice day. Thank you for the package."

[Laughter]

And in that moment, you've become eternally linked to that being. They might show up in your dreams, in your prayer and meditation. You'll be linked to them in what you call "forever" until that being also chooses to awaken and allows their experience to be reshaped by the One sent of the Father who knows exactly what you need, as learning lessons that come and go (they're all temporary), so that *you* can discover the *power* of choosing *only* the Voice for Love.

And as you grow in Christ, you will outshine the body. You will outshine this entire dimension, and you will feel that you are bigger than this whole (what you call) your physical universe, because your Love, the remembrance of that Love, will need that much space. Hm?

As you awaken to the discovery that there is nothing outside of you, you will know why I could make a decision to accept responsibility for the Atonement. What other choice would I have, once I recognized that there was nothing outside of me and that all power under Heaven and Earth was available for me to teach only Love, to find ways to create communication devices that bring the universal curriculum of Reality to each and every temporarily fragmented aspect of myself? What I do through this, my beloved brother, through all of you—what I've done through what you call *A Course in Miracles,* and many other teaching devices—is, you see, quite selfish of me. I want me, who is you, to be awake.

So let no one tell you that I sacrifice, for in Love, there is no sacrifice. Please do not look upon me as some great savior who, "Boy, Christ, *amazing* Love He has that He would just devote Himself ceaselessly to helping poor little me." Please understand, I'm just helping myself—because you *are* myself. You are myself. And as I am One with you, you are One with me, and I'm not about to go anywhere until you remember that *you are* Christ and that only Love is Real.

There will be a day and an hour in which the Atonement is completed, even on Earth as it is in Heaven, so to speak. And in that moment, temporarily, everything will be transformed, and no one will walk upon this planet with a single fearful thought, and no mind upon this plane will entertain the thought that it is separate from another. And Christ will gaze upon only Christ, and then the purpose of this world will have been translated, transformed, and completed. And the oceans, and the land, the trees, and the flowers that have come as angels to remind you of the Truth, the sparkling rays of light that create what you call the crimson sunset, all of these angels will disappear. The world will disappear just like it once began: as the result of a thought, the outcome of a perception.

And when only the Real World is chosen as a perception in all minds, this world will cease to be—*but Creation will go on eternally*, for the Father does not create that which ends. Hmm! Do not think that in that day and hour, you're going to disappear into an amorphous blob of consciousness. For here is the great delight of God: to create that which is likened to Herself. I hope that's okay, hm? And you are That One.

Never think that individuation means separation, but imagine existence as consciousness in which you have a sense of your individuation with no trace or sense of separation from anything, no brother or sister. Relationship is the means of your salvation, and the final step of your salvation is ongoing celebration and extension of the good, the holy, and beautiful.

So please do not pray to be dissolved in Light. *You already are Light.*

Pray only that you will release any obstruction to *extending* Light. And you might want to add that you'd like to have fun doing it.

[Laughter]

Please remember that your Creator is the simplest of Beings. Your Creator says "Yes" to everything. Every thought you hold receives an automatic, "Yes, it's okay. Have a nice time."

And please again remember that you will not leave this plane, and do what is called death, only to sit in the lap of God and have Him explain for you why He did all those terrible things to you. He'll merely welcome you home and say, "Yes. Yes. I love you. What would you like to do today?" And as you lay there, you might say, "You know, I think I'll create another universe and go get lost again."

[Laughter]

Now please, I know that all that I've shared with you so far in this hour is not quite what the world has taught you that I taught—not quite. But I can only teach you what you already know. And there is no one in this room who has not experienced, in this hour, hearing words which are merely symbols of symbols pointing at Reality, and had at least once in this hour felt an "Aha!"

Now, if you recognize the Truth, the *content* within the *form* of the words that have been chosen *carefully* in this hour, and have recognized the Truth of that content somewhere deep within your being, it can only be because the Truth is *already* inside of you. Truth can only be recognized by Truth. Love can only be known by Love. As you have your saying in the world: "It takes one to know one."

And so we would complete this short message, and then we'll continue on, with this simple thought:

Whatever the means or mechanism through which you believe you have come to discover me, whether through what is called the Bible, whether through *A Course in Miracles* or any number of the other forms of the universal curriculum, whether you have come to know me as I have appeared to you in your dreams, as I have caused energy, a little of what you call zapping in the heart to get your attention, through whatever means you have come into relationship with me as my *equal* and as my brother or sister, please remember that if you see a trace of the Love and Reality of Christ in me, it is only because you have looked *through* the eyes of Christ at me. It does take the One to know the One.

And this is true for anyone in relationship with me, whether they be what you call a pauper in South America, holding the rosary, hmm?—who thinks on me and knows that Christ dwells in fullness within me. That one is seeing through the eyes of Christ. They may not quite know that yet, but they will.

You are the One who sees Christ in another. That takes unlimited power and perfect freedom to see with the eyes of Reality and not with the eyes of the world. And the one being that many of you have failed to appreciate the deepest is yourself.

Self love, is absolutely essential if you would heal and awaken every obstacle or trace, of anything unlike love. You cannot love your brother while hating yourself, but by loving yourself your cup overflows. Therefore, as you would embrace another, include yourself in the circle. As you would give service unto another, include yourself as one worthy of being served by your love. As you would teach another, teach first yourself. As you would long to heal another, long equally that you be healed.

For the only thing a teacher of God, and that is what you are, you didn't even know you signed up, hmm. The only thing as a teacher of God that you need to do is to accept the Atonement for yourself.

> *"I am that light, I am that truth, I am that one, I love that which I am, for I am my Fathers creation. And my Father creates only the Good, the Holy, and the Beautiful."*

How deeply are you willing to cultivate the ability to receive that truth? For the depth will determine the fruit which springs forth thereof. Mmmm.

I love you. Your mother loves you. Your father loves you. And everyone to whom you've given a smile loves you. And everyone who has come to you in your relationships, and you've looked past their mistakes, loves you. You've been there redeemer. Isn't it about time you extended the same courtesy to yourself?

So, with that I want to suggest that you… 'tis an interesting word, your language is so peculiar. You're going to *take a break*. I don't understand this. Where will you get it to take it from and when you break it what will you do with it? Hmm, strange language. But it is a reflection, is it not, of how insane the world has gotten. So we make do with what we have.

Take what you call *a break* but as you do so, as you begin to raise the body from the chairs, if you do so in love you've just raised the dead. [Laughter] Notice as you, another good word, "mill about", notice if you have a tendency to avoid eye contact with another, whether the body gets a little tense. Decide otherwise and let the eyes linger for at least a moment or two. Let yourself relax and deliberately choose to see Christ in front of you and see how you feel. And enjoy it.

When we return, if you wish to return, we will spend some time with what you call the questions and answers so we can all entertain ourselves. That's when we pretend that you don't know the answers.

[Laughter]

And we will come back and abide together.

It is a great joy to communicate with you in this way. When I left this plain I did not do so with a hatred of the body or of this earth, only with a transcendence of this world. Therefore this medium of communication with you is delightful for me as well. And I cherish the opportunity to be with you, for you are my love.

Therefore enjoy your break and we will come back together. I suppose when something is broken it is good to put it back together. Be you therefore at peace and know how much you are loved. How much light fills you and how much there is within you waiting to be given to this world.

Be you therefore at peace beloved friends.

Amen.

Participant: Well, this is a question that's bothered me ever since I read this statement in the Course, and every time the expression consciousness was used tonight, I still had that same questioning. The statement in the Course that concerns me says "consciousness is an ego function". And yet it seems to me that we talk all the time about a God Consciousness and a Christ Consciousness, and so if we are talking about a God Consciousness and a Christ Consciousness, I can't somehow reconcile that statement in the Course that "consciousness is an ego function".

Beloved friend, that simply makes God the ultimate ego trip.

[Laughter]

First, reconciliation between forms of the universal curriculum is not always possible, for reconciliation would require that each form of the universal curriculum use the same terminology, and use terminology in the same way. Remember always, that words are symbols of symbols, and therefore are twice removed from Reality. Words are symbols of ideas, words can be used and must be used in this dimension, to direct the mind toward ideas which more clearly reflect Reality, but ideas themselves are not Reality.

Therefore, place value on the Reality toward which ideas and words about ideas would direct you.

Love, for example, is a word. It is a symbol of an idea which is a reflection of a Reality which is beyond form. For Reality is content. If you struggle to reconcile the form of a universal curriculum -

which I did in fact help to give, called *A Course in Miracles*, with terminology that maybe utilized here or elsewhere -, you will actually cause yourself to waste time. Time which could be better spent in that which "love" is a symbol of. By being the Presence of that which extends the good, the holy and the beautiful.

If it were not necessary to present the universal curriculum in a multitude of forms, there would have only been one text ever written, and it would have occurred several thousands and thousands of years ago, and no other form of teaching would have ever arisen. But in the fragmentation of the One into the many, levels of consciousness are created. Each mind can be reached through certain vibrations which are words which represent ideas, and each mind has a certain language which is all its own. Therefore, the wise teacher learns to speak the language of the student, in order to convey or to communicate the Truth.

When *A Course in Miracles* was given, it was given in the context of the students. Hm? Therefore, the universal curriculum and its content were structured into a form that could best serve the needs of the students. And those that have resonated deeply with *A Course in Miracles* and gained great insight and healing from it, are merely those who are in close resonance with the minds of the students who first received it.

Likewise, I do not choose my channels wrongly, nor do I err at the structure of language that is used through them. And why? Because although I participated in the creation of *A Course in Miracles* as a teaching device, I'm well aware that not everyone will receive that form, and because my desire is to join with my brothers and sisters, I seek out modalities of communication that allow me to reach out to more minds.

"Consciousness is a function of the ego." Within the context of *A Course in Miracles* this is perfectly consistent. Consciousness is a word which is related to an idea that reflects something about Reality. Again, beloved friend, whether with the Course or any other form of the curriculum, do not place as much emphasis on the form, but rather on the content to which it would direct you.

The purpose of *A Course in Miracles* is to leave you in the Hands of your Internal Teacher, your union with the Holy Spirit. In this sense then, your curriculum begins where the teaching device of the Course leaves you. It is not designed to answer every question a Teacher of God will have, for only your Internal Teacher can do so. No form of the curriculum could ever hope to be conclusive enough to satisfy an answer to every question. For this would place the source of your guidance outside of you.

Therefore, simply relax the struggle to reconcile terminology, but rather learn to feel - as you do very well - the content toward which it directs you, and then live from that Reality. And the Holy Spirit will guide you and the use of what terminology can convey the Truth to a brother or to a sister.

Does that help you in regard to that question?

Participant: Mm, thank you very much.

Thank you very much.

Participant: May I ask a question?

Absolutely not.

[Laughter]

Participant: Yeah, thank you, this isn't a question. Thank you for being here, and somehow contacting me, and sort of getting me here.

It took quite a lot of doing.

Participant: I wouldn't be surprised if that were true. I've got sort of what to me is kind of a central question, and I am not sure exactly how to phrase it. I guess my question is: why all this pain? Why all this... I've heard the stories of separation, and even that the separation is a positive creative act, an expression of our creativity to imagine ourselves as alone and all that... But still there's the idea that well, geez if we can even conceive of the idea of asking a question about pain, how does that reconcile with an all-loving God? I know this question sounds simpler, the way I am putting it, than the way I thought about it, but maybe you can answer it anyhow... I'm sorry I didn't mean to interrupt, I remembered how I wanted to ask it. How does it serve God, for what sake is it to Him that we've imagined all this, that we have gone through all this illusion, and if there's no sake, then what the hell is going on? [Laughter]

Beloved friend, the answer to the question what does all of this pain do for God, what's it all about, is this: it does absolutely nothing for God, and He did not create it. God's Creation is You. Not you as you know yourself or think yourself to be a particular body-mind, who has unique forms of experience that are perceived and judged as painful, insufferable. This world is not God's Creation. You are. And the You that Is You is Spirit. Infinite, unbounded freedom to create and experience. *That* is God's only Creation, You.

This world - please, listen carefully - holds no value or purpose except that which the Comforter, the Holy Spirit, the Bridge back to God can bring to it. Illusion can have no meaning until Love translates it into that which can serve the awakening of God's Creation, You - which is really just an act of turning your attention from perceptions, and ideas, and beliefs that are untrue toward the decision to accept the Truth that is true always, and to begin to use the power of the mind, the power of your being, to extend from yourself only the good, the holy and the beautiful.

A thought of self-judgement is like a disturbance in an infinite field of possibilities that creates a distortion, and twists the extension of energy. And you experience the outcome of it.

You are free to use time constructively, not to wonder why things are as they seem to be, but to discover how they can be created differently.

For instance, it makes not a very good use of time to ask why the ego, rather ask:

> *How can I utilize time differently so that only Love is extended to me, and only Love is allowed to settle into the field of my being, into my mind, that I accept nothing but Love?*

Imagine by way of a picture if you were a field of energy and your real boundary was about here, all around the body - actually it's much much much bigger than that - what if you decided that anything that comes to touch the entrance to your energy field which is unlike Love, doesn't get to come in, and only Love can come, and also only Love can be extended out. Gradually, the whole nature of your experience would be transformed.

This process of transforming the mind, renewing the mind, begins with one decision:

> *I have no idea what's going on here, I don't know where it all came from, but I'm going to assume complete responsibility for how I choose to use my mind.*

To be vigilant about what thoughts you choose to think. To will yourself in a sense to direct the mind toward only loving thoughts. To cultivate it on a daily basis, and to trust that the universe is going to show up in a way that's certainly going to challenge you to do what you say you are committed to.

Here, beloved friend, is the certainty of the end of all pain. For when the mind wants only Love, it will see nothing else. And it will see beyond all boundaries that seem to separate this dimension from another, which seems to separate you from the ones that you love. All feelings of loss will disappear, and you will know that only Love is real. You will literally embrace in your - pardon the use of the language - consciousness *[Laughter]*, in your awareness, in your beingness you will embrace the infinity of dimensions of Creation that are even now present. You will know that there's nothing outside of you. And you will know that only Love is real. Pain will no longer be a possibility in the field of your awareness. But that does not come by the act of someone else doing something to you, it comes from assuming responsibility for no other reason than this: it's the only way to change it.

Again, spending time wondering why it is and how it got here is a waste of time. It will merely keep you sitting in the same spot of consciousness. Rather, decide what it is you want. You could say that the greatest of questions that you could ever ask yourself is this:

> *What do I truly want?*

And know that it's perfectly OK to have what you want. You will come to want only Love, for nothing else can satisfy the soul.

And when Love is thoroughly established, you will see and experience nothing else. And paradoxically that state of awareness is possible right here, now. It's not that you have to leave this world, and go somewhere else to get it. It is essential to get it here. For the body is not what you think it is. The world is not what you've been taught to think it is. There is something else present right here that can be perceived and known, it's called the real world in which pain no longer exists. The body arises, it passes away, events occur, and yet awareness is never pained by any of it. It is too busy being the Presence of Love. And that is what must be cultivated. That is what requires utmost responsibility and commitment and Self-Love.

To go through the day, asking only:

> *How am I choosing to use this moment? To love myself, to allow healing to occur, to look into the eyes of another and bless them with the Presence of Christ, or to convince myself that there's something amiss.*

Consciousness is everything, and out of it immediately [snaps fingers] you create what you call reality. You'll discover, beloved friend, the Power and the Majesty within you as you come to see that by changing a thought you change your world.

Within you is the power to awaken to Love, to act only from Love, to see only Love, to feel only Love, to be the embodiment and the presence of only Love. And then you will one day look back upon an *old* memory of something you once called pain, and you will chuckle within yourself and say:

> *Wow, I am pretty amazing! Once upon a time I convinced myself that something besides Love was real.*

The journey from there to there is a journey without distance to a perfect remembrance of what has never changed. Call it the spiritual journey if you will, call it the journey of mastery, it goes by many names, it is a journey that everyone must undertake sooner or later. You can delay it, but the journey will be taken. Why not begin now, by simply deciding not to waste the power of consciousness looking for answers to questions that in themselves change nothing? But ask only:

> *What do I truly want?*

And if it is an end of pain, then turn it into the positive by saying:

> *I want only Love, and I choose to be as a wise farmer who cultivates the garden of my own awareness so that only the seeds of Love are planted, and what is planted in good season will indeed bear forth great fruit.*

Plant the seeds, beloved friend, of only loving thoughts and it will come to pass that you will reap the harvest.

That was a very, very important question to ask, not just for you. So thank you.

Participant: Thank you for your answer.

What is the link between the answer that you gave and social problems or planetary problems like overpopulation or the spoiling of the planet's resources? What I heard you say brings personal peace but what happens to the physical world that we're in?

Beloved friend, as you make the decision for personal peace, remember that you are indeed joined to all expressions of Creation. You are inseparably linked to what you call your planet, your beloved Earth.

Now, imagine that your awareness is like an ocean, or a pond. When you drop a pebble into it, it creates a ripple. When you drop the pebble of the '*choice for peace*' into the pond of your c-word, consciousness [Laughter], you send a ripple out.

Now, if you create a sound through what is called the megaphone, and the pebble is dropped once, that is you sing a certain note, it creates a ripple, a sound effect, that goes out and has so much power, and then it finally seems to drift away. But if you keep singing the same note over and over, a momentum or a wave is created, and that ripple, that sound effect goes farther, and farther, and farther and more, and more powerfully. That ripple touches everything, everything in Creation.

Currently, as you look out through your eyes, and look out upon the world, you see an interesting mixture of beauty and insanity, of Love and fear. You're literally watching an armageddon being manifested through human consciousness.

When I walked upon this planet of yours, it was not easy to awaken. Why? Because most minds were sending out ripples of fear. It created a density that was much more difficult to get through, but the quickening that has occurred on your planet from the time that I was a man until the time that you exist, has been quite phenomenal. Today there are minds that are awakening daily. And I don't just mean getting a little insight, I mean awakening. That creates an acceleration in the way that a new ripple, if you will, the Reality-ripple, is being sent out through this ocean you call Creation.

Yes. Currently there are children who will starve to death by the time this evening is done, because the world-mind believes not only that there's no way to do anything, but that nobody's responsible. Nobody wants to take it on. There are toxins being dumped into rivers and oceans. Absolutely true. These things are the reflection of the toxicity that has been settling in the past into many human minds, since the world is a reflection of what awareness or consciousness has allowed itself to value.

The connection between your personal peace, your decision to be the embodiment of Love and what is occurring in what appears to be outside of you, cannot be possibly overstated. It is crucial because there is nothing outside of you. As you choose - regardless of what you see around you - to be the embodiment of Peace, to practice forgiveness, to look lovingly and to find the essence, the sanity, the Christ Mind in everyone, regardless of what they seem to be doing, you are sending out a ripple that touches that mind.

And because there are many, many, many beings awakening daily now, there will be a point, what I believe your scientists call a critical mass... Hmm. How about a loving mass? That's much better. Hm.

[Laughter]

A loving mass will be reached - and please, listen carefully - there will be a transition that occurs, that affects literally, you will see in other words in the waters, in the air, in your forests, in the lives of your children. And it will occur in the twinkling of an eye [snaps fingers]. Because that's how experience happens: ripples are sent out, when the momentum is enough, bang [snaps fingers], experience takes place.

The wave that is now occurring on your planet, is growing by leaps and bounds, it can no longer be slowed, and it cannot be prevented. Your political parties are going to go into obsolescence.

Participant: Thank God. [Laughter]

Hmm. And there will be a day on this planet when those who have been given the power and the responsibility to direct the large guns and bombs, will look upon their creations and simply withdraw their value from them. They may have never picked up *A Course in Miracles*, they may have never what you call "the standing on the head", they will awaken because a loving mass has chosen to awaken previously. And just like that, it will occur within them. And they will look upon their creations and realize: This is not what I want. And the war will cease, because the consciousness, the awareness that is shared by the One Mind, will have become wholly committed to a different thought. A thought held in unity, a thought that desires only the reflection of the extension of Love.

It is not what you call "*pie in the sky*". It is the natural outcome of the correction of how the mind is used. Your decision for personal peace is critical.

Therefore, when you look upon what you call the logger who has just cut down what you call the old growth tree, love the tree for the beauty it brought, find the essence of the one who is called the logger, and love that one. That is what is critical.

And when one performs an insane act on this planet, remember, that it is only a cry for help and healing. No act, which has been an unloving act, has ever been done from a loving place. It has been done because the soul of that one simply sees no other way to cry out for the attention required so that healing can begin.

Somebody must make the decision for Love. Fortunately, this room is filled with the multitude who understand that, and that definitely includes you.

Therefore, beloved friend, please, cultivate your personal peace, even as you act lovingly in the world. You'll know where to be, what causes to be a part of, what action to take. But see it not as a fight against something, for that only ensures that the opponent will always remain. See it as an opportunity to teach only Love, and thereby learn that only Love is real. And the ripples that you create, you cannot begin to comprehend the effects of them. Give everything, to the creation of those ripples within the field of your personal peace.

The Earth is an entity just like you. It is a consciousness, an awareness, filled with Love. Nothing that mankind could ever do, could possibly destroy the life of this Earth. That is like a tiny little fly thinking that it has the power to destroy the horse upon whom it's riding. It is only because the horse has tolerance and love for the fly, that the fly gets to be there in the first place.

[Laughter]

This Earth is a great loving being who knows exactly what to do to maintain itself. Its compassion is great.

And the waters of the Earth will run purely, and the skies will be clean, and no child will starve. That wave of probability cannot be stopped now. The dream of separation is playing itself out. Simply focus on Love. And thereby take up your rightful place as part of the solution, instead of part of the problem. You're doing rather well, too, beloved friend. Simply continue to know that you are worthy of Peace. Does that help you in that regard?

Participant: Yes, thank you.

Hi.

Hello.

Participant: I have a question.

Long time, no see. *[Laughter]*

Participant: Yeah. I have a question about my body. I've read in the Essene Gospel of Peace that...

All lies, don't believe them. Just kidding.

Participant: ... that we need to purify our bodies, and keep our blood clean, and then I read in A Course in Miracles that the body's not real, and that the mind creates the discomfort in it. And a lot of drama that I've had in my life has been around illness in my body. And I'm a bit confused as to how to heal what I'm experiencing right now which has just been chronic for years... And if it's not one thing, it's another. And if that goes away, it's another.

Beloved friend, what is the manifestation of dis-ease keeping you from?

Participant: Peace and joy.

Hm. As I said a few moments ago, when you want only Love, you will see nothing else. Even in the body. Therefore, look well, beloved friend, for beneath the surface of your awareness, there is a conflict within the soul about its very worthiness to have peace and joy. There is a struggle within the soul, an armageddon between the part that would want it and the part that seems to have its grip on you, that says,

> *no, you're not yet proven yourself worthy. You have erred in the past, and therefore carry a certain guilt.*

That guilt keeps you from allowing the peace and joy to enter into the field of your being, and thereby bring about the correction of the body that you would desire. There is a pattern in the mind that keeps the energy or the vibration of disease in your consciousness.
Healing will occur when you've withdrawn all valuation you have placed upon disease. And as long as you perceive that there is something within you that justifies a sense of guilt, a sense of failure, you will keep valuing dis-ease as a way to reflect back to you the truth of your guilt.

This guilt is deeply embedded, I don't mean by that to frighten you, saying it's underneath 40 tons of concrete, it just means that it's old, and it has been pushed down.

There is a feeling that comes up for you from time to time, you feel it generally right about in this area of the body, it is a very old sadness. Give yourself permission when next it comes, to set aside everything, and give yourself permission to abide with and feel that sadness. It is called embracing it, it's a feeling in your world because you have a body, that is to embrace what is unlike Love within you. And by doing so, that guilt will begin to dissolve as a weight within your field of energy, your field of being or awareness.

Disease has served you, in the sense that it is kept in place the deeply held belief that your guilt is justified. As you come then to the decision to love yourself, to truly understand that you have never sinned, and you have never failed anyone at anytime, that you indeed remain wholly loved, wholly loving and wholly lovable, the guilt will be dissolved from the mind, and the body will begin to reflect the change that has occurred. Listen carefully to those 3 words: you are loved, you are loving and you are lovable.

As you go to your home this evening, say those words over in your mind, and discover the one that is the hardest to accept, and there is your doorway to the guilt. One of those words is a symbol of an idea of something which is very real, that is difficult for you to truly accept into your being.

There, beloved friend, is a very important doorway for you. And as you choose to discover it - and please listen carefully - I will come and abide with you, we will go through that doorway together, and that which is the guilt held as an ancient sadness in the depth of the soul will come to be wholly dissolved from within your being. I am your friend, and I will walk with you, because I love you, and I recognize your lovability.

Therefore, look well, and simply decide, you don't have to know how to do it yet, just make the decision that it is time to heal an ancient sadness that has birthed the residue of guilt from which disease is merely the reflection that the guilt is justified. Indeed it is time to heal. And something within you knows this now, or you would never have come to this place this evening. For well does a part of you that knows that you know me and I know you. Accept what you feel in the depth of your being. You've known me before, you'll know me again. And I am your friend. And it is time to heal, so it's no longer one thing after another, but just one thing.

Indeed. I love you. I love you.

I feel it would be important here to let you know that once you invite me in, I'm like the guest who comes and does not leave. [Laughter] But I'm not such a bad guy. [Laughter] And I will never demand anything of you, save the opportunity for you to release the grip deep in the heart so that I can enjoy loving you. For only Love heals.

Blessings. My blessings I give to my ancient sister. Be you, therefore, at peace, and I will be knocking. Fair enough?

Participant: Thank you.

Hm. Beloved friend, thank you for the courage to come here this evening, in front of all these other minds, admit the truth that you are tired of the weight of an ancient guilt and sadness. That ensures that healing occurs. Hm. You are courageous one. You do not yet know the depth of your courage, but you will. Hm.

So, I'll be seeing you. *[Laughter]* Hm.

Participant: Thank you.

Indeed.

By the way, I do look forward to the day when all questions have been answered.

[Laughter]

Not because they are a burden, but when you realize that all your doubts have been solved, and all questions have been answered, it simply means that you'll know that you're Christ, and that the dream you've chosen to dream no longer holds any value. And then we can - what is your term here? Then we can truly begin to rock and roll. *[Laughter]* Rock and roll. Hm. Hm. I do love your language, it is rather fun. *[Laughter]*

Participant: Hi Jeshua.

It's about time.

Participant: [Laughter] I have lots of questions, but there's one...

Do you?

Participant: I guess, they do come up from time to time, and then they do seem to get answered. But so nice to have you here, because it's quicker this way, it seems. [Laughter]

Beloved friend, I'm always here. It is you that goes away. [Laughter]

Participant: [Laughter] Fair enough. The last time I talked to you, I talked to you on the telephone, and... well... no... [Laughter]

Don't tell anybody! [Laughter]

Participant: [Laughter] And I happened to mention that I was writing something...

Happened to mention?

Participant: It's a very important thing that came up.

Yes.

Participant: And I said that I was writing something, and I was feeling doubts that it was very important, and that my feeling was: why bother when obviously there are more important things being written, and who knows who might read it? So... you became very... well, you said very clearly in a very assertive voice that everything that people do... well, that this was soul work, in other words, that this was a piece of art or whatever, and it was soul work, and that it was very important to finish it. And as I remember, the one reason it was important was that "you didn't want to have to come back and finish it another time perhaps". And also that it didn't matter if anyone read it or not. So I continued, and finished some stories expecting in some way that at the end of it I would feel, you know, excited or that I had created something, you know, special, or whatever... Well, I've had a few little feelings like that. But at the same time...

Heaven forbid that they should grow into large feelings...

Participant: [Laughter] That's my next question actually... When obviously doubts come up, because one feels that the ego is speaking when one is writing as opposed to the deeper sense of Spirit... I guess my feeling has been that if it were deep Spirit, I would have an incredible joy of completion. And obviously I'm looking for ways... I don't wanna just write from an ego place, I wanna write what's true, and I wanna write with the feeling that in a sense something's coming through me, which does happen, you know, at times. But is there a way for me and others - for people who write or create, whatever - to be more in touch with allowing that to happen? I mean I know there's meditation and etc, but is there something, is there some other way? Something that I haven't been able to open up in myself?

For you there is no hope. [Laughter] You might as well throw in the towel. And someone, have so much you call hemlock to give to this one! Hm. I'll make sure that my Father erases your name out of the Book of Life. After all, you're certainly not capable of bringing through anything remotely resembling Spirit or Love. *[Laughter]* Ahhh… A scourge upon the Earth. *[Laughter]*

Participant: [Laughter] You said that whatever I ask for, I would receive. You said that quite a few times. And I've been asking, I have been receiving lots of things, I don't wanna say that… you know, that's not what I'm saying. I really do feel wonderful basically and blessed. It's this one little thing… [Laughter]

It's always something. One thing after another. *[Laughter]*

And that way, beloved friend, you can keep the feeling little. A feeling of Reality and of Truth.

Beloved friend, it is soul work. The greatest soul work, the content of soul work regardless of the form is Self-Love. Complete Self-Acceptance. The recognition that only the Truth is true. That your gift, your desire to take a blank piece of paper, and form words as symbols of that which point to a Reality beyond themselves, beyond the power of the mind to ever truly comprehend it intellectually, that which sets the heart soaring, that which touches the hardness of the mind, that which brings a lesson to remember Love.

That gift, some would call it, you've cultivated over multitude of lifetimes out of the huge, huge, compassionate heart, that so loves this Earth and every being who walks upon it, flies above it, crawls upon it, or swims in its waters, that if you could, you would stretch even that physical body wide enough to give them all a home to live in. You, oh, compassionate one, have cultivated that gift, and you can only mock yourself by not letting it be utilized to express the good, the holy and the beautiful, that you know - and we both know that you know - is the Truth of your being.

You're yet struggling with the fear of what would transpire if you fully accepted that only the Truth can be true, and you withdrew the value you placed upon your belief that you must remain little and small within yourself in order to be accepted by the world. That is the creation of the tension and the struggle.

Now, I let you in on a little secret. The opinion of the world, which is a collection of the insane thoughts, does not hold very much merit. But the Truth, that you know to be true, holds all merit. Therefore, write as though your life depended on it! And Life will more and more inform the form of your stories and your sharings so that the words which are symbols of ideas will more and more reflect the Reality that you know perfectly well is true.

The only question here is: When will you decide to live it? By releasing the perception that you must dim your Light in order not to offend the insane. Hm.

Write, beloved friend! Dance, beloved friend! Ride upon your horses, beloved friend!

[Laughter]

And enjoy the hell out of all of it! *[Laughter]*

Do not fear your passion! Do not fear your aliveness! Show it forth to the world! Stop hiding your Light under a bushel! Become a little what you call crazy in the head, as though the opinions of the world meant nothing! Let yourself be a little giddy, light-headed! Let the body dance! Go and find a waterfall, take off the clothes, and dance and sing in the waterfall! You know, you love those things. *[Laughter]* And then go back and sit and look at that blank piece of paper, and recognize that Christ is looking at that paper! And Christ loves, loves to create forms that reflect the good, the holy and the beautiful. Not in order to be approved of, but out of the sheer delight of extending the Reality of God's Love.

Christ, you see, is that energy which will create the good, the holy and the beautiful simply for Christ's delight. And you and how many others in this room block that from occurring because they hold the thought that perhaps no one will notice. You can notice. And when you notice it fully - listen well -, when you step into the willingness to create the good, the holy and the beautiful for yourself, not giving - what is this word? - a hoot whether anybody else on the planet ever knows about it, you'll be tapping into the supreme secret that there's no way in Reality that it cannot be noticed, because all minds are joined. And when you write and extend your love and your beauty and thoroughly enjoy it, it is impossible for other minds to be unaffected.

Therefore, the sage transforms the world without ever leaving his room. Hm. Except perhaps to ride the horse *[Laughter]* or to what you call "the making love", the dancing. In other words, beloved friend, enough is enough! *[Laughter]* You have to pardon the levity here, we've known each other a very long time.

Are you willing to love yourself so much that you give up expending energy creating the perception of doubt in order to keep your Light small out of fear of what someone else might think?

Participant: Great question.

Tis the only question. You know the answer. It's just a question of when you'll answer by saying: Screw the small stuff! You know, it's one way to say it. *[Laughter]*

Participant: I do need to hear it. I did need to hear it tonight. So I thank you.

Hm. I will send you a bill later. *[Laughter]* Rest assured, beloved friend, you just never know, who's going to show up to help form the words on the page.

Participant: Exactly. And now that's my next question. Haha. Just come and be there with me, just looking over one shoulder.

I see if I can have it scheduled into my…

Participant: ... busy busy schedule... [laughing, and speaking at the same time with Jeshua]

… itinerary.

Participant: Thank you, Jeshua. I do love you very much.

I know that, beloved friend. When will you be willing to accept how deeply I love you? Hm.

Participant: Now.

Very good idea. *[Laughter]*

Participant: Thank you.

Hm. Have you thought you could escape me by skipping into another timeframe or two?

Participant: Haha. Not on your life!

Hm. Right. [Laughter] Hm.

Participant: Jeshua, my heart is pounding, and I guess I need to hear it from you, too. And I wanna know what blocks me from using my artistic ability to capture you.

Beloved friend, if you seek to capture me, I will prevent you from using it. *[Laughter]* Hm.

If you allow that communication to transpire, and then express it, you know that you will have created something that can be seen by others, and it triggers an old fear by which someone in the world can point and say:

> *"She's one of them. I believe she's part of that Essene community where this saviour of the world came from that we've just got rid of."*

Fear not persecution this time around! Therefore, beloved friend, if you would well entertain it, I would be most pleased to, shall we say, sneak into the corners of your awareness in order to - how shall we say this - transport an image into your awareness that will stay with you, and can be easily translated through the artistic medium.

If it's OK with you, I mean it's OK with me, if it's OK with you, you can put it into your closet.

Participant: [Laughter] I don't think so.

Indeed. Beloved friend, it is just an old fear. Where once you felt you needed to conceal a certain relationship, so that you aren't marked.

Participant: I, too, have been with you many times.

Indeed. Rest assured, in this timeframe there's no secret police, so to speak, seeking you out, and persecution will not occur.

Participant: Thank you. Please, be with me in that art room!

Very well. *[Laughter]*

Participant: Well, you have a lot of places to go.

When one knows they are thoroughly unlimited, there is no place they cannot be. And when one has mastered fear, there is no place one would not want to be. Just something to consider. Hm. I will be with you.

So, we will entertain one more question.

Participant: Jeshua, I've been sitting here asking...

No, I've changed my mind. *[Laughter]*

Participant: [Laughter] I've had a lot of questions, and I've narrowed it down to one. In A Course in Miracles what is meant by "the Father will take the final step"?

That's a very good question. I don't know where that one came from. *[Laughter]*

Never let anyone tell you that *A Course in Miracles* is purely a rational spirituality. There's much of mystery within it, much of poetry, much of mysticism. It must be this way, because again, words, no matter how they are structured, are symbols of symbols which are hopefully effective reflections of Reality. And no symbol, word or idea, can comprehend, wrap itself around Reality.

When I shared the thought with Helen that "*the Father will take the final step*", there were many levels of meaning contained, hidden, veiled in that statement. Why?

Remember always, that *A Course in Miracles* was given within the context of the students involved. Therefore, teaching is an art, and not a science. When to nudge, when not to nudge, when to lay it on the line, when to be a little sneaky. *[Laughter]* Hm.

I could not say to Helen at that time that as correction comes to the depth of the mind, there is a point when the self one thought one was is revealed to be only God. The entire language of the Course then is based on a fundamental duality between Creator and Created, Spirit/matter. This was a language that she could understand and accept without it causing fear.

Therefore, to say "*the Father will take the final step*" allowed her to continue the process, and by the way we would say here that she was a bit of a stickler *[Laughter]*, it was like walking on what you call cosmic eggshells to make sure that I did not upset her.

Now, when I said "*the Father will take the final step for you*", that allowed her not to be fearful for she had not yet truly completely healed her own armageddon over the form of the universal curriculum called christianity that she experienced early in this life. It kept in place within her mind the perspective that there is an internal gulf between

Creator and Created. At the same time I simply told her the Truth. Of course "*the Father will take the final step for you*". The final step is the complete realization that *there is only God*, that the one doing the stepping is the one toward whom you wish to step. Hm. 'Tis something to consider now.

Grace comes from yourself, for I and my Father are One. You cannot tell where the Son begins and the Father ends. Who can find such a boundary? In Truth, it does not exist. We speak this way only because teaching is an art. And communication without the creation of fear is always the goal.

Helen could accept that statement. Had I said to her:

> *"Look, it's very simple [Laughter], you think you're something you're not, and there's only God. Wake up!"*

There would be no *A Course in Miracles. [Laughter]*

And for you, too, the Father will take the final step. Merely love yourself, and illusions will dissolve from the mind, from the emotions, from the body - gently, lovingly, following a path that you have set amidst the stars. The end of the journey is certain. For the One you walk toward is doing the walking, and That One knows the way. Through you, indeed.

Thank you, sweet and benevolent soul, for your Light is a blessing to all who know you. Time to accept it. *[Laughter]* Hm.

When next you'll see one of your friends, just go: "I know, I know, I'm a blessing." *[Laughter]*

Participant: There's a lot of them here, so they can help me practice.

Indeed. So, since the final step is the final step, that's a good place to end. How are you all doing?

Participant: Great. Good.

Has this evening been worth your while?

Participant: Yes! Oh, yes!

Well, I hope so. You're the one that created it! If it is not worth it, then you wasted your time. *[Laughter]*

Hm. So, please understand that I am not within this body, just as you're not within yours. The body emerges out of your own awareness, it is within you. I cannot be localized here as opposed to there. I did that once, and found it quite unfulfilling. 'Tis called a body.

I love you. And any of you do not yet truly know how deep that Love is. You've only begun to touch upon the enormity and the depth of the Love that I feel for you, because that Love is the Love of the Father who calls Himself back to Himself in and as you.

If you try to comprehend the vastness of your physical universe, and then compare that to the depth and width of my Love for you, it is like taking a grain of sand from the beaches of your world, and say:

> *Here, this is all the sand in the world.*

I love you so much, that I can't even imagine wanting to be anywhere where you are not. And I will never cease in giving you my strength until yours is as certain as mine.

I know Who You Are. And you can't fool me. *[Laughter]* Be you, therefore, the Light that you are by choosing to teach only love, by choosing to use time constructively, to become the master of the only thing that exists: the Mind. And you are, wherever you are, the Light that lights *this world* while it lasts. What else could you possibly find that will be better to do? You need go nowhere to redeem this world. Merely turn each moment over and ask,

> *What would you have me do? Oh, call Mary. OK. Ride a horse. OK. Have some ice cream. OK.*

Hm. Thank you. And when I say thank you to you, I mean it. It takes great courage to choose the unique form of attention called incarnation into this, the most insane dimension of Creation that exists in order to translate it into that which reflects Reality.

That is why you come. Look no further to find your purpose. You know perfectly well what it is. So get on with it! And never think you are alone. This is maybe horrific to some, there is no such thing as privacy. *[Laughter]* Hm.

And when next you're doing that which is called the making of love, know that the whole universe is watching. *[Laughter]* Some beings are saying you know her body wasn't so bad. *[Laughter]* Hm. Hm.

So, go you therefore into your evening, but do this one little thing, just for the fun of it. When you rest your head upon your pillow, let your last thought be this:

It is true. I and my Father are One. And now would Christ sleep.

Peace be unto you always, precious and holy and innocent and guiltless Child of God who is but Love.

Amen.

Epilogue

In the classic American film, *The Wizard of Oz,* the main character, Dorothy, transported suddenly to a new world, spoke for the soul when she said to her small dog and faithful companion: "Toto, we're not in Kansas anymore!"

My experience, related in *The Jeshua Letters,* was much like Dorothy's. I still notice twinges of disbelief at times – it was as if I was swept up and deposited on a different planet! Of course, I *was* swept up, turned inside out, and deposited back on the very same planet, emerging as a radically different 'me' in the process.

The call of ceaseless surrender – no matter what – leaves no room for the mind to reasonably assess things, as it comes to release the one thing the small ego mind wants: control!

It seems as if it was yesterday when Jeshua gave me such a key statement of universal wisdom: "My brother, what would you control save that which you mistrust?" Every step on the path of healing, and every call to incarnate more of Christ Mind has required me to rest first in this Truth, learn to see the fear underneath my desire to control, and then surrender it and leap!

My mind still cannot fathom how all that has occurred in the last thirty-plus years was possible, unless, of course, it is true that God's Love does collapse the need for time...and that we are truly supported in our willingness to submit to the alchemy of the spiritual journey, so that we become conduits for what Jeshua calls in *The Aramaic Beatitudes*, 'God's new creations.'

We cannot experience these 'new creations' unless we surrender and become willing to engage our inner demons, learning more deeply how to become the Presence in which our deepest drives, fears, doubts, sense of unworthiness, and guilt are healed – unless we allow all of the structured ideas and perceptions we carry about ourselves, others, and life itself to be flushed up into awareness, there to be dissolved in a Love that far transcends the limits of 'reason.'

From *The Early Years* channelings, onto *The Christ Mind Trilogy*, the years of diving deep into, and creating with Him *The Living Practices*, discerning under Jeshua's guidance *The Aramaic Beatitudes*, living homeless, traveling the globe to share and learn from others (like you!), making eight pilgrimages to Israel and many other pilgrimages to sacred lands, ten years founding and living in an ashram in Bali, birthing The *Jewels of the Christ Mind* program and many other online courses, and so much more...Jeshua has led me throughout.

Could I have known any of this would unfold? Of course not! And, boy, did I ever put up a good fight attempting at times to resist every bit of it! And clearly, it was not "me" doing it. Rather, God was having His way with me, and I have learned from it all one crucial, essential, vital thing: we simply cannot unfold God's life for us, which is what our life really is. Only God can do this, and this life will unfold only when we have truly said "yes," when we have surrendered our need for control, and allow ourselves to BE unfolded – then, and only then.

The entire body of teachings that comprise *The Way of Mastery Pathway* are astounding in both depth and breadth. We remain free, however, to elect just how far along the steppingstones Jeshua has set before us we will walk at any time.

What I have seen now, very deeply in myself and in the journeys of the thousands I have been blessed to grow with (even when such growth seemed a torment for ego) has revealed for me this truth: together, we are the makers of the 'world,' which is a projection of fascinating 'frequencies' made by 'bending' Light into distortions, so that what we see, feel, and believe is the opposite of Reality. That is our remarkable creation, called by Him "the dream of separation." But separation does not – cannot – exist.

What, then, an astounding thing we have done, experiencing what cannot exist! And still, Love calls us home, and however real the dream may seem, still, only Love is real. Indeed, the dream exists only in what we project upon reality, veiling the shimmering, extraordinary, infinite, and astounding Presence of God from ourselves, then using our creations in an attempt to regain what we threw away without having to remove those veils!

While only loving thoughts are real, until we heal beyond thoughts themselves and come to rest in the field of Love itself, often our 'loving thoughts' merely veil what remains to be healed into wholeness; we are hallucinating, still lost in the dream. And yet, Love is shimmering and smiling at us through all that we see, and we can come to see this Love infinitely, if we choose to. The "problem," then, isn't out there, it is with the nature of the seer. Turn within, then, not to escape, but to discern the veils that color reality, bringing all to Love for healing and correction.

Once we do this, we no longer hold onto the belief that, "If I just 'wake up,' I can finally escape this damn world," because we no longer have a desire to escape.

Waking proves that we have been utterly wrong about awakening itself, for the result is just the opposite – it is not about escaping at all but about embracing and loving our 'enemies.' For as we are free to choose what we put our attention on, and thereby create our experience, we see that our true 'enemies' are merely the veils we have allowed to cloak our minds, express through our bodies, and warp our very use of life and time.

That even thought arises from a far more primary field of energy, of frequencies made of Light that can veil Light from operating not just as thought, but as feeling, as the true power and potential of Love—this profound realization is what sets the fullness of *The Way of Mastery Pathway* apart from most forms of spirituality.

We are 'the world.' And it changes only as we choose to change. Until we become conduits for the transfiguring power of Love exactly where we have thought we were trapped – like Dorothy in Oz – there is no completion in Christed Being.

As these realizations truly began to dawn for me as a result of my journey under His masterful guidance, Jeshua led me to a statement in *A Course In Miracles* that I had not heard anyone teaching the *Course* refer to, let alone emphasize: "Heaven and earth will pass away means only they will cease to exist as separate states." Yes. There is no room for the hope of getting 'beamed up,' or shirking total commitment to our own transformation and serving the healing of all, nor can we justify ongoing distraction (which most of the world is designed to be – just go shopping!) if our deeper desire is awakening to Truth, Love, and Reality!

Jeshua makes it clear: "Christ assumes responsibility for the whole of Creation."

The Christ Path is one of radical death to self, rebirth, *and* a call to see that 'there is no other, you see only your Self,' a call to fully participate in the very process of coming to experience heaven and earth as ceasing to exist as separate states.

All we need do is humbly, fully, devotedly, allow Love to guide our own unique journey from fear to Love, under all conditions. All the rest will unfold from there, exactly as the creations of 'my life' have unfolded from the willingness to be 'taken all the way, no matter what.'

The Way of Mastery Pathway is a vital part of such an unfoldment for many, and though we may never meet face to face, we journey on it together, and I want you to know I am grateful for each time you choose forgiveness, or are willing to look within and question the little mind, open to new revelations, and are moved to new creations and choices to extend Love to one and all.

What Jeshua says is true: "This we do together, until all of Creation is returned to being only the praise of God's Presence." Peace comes when, truly, this is seen and known, and we see that the bringing of fear to Love, and the bringing of illusion to Truth for healing and transformation, for seeing the remarkable, joyful journey that this includes, is the only truly worthwhile use of time.

Blessings to you!

Jayem
July 2021

The Way of Mastery Outline

Pathway of Enlightenment

The book you hold in your hands is part of a larger body of work, namely *The Way of Mastery.*

The Way of Mastery is a pathway offering a profound and comprehensive theology and lived experience of love via a progression of teachings, exercises, and *Living Practices*, all devoted to a genuine – and radical – depth of living enlightenment.

This depth goes beyond intellectual belief or the acceptance of certain concepts and ideas. It guides the student into their essential and eternal Heart, into a radical, transfigured gnosis, a 'knowledge by being that which is known.'

The purpose of *The Way of Mastery Pathway* is threefold:

~ To create a pathway that can support any student from their first steps all the way to truly awakening into 'Christ Mind'

~ To restore the original Teachings of Jeshua (Jesus) given to His followers

~ To 'birth a million Christs'

The Way of Mastery Pathway is comprised of four essential and interconnected parts:

~ The Jeshua Channelings: *The Jeshua Letters, The Early Years, The Way of the Servant, The Christ Mind Trilogy: The Way of the Heart, The Way of Transformation and The Way of Knowing and The Later Years.*

~ The Living Practices: a series of alchemical trainings and Aramaic teachings, including *LovesBreath, In the Name* meditation, *The Aramaic Lord's Prayer, The Aramaic Beatitudes, Radical Inquiry,* the seamless life and more.

~ **Facilitated Teachings and Sacred Journeys:** deepening into a spiritual path often requires support; private sessions, workshops, seminars, on-line classes, sacred pilgrimages and a host of classes and gatherings are led by *Pathway* teachers.

~ **Temple Canyon Sanctuary:** sacred land near Abiquiu, New Mexico, miraculously purchased in the early days of the Pathway, and meant for future steps of development, as given specifically by Jeshua during the time of its purchase.

In summary, *The Way of Mastery* is a Pathway of Enlightenment that re-establishes Jeshua's original teachings, and in doing so, it offers a profound, in-depth roadmap to support any soul from the first inkling to awaken all the way into knowing their most essential Self.

The *Pathway* aims at nothing less than a radical shift of identity from 'Ego' to 'Christ,' aiding students to increasingly live in and create from Christ Mind, itself. Through His *Pathway*, Jeshua seeks nothing less than the birthing of "a million Christs" on this planet and the transformation of the experience of humanity from fear to Love—the manifestation of Heaven on Earth that 'completes the very need for Time.'

Jayem is the channel of *The Way of Mastery.*

Official Website: www.wayofmastery.com

Shanti Christo

'Shanti Christo' is a term mentioned often in *The Way of Mastery* texts. The meaning of Shanti Christo is 'Peace of Christ.' This term was first given by Jeshua to Jayem prior to the unfolding of the *Pathway* (as *The Way of Mastery Pathway* is often called) itself.

Shanti Christo was also the name given to the non-profit foundation that Jayem set up in the early years of his channeling with Jeshua. The Shanti Christo Foundation was established to disseminate *The Way of Mastery* teachings, and to steward the Temple Canyon Sanctuary land near Abiquiu, New Mexico, until time for it to be developed further.

In 2002, Jayem received guidance from the Holy Spirit related to the foundation and his role within it. Following this guidance, he resigned as its director and continued his own deep immersion with Jeshua. It feels important to share the portions of the guidance related to Jayem's role for you to read directly:

> *"First, you* [referring to Jayem] *must step aside completely. You have successfully completed the stage of vision. The twofold purpose of the entity* [Shanti Christo] *is fully revealed and given: the teachings, which began with* <u>*The Jeshua Letters*</u> *and ended with the three works entitled* <u>*The Way of the Heart, Transformation, and Knowing*</u>*. Second, the physical setting has been attracted, discovered, purchased, and its design features openly shared* [the land near Abiquiu].
>
> *"The next stage, implementation, is not your role or your concern.* [Jayem interjects at the time of the channeling: 'And frankly, this is a surprise to me in big doses.' The reading continues:] *Remember, you can only be what your Creator would make of you, not what you may perceive you should be."*

Holy Spirit later goes on to share:

> *"Your only role* [speaking directly to Jayem], *the essence of your existence, is to bridge vision and the teachings of Christ mind to others, thus fully learning them yourself."* ★

As a result of Jayem's continued immersion with Jeshua, further stages of the *Pathway* developed after his departure from the foundation – namely the *Living Practices* (*Love'sBreath* and *Radical Inquiry*) and *Facilitated Teachings.* Also included in this unfolding was what Jeshua states as a primary purpose *of* the *Pathway*: "to restore My original teachings." These unfolded under His guidance and are known as the *Aramaic Teachings*, which in themselves express the soul, depth, and heart of the entire *Pathway*.

Interestingly, this development was 'predicted' in Lesson 10 of *The Way of Knowing*. Jeshua revealed that much more would be coming forth after the completion of what came to be known as *The Christ Mind Trilogy*:

"...as we enter these last days of this *Way of Knowing*, we have come in this hour to share with you that we do not so much come to a culmination, or an end, but to a *springboard* for what shall be."

To this day, Jayem continues to develop teaching tools that provide valuable assistance to thousands as they engage *The Way of Mastery Pathway*. He has gone on to become a masterful facilitator and continues his dedicated servantship with Jeshua – holding His vision for the *Pathway* as sacred.

Notably, after Jayem stepped away from the Shanti Christo Foundation, its board elected to publish only three of the five core teachings: *The Way of the Heart, The Way of Transformation,* and *The Way of Knowing.* Substantial sections of these texts were edited and removed, including the questions and answers that followed many lessons, and the trilogy was published within a single book entitled *The Way of Mastery* (referred to by many as the "blue book").

While this publication served to disseminate the teachings to many, identifying the trilogy under this title has also created confusion for many students who have come to equate *The Way of Mastery* with a single book. The *Pathway* is far from complete without *The Jeshua Letters* and *The Way of the Servant* texts (which the Shanti Christo Foundation chose not to publish), and the crucial experiential components that Jayem has continued to develop—*The Living Practices, Facilitated Teachings,* and *Aramaic Teachings.*

~

This series of books—the only authorized and complete version now in print—has been published to ensure that students understand the broader context in which *The Jeshua Letters, The Way of the Servant*, and *The Christ Mind Trilogy* were given, and that they are only one part of a comprehensive 'pathway that can carry anyone from the first inkling to awaken all the way to Christ mind.'

May *Shanti Christo*—the Peace of Christ—be with you.

* *The complete text of the 2002 Message is available on our website: wayofmastery.com*

WAY of MASTERY
www.wayofmastery.com

www.ingramcontent.com/pod-product-compliance
Lightning Source LLC
LaVergne TN
LVHW040825090826
845145LV00001BA/177

* 9 7 8 6 0 2 9 1 8 9 1 4 8 *